BENGT HÄGER

ADDITIONAL TEXTS BY

Isaac Albéniz, Hans Christian Andersen, Georges Auric, Riciotto Canudo,
Alfredo Casella, Blaise Cendrars, René Clair, Paul Claudel, Jean Cocteau, Claude
Debussy, Arthur Honegger, Jean Hugo, Désiré Émile Inghelbrecht, Louise Labé,
Daniel Lazarus, Fernand Léger, Rolf de Maré, Darius Milhaud, Gerald Murphy,
Francis Picabia, Luigi Pirandello, Francis Poulenc, Maurice Ravel, Erik Satie,
and quotations from Colette, Raymond Radiguet, Maurice Raynal, Henri
Sauguet, and other contemporary artists and critics

SETS AND COSTUMES BY

Aleksandr Alekseev, Pierre Bonnard, Giorgio de Chirico, Jean Cocteau, Paul
Colin, Nils Dardel, Foujita, Gunnar Hallström, André Hellé, Jean Hugo, Valentine
Hugo, Irène Lagut, Jeanne Lanvin, Pierre Laprade, Fernand Léger, Mouveau,
Gerald Murphy, Einar Nerman, Andrée Parr, Hélène Perdriat, Francis Picabia,
Alexandre Steinlen, Louis Touchagues and Maria Vasilieva

TRANSLATED FROM THE FRENCH
BY RUTH SHARMAN

HARRY N. ABRAMS, INC., PUBLISHERS, NEW YORK

BALLETS

SUEDOIS

(THE SWEDISH BALLET)

TO MY BELOVED WIFE, LILAVATI

The publishers wish to express their profound thanks to
Stockholm's Dance Museum. They would also like to express
their gratitude to the cultural department of the French
embassy in Stockholm, the director of the Swedish Cultural
Centre in Paris, and Gérard Bourgadier, without whose
enthusiasm and support this book could not have come into
being.

Conceived by Jacques Damase
Designed by Patrick Lébédeff, Arbook International

Library of Congress Cataloging-in-Publication Data
Häger, Bengt Nils Richard, 1916–
[Ballets suédois. English]
The Swedish Ballet / by Bengt Häger ; texts by Isaac Albéniz . . .
[et al.] : designs and costumes by Aleksandr Alekseev . . . [et al.].
p.   cm.
Translation of: Ballet suédois.
ISBN 0-8109-3803-0
1. Ballet suédois—History.   I. Albéniz, Isaac, 1860–1909.
II. Alekseev, Aleksandr, 1901–   . III. Title.
[GV1786.B315H3413   1990]
792.8′09485—dc20   90–30453
CIP

Printed and bound in Italy

CONTENTS

STOCKHOLM

PARIS

A FIVE-YEAR REVOLUTION

'What ballet company has ever put on such a display, bringing together at one time the most famous musicians and the cream of contemporary French artists? . . . What theatre has staged, in so short a space of time, such a great number of national works, in décors created by French artists?'

When Louis Handler wrote these lines in *Comœdia* (15 February 1921), it was scarcely five months since the Ballets Suédois had reopened the Théâtre des Champs-Élysées, built in 1913 but closed down for the duration of the war. It had taken the company only a matter of weeks to turn this theatre, regarded at the time as 'the most beautiful in the world', into 'the most active and the boldest: the one indispensable theatre in Paris'.

For the next five years, the Théâtre des Champs-Élysées was to be the scene of an incredible adventure, thanks to a group of young Swedes: a choreographer born near the Arctic Circle, forty or so dancers from an opera house which had gone rather unnoticed since the eighteenth century, and a director who had no previous experience of the stage. They were to uncover as yet unknown geniuses of French artistic life – poets, painters and musicians – and transform an abandoned theatre into a forum of avant-garde art; this, in the cultural capital of the world, and during a decade which was creatively the richest this century has seen.

The fact that they were Swedes is of no significance in itself: the Ballets Suédois, born in Paris, were immediately 'naturalized', becoming not French, but Parisian – in other words, universal.

Pre-war values no longer held good, but what were to be the new targets? No one could tell. The mark of the twenties was a kind of general uncertainty combined with astonishing mobility: monarchies were transformed into democracies or communes, princes turned into taxi drivers, newspaper vendors became millionaires and their daughters duchesses. Politics was currently a free for all and art could bring world acclaim overnight; inflation dissipated the soundest fortunes and new financial empires sprang up in the most unexpected ways; the sexes switched roles and love proclaimed itself free; uncomfortable clothing was thrust aside and prudish concealment gave way to open display – morality foundered as conventions were swept away.

The most ambiguous of all the arts, ballet, made its entrance and henceforth led the dance.

In this new society, where respect was said to be a forgotten word, dance became a respected art and the fine salons opened their doors even to dancers. On the dancing scene, all the arts united to create one total art, which was to reflect in depth the reality of life and seek to mark out the routes of the new world.

The motto of the Swedish painter Nils Dardel was: 'Why not the other way round?' This ironic gesture of his gave the Ballets Suédois their cue: what was no more than a talented artist's passing whim immediately assumed the form of an artistic laboratory where ideas were generated, assembled and tested.

At the beginning of the century, there were only a few ballet companies in existence, and all of these were attached to opera houses, trapped in a rigid system which segregated them from contemporary art. Today, the world is full of independent companies. In the space of a period no longer than an average life span, dance, more than any other art, has experienced an absolute explosion. This development, destined to turn a minor art into one of the most important, one of the most representative of our age, began through the initiative of a few private individuals who took the bold step of forming a dance ensemble, itinerant, living from day to day, autonomous, in order to be able to express itself with the utmost freedom.

The first innovative company to astound Paris, in 1909, was Diaghilev's Ballets Russes, with which the brilliant Fokine and the legendary and ill-fated Nijinsky were associated. A more modest company was also created by Pavlova, whose personality was adored the world over.

The third independent company, that of the Ballets Suédois, seems to be forgotten today. Which of us now remembers those Swedes who, for the first half of the twenties, held the centre stage of artistic life in Paris, and caused waves throughout Europe and America? Or the director, Rolf de Maré, who brought together Claudel, Cocteau, Picabia, Cendrars, Satie, Debussy, Honegger, Milhaud, Léger, Bonnard, de Chirico, Dardel and, not least, René Clair, in order to create that 'total art' so representative of the twentieth century? Or Jean Börlin, the choreographer who abolished the traditional frontiers between different types of dance and widened its scope? What does posterity remember of the richest, the most startling, theatrical adventure of the twenties?

MICHEL FOKINE

It all really began in 1913, when Stockholm's Royal Opera engaged Fokine as director of ballet, giving him *carte blanche* to organize the company as he chose (he had just fallen out with Diaghilev, with whom, over a four-year period, he had created the immensely successful Ballets Russes). Arriving in this sleepy little corner of Europe, Fokine found a ballet company that was trained along the lines of the classical French tradition. Thanks to their high level of technique, its dancers represented an artistic potential, but they were stagnating in a complete cultural backwater and their reputation was non-existent. Lacking for generations past a choreographer of real talent, they had principally been employed to appear in the ballet portions of the operas.

Fokine immediately set about modernizing this ballet company, establishing his own new, dramatic and much freer style. His *Cléopâtre* and *Les Sylphides* were an instant success and the following year he consolidated this triumph with *Sheherazade* in a décor by Bakst: the whole of Stockholm was suddenly in love with ballet.

Asserting that the Swedes were by now superior to the Ballets Russes (who, since his departure, he said, had been performing his masterpieces less well), Fokine then suggested to the Opera management that the company might go on tour to show his works abroad. He hoped thereby to provide serious competition for Diaghilev, whom he had not forgiven for preferring Nijinsky to himself. But the Royal Opera's conservative management balked at such a daring project: the company had never yet ventured outside its own theatre!

Fokine's career at the Stockholm Opera was in any case interrupted by the war, to which Sweden reacted by isolating herself in a prudent neutrality. Nothing came of his proposal.

ROLF DE MARÉ

During his time in Stockholm, Michel Fokine and his wife Vera were very much in the public eye and naturally received into high society. It was here that the couple met and struck up a friendship with Rolf de Maré, a great traveller and collector of contemporary Parisian art. He was grandson of a Swiss nobleman, Count Hallwyl, who had emigrated to Sweden and married the daughter of a very rich middle-class family. After the Russian revolution, the Fokines returned to Sweden, crossing the frozen Baltic by sleigh. But at that time the Opera preferred to stick, as an economy measure, to a ballet mistress from its own rank and file. The famous Russian couple were reduced to making a living for a while touring the provinces with a recital programme. Rolf de Maré invited them to stay on his estate in southern Sweden, within easy reach of Copenhagen. There Fokine told him about his project for a foreign tour, stressing that Stockholm possessed dancers of world-class ability: notably, Carina Ari, Jenny Hasselquist and, above all, the highly talented young Jean Börlin, whom Fokine had made a soloist in the Opera ballet.

De Maré was intrigued by the notion of a Swedish ballet company. But he went a step further – did not a Swedish ballet company require a Swedish choreographer? So he asked Nils Dardel for advice and, through him, made the acquaintance of Börlin. De Maré helped Fokine to open his own dance school in the vicinity of Copenhagen and persuaded Börlin to leave the Stockholm Opera, promising to pay him a salary while he was studying choreography with Fokine. During vacations, Jenny Hasselquist and Carina Ari, who had found themselves patrons, joined Fokine at their own expense.

De Maré had many friends in Parisian artistic circles, into which he had been introduced by his childhood pal and fellow aristocrat Nils (von) Dardel, who was to become one of Sweden's most important painters. Rolf de Maré's sole talent was his remarkable intuitive ability for discovering talent in others; in him, this had reached the level of virtual genius. During his lifetime, he was rarely to be mistaken about an artist's quality and future: practically all the young unknown painters, musicians, etc. to whom he drew attention would eventually be reckoned among the greatest.

De Maré was born in Stockholm in 1888. He was poorly educated and never learnt to write well. From earliest childhood he suffered from chronic asthma and, since it was thought that he would be unable to attend school normally, he was entrusted to the care of a tutor. He had musical skill, he could read a score with ease and was a good amateur piano player. In 1918, though he knew little about ballet, he was interested in folk-dance. Popular, spontaneous dancing had already more or less disappeared from the Swedish countryside, to crop up again as a fad in student circles. Since university students mostly belonged to the better-off classes, folk dancing became, on country estates, an entertainment for the masters. De Maré learnt the steps at his own manor and at those of his neighbours.

His delicate health meant that already when young he had to depend a great deal on his own resources. His mother, a gifted sculptress, divorced his father, an officer and courtier, and married her son's tutor, who was closer in age to the boy than to the mother. It was to be a happy marriage, the young husband eventually taking up the chair of history of art at the University of Stockholm. But the divorce caused a considerable scandal in good society. Rolf suffered as a consequence of this, maybe even more than as a result of his enforced isolation during periods of illness. He was always to maintain a sort of distance and reserve in relation to other people, though he also acquired exceptional will-power and great leadership abilities. Once he had decided on a project, he executed it with perseverance, skill, and generally success, oblivious of the opinion of those around him and of any difficulties which might arise.

He decided to open a dance theatre in Paris which would reflect the new French artistic spirit but whose members would be recruited in Sweden following Fokine's recommendations. He focused his attention on Jean Börlin, convinced of his talent. In this, he was influenced not least by the opinion of the master himself: Fokine (later) described how Börlin 'crossed the stage with great bounds, landed with all his force and glided over the boards among the group of bacchantes. What character! What ecstasy! . . . It was a revelation to me' (C.W. Beaumont, *The Complete Book of Ballets*, London, 1937). De Maré suspected that Fokine had already said all that he had to say, that no great innovative ideas could be expected from him – and time was to prove him right. Fokine was no doubt disappointed, though he never said or wrote a word to that effect. On the contrary, on Börlin's death he paid him the finest compliment he could ever have formulated: 'Börlin was the one who resembled me most.'

When Börlin prepared his first solo recital in Paris, Rolf de Maré discreetly set about putting together a company, while avoiding publicizing his plans for as long as possible. He needed a front man to hire dancers or, rather, lure them away from the Royal Opera, and in Jacques Hébertot he met just the man for the job. Hébertot was an ambitious young French journalist who had come to Stockholm at the head of a touring theatrical company. He became de Maré's private secretary and established contact with those young *danseuses* from the Royal Ballet whom de Maré and Börlin had singled out. Despite their competence, most of these girls had little hope of establishing a career, since they were pushed aside by a group of older dancers with powerful patrons; what is more, their salaries were meagre, and the ballets both few and far between, and inferior. All the young dancers with an artistic ambition felt frustrated by the fact that Fokine's brief renaissance had come to nothing. Hébertot turned this mood of discontent to account by offering double their current salaries. What he could offer above all was adventure, the opportunity to go off and conquer the world by dancing. With the exception of a couple of faint-hearts, all those who had been approached signed the contract right away. Hébertot then completed his task by hiring a number of first-class male dancers from the Royal Theatre in Copenhagen, which always had, and still has, talented dancers to spare.

Confronted with a stream of resignations, the management of the Stockholm Opera was at first panic-stricken, then furious: someone had had the temerity to take an interest in dancers whom the Opera itself held in the utmost contempt and to whom it refused any kind of promotion. The management brought its influence to bear on the right-wing press and, when it was discovered that the young aristocrat Rolf de Maré, an unknown in the world of theatre, was behind the whole thing, a violent smear campaign was launched against him. The theatre hired spies to operate in Paris, conveying back to Stockholm every smallest hint of criticism concerning de Maré and even inventing scandals. Rolf de Maré was thus persecuted in his own country, where the Ballets Suédois were described as a total fiasco. Swedish officialdom in Paris also did what it could to bring the Ballets into disrepute. The management of the Stockholm Opera published a lofty communiqué declaring that M. de Maré's private ballet company had no affinity whatsoever with the Royal Ballet – which, in itself, was perfectly correct. Exiled from the country of his birth, Rolf de Maré could scarcely show his face there again: obliged to set up home in Paris, he was to remain domiciled abroad for the rest of his life.

JEAN BÖRLIN

Jean Börlin was born in 1893 in a little town in the far north of Sweden. His father, a master mariner, travelled the seas far and wide, and it was from one of these voyages that he brought back a French Christian name for his son. Jean's mother suddenly left her husband for another man. A relative living in Stockholm, offering to bring up one of the numerous Börlin children, adopted Jean. His new family's means were slender, and since Jean showed a gift for music, he was enrolled at the Opera's ballet school, where the instruction was free; students could also make a little money for themselves by appearing as extras in the operas. As an adolescent, Jean gave up dance for a while in order to study singing, then later returned to ballet, which ensured modest but more frequent fees.

Jean Börlin was witty and fun-loving and the girls adored him. He was straightforward, loyal, hard-working and brimming with new ideas. His receptiveness and his thirst for knowledge were something quite out of the ordinary. He read a great deal and studied foreign languages untutored. He had a gift for adapting to new situations or different ways of thinking. In this respect, he was very like Rolf de Maré, five years his senior, but, in contrast to de Maré, Jean was jovial and easy-going. During his Paris years, surrounded by the talented but frequently egocentric and pretentious people of the artistic milieu, the young provincial choreographer was completely in his element, transposing their brilliant conceptions on to the stage with an exactness of touch. In this respect too, Jean was valued, even if he remained unknown to some, so little importance did he place on his own reputation and so readily did he seek to enhance that of others. When it came to his own art, however, he rejected all compromise. Mastering classical technique to perfection, he needed no roots and no tradition: he was, on the contrary, a man of his time, ready to contribute to an artistic renewal which he sensed to be a necessity.

In 1918, Börlin was twenty-five. Like Fokine at the same age, when the latter was working at Saint Petersburg's imperial theatre, Börlin had not yet had the opportunity to direct a ballet at Stockholm's Opera. And yet, like Fokine, at twenty-five he was already an experienced choreographer: during the Opera's holiday periods, he had been responsible for choreographing several pieces for occasional shows or for his own recitals.

He spent the year before the inception of the Ballets Suédois travelling and studying throughout Europe, at de Maré's expense. His aim was to familiarize himself with the new artistic currents, emanating principally from Central Europe. In Stockholm, he had seen Isadora Duncan in 1906 and Émile Jacques-Dalcroze in 1911, when the latter was on the point of giving definitive form to his eurhythmics – it was precisely at this time that Börlin was pondering whether to devote himself to singing or to return to dance. Duncan and Jacques-Dalcroze exerted a great influence on him, as they had on Fokine, who would often refer to the importance these two artists held for him.

We do not know exactly where Börlin studied during his European odyssey. It is likely that he went to the Hellerau school, and Rolf de Maré later stated that Börlin had been at Jacques-Dalcroze's establishment, in Geneva, at the time when the latter was writing his fundamental work, *Le Rythme, la Musique et l'Éducation* (Rhythm, Music and Education), published the following year.

Jean Börlin was modesty itself, apart from which, of course, he was still unknown abroad. Mary Wigman vaguely remembered him, and that, in 1919, he came and stayed with her in Zurich, where she was just then enjoying a decisive success as a soloist, before going on to open her dance school in Dresden the following year. In Zurich, Börlin may have come into contact with the Dadaists, as Suzanne Perrottet (Laban's then wife) later claimed.

Rudolf von Laban, meanwhile, left Zurich in 1919 for Germany. Laban's conceptions had been influenced by the dances of the whirling dervishes. Börlin had witnessed these in North Africa, and it was on this same theme that he created a five-man ballet, one of his successes in the Ballets Suédois' opening programme in Paris in 1920. Börlin's researches also included Spanish dance, which he studied with the great Otero and which was to be reflected in his ballet *Iberia*. El Greco's paintings in Toledo and Madrid completed the impressions he would have formed of the four paintings (either by the master or by his school) in Rolf de Maré's collection. And, finally, the art dealer Alfred Flechtheim opened Börlin's eyes to abstract and futurist Expressionist painting, which provided the inspiration for his pioneering Expressionist ballets.

We can find numerous traces and indications of the contacts Börlin made during this year of intensive foreign study. He orientated himself on contemporary tendencies in the art of dance, certainly, but, profiting from what Fokine had taught him, he used his knowledge as a springboard from which to create his own distinct and original work.

In the first interview given by him in France (*Comœdia*, 1920), Börlin expressed his admiration for the Russians and rendered warm homage to Fokine: 'I owe him so much and dance today owes him everything. He has truly been my teacher, and one who was kind enough to look upon me as a friend and collaborator.' But, more precisely, he said that he was looking for a path 'that I want to be personal and which I hope is original'.

LES
Ballets Suédois
ROLF DE MARÉ
DIRECTOR

THE SNARE by Hélène Perdriat and Germaine Tailleferre — THE FOOLISH VIRGINS by Kurt Atterberg and Einar Nerman — DANSGILLE by Jean Borlin and Eugène Bigot — IBERIA by I. Albeniz and Steinlen. — CREATION by Blaise Cendrars, Fernand Léger and Darius Milhaud — MIDSUMMER NIGHT'S REVEL by Hugo Alfvén and Nils de Dardel — L'HOMME ET SON DÉSIR by Paul Claudel, Andrée Parr and Darius Milhaud — THE TOY SHOP by Andre Hellé and Claude Debussy — SKATING RINK by Canudo, Fernand Léger and A. Honegger — EL GRECO by Jean Borlin and Inghelbrecht — THE NEWLYWEDS ON THE EIFFEL TOWER by Jean Cocteau, Irène Lagut, Jean Hugo and the " Six " — JEUX by Claude Debussy and Bonnard — THE MADHOUSE by Jean Borlin, Viking Dahl and Nils de Dardel — LE TOMBEAU DE COUPERIN by Maurice Ravel and Laprade — WITHIN THE QUOTA by Gerald Murphy and Cole Porter — DERVISHES by Jean Borlin — and Glazounow —

IN PARIS — LONDON
STOCKHOLM — GLASGOW
NICE — MADRID — GOTHEN-
BURG — BRUSSELS — BORDEAUX
BUDA-PEST — COPENHAGEN — MILAN
DUSSELDORF — CHRISTIANIA — VENICE
BERLIN — BARCELONA — FLORENCE
HAMBURG — VIENNA — COLOGNE — NANCY
AND OTHER EUROPEAN CITIES

1 9 2 0

PARIS DÉBUT

On 25 March 1920, the Parisian public had its first taste of Börlin's talent when he gave a solo performance at the Comédie des Champs-Élysées. The programme, which was repeated on three consecutive evenings, comprised seven compositions performed without décor of any sort, against a simple, neutral backdrop. The only outlay was for a forty-five-piece orchestra conducted by D.E. Inghelbrecht, which also played musical interludes to give the dancer time to change costumes.

The most startling piece of this first performance appears to have been *Sculpture nègre* (Negro Sculpture), with Börlin, dressed in a costume imitating an African statuette carved in wood (of which an echo was later to be found in *La Création du monde* [The Creation of the World]), dancing in ponderous fashion: 'The body's flexible points all bend as if under the weight of an abominable compulsion.... It rose up, slowly and as if ossified by years of contemplative immobility. And what this god unveiled before our eyes was the primitive eurhythmics of the first beings: an extraordinary vision in three-dimensional form', commented the critic Pierre Scize.

In another composition, *Devant la mort* (Facing Death), Börlin appeared 'like a Christ descended from a medieval cross' (Paul Sentenac, in *La Renaissance*). 'The body burnt and emaciated, movements angular and distorted, contours sharp as if chiselled, he conveys an impression almost like [that of] a hieratic super-reality' (Paul Abram, *Eve*, 29 March). This was a fully fledged Expressionist essay, later enlarged in the ballet *El Greco*.

Danse céleste (Celestial Dance) was inspired by Siamese dances. It was well received, generally considered just an 'exotic' piece of choreography, in the genre launched by Fokine. But it was a more conscientiously studied work than it seemed. Ten years earlier, Rolf de Maré had filmed court dances in Bangkok. Börlin studied this and other material. His dance was moulded on authentic choreography and executed throughout in a low 'plié' (a seemingly sitting position), which expresses the 'proximity of the earth' in Hindu dancing, and which has also become a fundamental ingredient in modern Western dance.

Börlin's programme also included a Swedish Folk-Dance. Folk-dances are in themselves monotonous and repetitive, conceived with participants rather than spectators in mind, but, once again, Börlin attempted a new approach: a choreographic composition which, under its theatrical garb, still retained a dimension of authenticity. He would return to this idea in a more ambitious way in his later work *Nuit de Saint-Jean* (Midsummer Night's Revel), which represented a truly new dance genre: the first modern folk ballet.

Despite a few critics who vaguely complained of the musical interludes, finding the performance too long, Börlin's Paris début was a resounding success: 'We need merely consider that Jean Börlin is the sole hero of an evening's performance . . . in order to grasp the astonishing wealth of his resources, his undeniable personality and the exceptional quality of his authority. The general history of theatre is marked out by a handful of important dates: Jean Börlin's performance will mark one such date in the evolution of dance' (*Paris-Journal*, 3 April 1920); 'This dancer, whose sensitivity, intelligence and technique are incomparable, takes his place with dignity in the illustrious family of the Duncans, Nijinskys, Pavlovas and Fokines' (René Bruyez).

In *Le Figaro* (27 March), Antoine Banès wrote that Börlin's artistic contribution was 'of major importance . . . in no way surpassed by Russia from a choreographic point of view.... Jean Börlin is a truly extraordinary person, much inspired – though with the addition of a personal note – by the theories of Isadora Duncan and Nijinsky.' Louis Laloy, in *Comœdia* (6 March), recalled that, in her time, Isadora Duncan had been capable of 'maintaining interest in an evening programme entirely by her own efforts', a feat even Pavlova had not dared to risk; and, stressing Börlin's similar success, he remarked: 'With no other back-up than that of an orchestra, he succeeds in holding the interest of an entire auditorium for two hours . . .'.

The critics immediately seized on the notion of Börlin's 'originality', and in *Bonsoir* (26 March) Pierre Scize offered what he himself called 'a very rare piece of praise' when he wrote that 'Jean Börlin's stylistic researches are launched in a highly modern direction. . . . His dancing is characterized less by virtuosity, for all that it recalls the supple contortions of the Russians, than by a certain heaviness which appears to be deliberate . . .'.

The critics were surprised by this unfamiliar kind of dance, the emerging 'free' or 'modern' dance, which did not aspire to a light and airy grace, but sought to develop like a plant pushing up from the soil. It treated the ground as a partner and emphasized the natural heaviness of the dancing body instead of trying to disguise its weight. When we look back today on the evolution of modern dance, it is easy to see the place which Börlin occupies as an innovator. He based his ideas on the 'natural' movements of the emerging Central European school, distancing himself from the classical and academic discipline of the style which he had practised at ballet school. This total, free and supple expressivity centred round a mobile trunk was something Fokine had narrowly failed to discover. Laban was in the process of experimenting but had not yet fully conceptualized the new aesthetic (*Die Welt des Tänzers* [The World of the Dancer] was about to be published, in 1920). In his choreographies, Börlin, at that time, was putting such theories into practice in an accomplished form.

Thus, before the inception of the Ballets Suédois, Börlin had already found a direction of his own, and his solo recital of spring 1920 embodied characteristics of his later fully articulated creations. During the next five years, he would present the new 'free dance' and its totally expressive body language in the form of large-scale ballets – one of the first to do so. He was finally to push still further beyond the limits of what had previously been defined as 'dance'. Börlin's first bold initiative was taken up by others after the war and is one of the characteristic features of today's modern dance.

25 OCTOBER

Rolf de Maré had chosen a good moment to acquire a seven-year lease on the Théâtre des Champs-Élysées, which was having great difficulties starting up again after its closure during the war. He decided to keep Hébertot on, in an administrative capacity. The huge theatre, one of the finest examples of early nineteenth-century architecture, decorated with numerous bas-reliefs and sculptures by Antoine Bourdelle representing Isadora Duncan, offered the Ballets Suédois spacious premises for their performances. When the company was on tour, de Maré hired out the theatre to other companies, in particular to Diaghilev's Ballets Russes.

Rolf de Maré wanted his Théâtre des Champs-Élysées to become the centre of Parisian artistic life, with the Ballets Suédois as its pivot.

Monday 25 October 1920 is the official date for the Ballets Suédois' première. But, as was customary, the preceding Saturday was the occasion for the press preview, to which critics and eminent personalities – in short, all those responsible for forming public opinion – were invited.

IBERIA

Iberia opened the Ballets Suédois' programme with a wonderfully lavish spectacle. The old painter Alexandre Steinlen, adored by the French, created three immense Spanish sceneries and designed hundreds of brightly coloured costumes, not merely for the dancers (who each had at least three changes in the course of the ballet), but also for the swarming crowd of extras. The conductor, D.E. Inghelbrecht, made an elegant orchestration of a piano suite by Isaac Albéniz.

With *Iberia*, Börlin aimed at a synthesis of Spanish daily life and the atmosphere of Spain in a festival mood. The choreography, rather than comprising well-known popular dances, or flamenco, was based on the Spaniards' natural movements, reflecting a human behaviour and body language that is characteristically Iberian. Only when the action demanded it were authentic dances inserted. Börlin and Carina Ari were highly praised for their dancing abilities, but the critics were nevertheless disconcerted. For the past hundred years, dancers from Spain had regularly been performing in Paris, and Argentina was the darling of the Parisians. The previous year, Diaghilev's company had performed a ballet by Léonide Massine, *Le Tricorne* (The Three-Cornered Hat), comprising authentic Spanish dances incorporated into a dramatic story. Now, *Iberia* was completely different: a broad and lush down-to-earth portrayal of a Spain which Börlin adored, in which the action itself was relatively insignificant. This result was obtained by a complex but well-concealed choreographic scheme. Börlin's realism was subtly stylized, just enough to suit the demands of the stage, without detracting from the verisimilitude. *Iberia* marked the beginning of a trend in choreography which might be called a realistic dance theatre.

JEUX (GAMES)

The inaugural programme continued with *Jeux* (Games), Debussy's final masterpiece, which Nijinsky had choreographed and danced for the Ballets Russes' 1913 season at the Théâtre des Champs-Élysées.

There were several reasons which led Rolf de Maré to take up a work created by his predecessor Diaghilev. His most influential artistic collaborator after Börlin was the conductor Inghelbrecht, who had been a pupil of Debussy and had been present during the composition of *Jeux*. Like the rest of the young musical world in Paris, he keenly regretted that this masterpiece was given only a very few performances, and had not been played at all for many years. The reason was simply the highly personalized choreography which Nijinsky had conceived for his own part, and which nobody but he could dance.

From a historical point of view, all of Nijinsky's four ballets represent important moments in the evolution of dance. Predating Börlin's work by six or seven years, these ballets were extremely advanced and, at the time, were accepted by few in the audience.

In *Jeux*, as Louis Scheider notes, 'he [Nijinsky] forced Debussy's music to signify I know not what bizarre civilization, where baroque characters perambulated in capriciously extravagant motion'. Pierre Scize found that Nijinsky 'made of *Jeux* a vast and violent canvas on which charm was partially submerged beneath I know not what barbaric, oriental cruelty... almost sadistic . . . interpretation'.

When he composed his music, Debussy had entertained a different vision, involving a realistic action: the libretto referred to a tennis game between a young man and two young women, with a background atmosphere and impressions that were subtle, sensual and fleeting. Inghelbrecht knew as much, having it from Debussy himself. In conjunction with other specialists, he regarded Nijinsky's interpretation as incompatible with the music and helped Börlin analyse the intentions of the score, which appealed to the dancer's deep musical sense.

Börlin accepted the task of re-creating the long-regretted ballet. He knew the risk he was running by taking on a role in which the incomparable, the unique Nijinsky had shone (though in fact he had never had the opportunity to see Nijinsky dance). But, in seeking above all to convey, with subtlety and warmth, a realistic game and the human emotions involved, Börlin's choreography uncovered new aspects of the work.

The lyrical atmosphere, marked by youthful sensuality and innocence, Debussy's elegant music and Bonnard's stunningly beautiful new décor – a subtle cameo of greens and blues – combined to make *Jeux* a huge success with the public. This ballet was to be performed twenty-nine times that first year, and the critics praised the Swedes for having saved Debussy's last masterpiece from unmerited neglect.

NUIT DE SAINT-JEAN (MIDSUMMER NIGHT'S REVEL)

So far the Ballets Suédois had in no way justified their name. However, to close the programme of the première, they did perform a ballet on a native theme, *Nuit de Saint-Jean* (Midsummer Night's Revel). The action revolved around the midsummer night's revels held in any little village in Sweden. Nils Dardel's splendid décor, involving peasants dressed in pastel costumes dancing around a maypole, was colourful and the whole ballet was elegant and sophisticated, lit with a gleam of humour.

Börlin, like de Maré, took an interest in folk-dance. Transposing on to a stage a dance form intended for performance rather than for viewing is not an easy thing. A hundred years earlier, a ballet master with Stockholm's Royal Opera had devoted his whole life to choreographing Swedish popular dances. Reviving the tradition, Börlin went to the root of the matter, exclusively using, for the choreography of an entire ballet, movements and steps from folk-dance, which he stylized by organizing and expanding them. He established the aesthetic principle of what one might call an abstract folk choreography.

Over the course of time, choreographers had inserted borrowed elements of folk-dance in classical ballets, but this was the first time that a complete ballet had been staged using nothing but authentic folk-dance steps: a novelty in Western ballet.

In 1937, a classical Soviet choreographer, Igor Moisseiev, was to follow Börlin's lead, without having access to his predecessor's works except through descriptions given by de Maré during conferences on official invitations to the USSR, in 1932 and 1936. This type of people's ballet was to enjoy great success and gradually set an international trend, with each country, and not least the newly independent, former colonies, creating its own national ensemble.

Nuit de Saint-Jean and *Dansgille*, created the following year, were typical of a new theatrical genre, representing an event which has been overlooked by historians of dance, although these two ballets were performed almost two hundred and fifty times apiece, in Europe and the United States, during the Ballets Suédois' five-year career.

Rolf de Maré's company had got off to a smooth start. There was as yet nothing shocking in its programme. The Parisians took to this début, but the press gave the ballets a rather cool reception: they were reserving judgment. The first bombshell was to explode two weeks later.

8 NOVEMBER
MAISON DE FOUS
(THE MADHOUSE)

The Ballets Suédois' second programme opened on 8 November 1920 with *Maison de fous* (The Madhouse), the first Expressionist ballet. The curtain went up on a décor by Nils Dardel: on the backdrop, a monumental creature held out a pair of immense hands, knotted and deformed with pain or madness. According to a long-established rule, a ballet décor should not distract attention from the dancers. Dardel did the absolute opposite. A particularly strong performance would be required if the choreography was to hold its own in front of the enormous painted monster, whose hands hovered over the dancers' heads.

Börlin took up the challenge, peopling the stage with creatures each of whom, through various movements, expressed a particular form of madness. These deeply disturbed figures, in the throes of some violent passion, manifested their despair or their aggression by silent gestures. Like lone wolves, they rarely found a moment's togetherness.

The narrative thread is as follows: a young woman, the only normal being in the midst of these lunatics, becomes attached to a young man who is obsessed with the idea that he is king; in the end, fear drives the woman mad too and the man she loves strangles her.

Each role was individualized, characterized by its own particular contortions. The internal drama of each of the personalities was simultaneously juxtaposed with that of each of the others. The spectators' attention was thus split and their eyes were drawn towards several parts of the stage at once, where as many mini-dramas were in the process of being enacted as there were characters on stage. The public was tortured by the difficulty of making a choice between these multiple actions all taking place simultaneously.

Poorly represented in France and England, Expressionist dance was developing at that time in Central Europe, and also in the United States, generally in the form of solos executed by the new 'free dancers' in recitals. Börlin was familiar with this type of Expressionist dance, as he was with the similar schools in painting and literature. In *Maison de fous*, he created a large-scale composition, drawing inspiration from his fellow-countryman the writer Pär Lagerkvist, from whom, like Dardel, he borrowed certain motifs.

Moreover, Börlin required the dancers themselves to participate in the creative act: they were asked to suggest their own movements according to their feelings about the roles. Then Börlin selected and assembled their individual choreographies into a unified, complete composition. It was a team-work method which was to be much practised in modern dance, particularly by Kurt Jooss.

Expressionist dance presupposed that the dancer gave free rein to those intimate feelings which were generally kept under wraps. The freer they were, the more interesting they were; and the more intense, the more readily they would find that sensitive spot in the spectator's emotions. 'Expressions' would elicit protest or pity, or, again, provoke secret, disturbing identifications. For the artists, the important thing was to discover that point of intersection between the raw material and the artistic discipline which teetered on the verge of the unendurable. In *Maison de fous*, Expressionism – which represented only one of the contemporary currents which Börlin's choreography sought to interpret – attained a high level of intensity.

During their Central European tour to follow, the Ballets Suédois were greeted with enthusiasm. Fellow dancers there viewed Börlin as a flag bearer, someone who had succeeded in exercising a new art at the head of an important company, enjoying the benefits of a large orchestra and having scenography of opera house quality at his disposal, while they had to be content with hiring a platform and a piano.

The musical score of *Maison de fous* was the work of Viking Dahl, a twenty-three-year-old Swede, an admirer of Stravinsky, as *Paris-Midi* (9 November) emphasized, adding, however, the criticism: 'Listening to this music, one is for ever waiting for something that never comes.' But, in reality, Dahl had deliberately sought this effect in order to reinforce the suffocating atmosphere of the ballet. In his lifetime, he was rarely played and appreciated even less; following his stay in Paris, he was to return to Sweden and bury himself as an organist in a small provincial town. After his death, his country finally recognized Dahl as one of its distinguished composers.

The name of Pär Lagerkvist did not appear on the programme, but *Le Figaro* devoted a few lines to him nevertheless: 'He is said to be quite a young man, recently come down from his mountain home in Scandinavia with the firm intention of taking the world by storm. So far he has only succeeded in making himself look ridiculous. . . . Let this catastrophe be a lesson to all who suffer from the sin of presumption!' Later, in 1951, Lagerkvist was to console himself by receiving the Nobel prize for literature.

An article by Lucien Dubeck, in *L'Action française* (15 November), makes a comparison which clearly reveals the criteria on which many contemporary critics based their judgments: 'If dance is not intended to show us beautiful rhythms, where then should we look for them? None of the Russian ballets, not even the boldest, not even *Le Sacre du printemps*, transgressed that law' – and he continues reproachfully to point out that this fault was an indulgence exclusive to the Swedes.

Rolf de Maré, for his part, regarded all the negative or even malevolent criticisms of which he was the brunt as proof that some of his ideas had managed to stick. His adherence to Expressionism represented the search, not for beauty, but for what he conceived of as a neglected reality: dance no longer expressed merely the pleasure and charm of life, but also its horror and suffering. The Ballets Russes had gained their victories by cultivating their classical inheritance and the aestheticism of the *Belle Époque*. Eleven years separated the respective débuts of the Ballets Russes and the Ballets Suédois, and, owing to the war, those eleven years had accounted for a new epoch coming to the fore.

In 1920, Diaghilev, now exiled, was searching for a new anchorage, a new *raison d'être*, in an alien world, a world in which Rolf de Maré felt completely at home, while Börlin, for his part, had never known any other. As for the dancers of the Ballets Suédois, they had been no more than children during the war, and were still very young.

Rolf de Maré had a deep respect for Serge Diaghilev. The two had much in common and ought to have become friends. De Maré would have liked to learn from his older colleague's experiences. But Diaghilev avoided him and was courteous but distant on the rare occasions when they met. (This was generally when the Russians needed to use the Swedes' theatre, or when Diaghilev came to see their performances – he saw them all, in fact.)

The première of *Maison de fous* was unanimously slaughtered by the French critics, who regarded the ballet as an affront. Their numerous articles are a veritable anthology of vicious, scornful and arrogant turns of phrase. Many critics were amazed that the audience remained silent during the forty-five-minute-long ballet and that no one whistled before the curtain fell, while several journalists noted that, in spite of everything, half the audience clapped.

One person made the ironic remark that the Swedes had succeeded in setting the public's teeth on edge, and that 'that's just what they want'. But this was not at all the case. The company was not experienced enough to realize that in the Paris theatrical world a scandal could serve their cause. Börlin was bitter: the critics were accusing him of incompetence, and no one seemed to understand that he was suggesting to them a deliberately new kind of ballet. The young ballerinas had worked hard to distort their naturally attractive looks and were mortified to see Henri Frossard write in *La Démocratie nouvelle* (11 November): 'If our ballets [at the Opéra] are no more intelligent . . . our ballerinas are a pleasure to look at. . . . If I were going to assemble a harem, I wouldn't recruit it in Sweden.'

LE TOMBEAU DE COUPERIN

The second new work on the programme, *Le Tombeau de Couperin*, was to cool the general excitement, however. It comprised a suite of six piano pieces, recently completed by Maurice Ravel, who was to orchestrate three for the Ballets Suédois: 'One might have expected this suite to be performed by the Ballets Russes. But, on the contrary, it was presented by the Ballets Suédois', remarked Adolphe Boschot in *L'Écho de Paris* (10 November 1920). Journalists were entranced by the music, commenting: 'the most exquisite of things', 'an absolute masterpiece: such nobility, style, quality, something really great, in short'.

The popular Pierre Laprade painted a French-style garden full of atmosphere, and was admired for his costumes, even if a handful of cultured critics reproached him for lapsing now and again from the Louis XV style, particularly in the case of Börlin's costume which, for no apparent reason, tended more towards the *Directoire*.

Börlin choreographed a forlana, a minuet and a rigaudon. These were style dances which he knew well, since the old, distinguished French dances were still being performed in Stockholm, whose ballet company had been founded in the eighteenth century – as it happens, by French dancers. With regard to Börlin's own interpretation, and the other dancers' as well, the critics were rather patronizing. No dramatic action was involved, just dances, pure and simple, 'imbued with a dream-like languor, a whimsical grace, a mysterious and enchanting softness' (*La Liberté*, 17 November 1920).

The dark forebodings expressed during the interval by a section of the audience, who feared that lunatics would soon be followed by phantoms, thus revealed themselves to be unfounded. Indeed, *tombeau* (tomb) has no sinister significance here: it was a term (no longer in use) employed in the eighteenth century to designate the work which a new Master of the Chapel Royal composed in honour of his predecessor, whether the latter were currently living or dead.

For the hundred and fiftieth performance of *Le Tombeau de Couperin*, the composer himself would be conducting.

The success enjoyed by this inoffensive work did not, however, manage to dispel the impression that the Swedish ballet company was an unwelcome upstart. The memory of the absent Russians still lingered in people's minds, and the fact that the Paris Opéra's ballet company was currently the object of ridicule, and that Paris could boast no other, did nothing to change matters: the Swedes continued to be treated as undesirable guests.

And then, suddenly, a surprising and rapid volte-face took place and, at the company's third première, on Thursday 18 November, the situation swung the other way. The signal for this reversal was given with *El Greco* and *Les Vierges folles* (The Foolish Virgins), which framed a traditional pas de deux set to music by Chopin.

18 NOVEMBER
EL GRECO

On 18 November 1920, the third première opened with *El Greco*, described in the programme as 'mimed scenes'. It contained nothing that was currently understood as dance. (Today's norms are quite different and no one accustomed to the post-modernists would hesitate to consider *El Greco* as ballet.) The scene was transformed into a three-dimensional painting by El Greco, or rather an all-embracing synthesis of his pictorial universe, for which the Paris Opéra's head scene painter, Mouveau, accurately re-created the palette and visual language of the Spanish master.

The painting of El Greco is full of movement, as represented by sweeping gestures, attitudes requiring the participation of the whole body and in particular that of the head and torso, and intense facial expressions. His figures appear to be on the point

of breaking out of the frame, ready to unfold their limbs in open space: there is no painter whose work is more akin to dance than El Greco.

He has in common with the twenties a violent expressivity, if not to say Expressionism in the modern sense. El Greco's art transcends the limits of narration almost to the point of becoming an abstract game, taking as its objective expressivity itself. His message is simply a feeling, an atmosphere, intense and impossible to define in words, a mystical emotion directly transmitted to the spectator. Like dance itself, El Greco's painting has the power to convey the artist's feelings to the spectator without resorting to the medium of words.

Börlin peopled the scene with figures from the great Mannerist painter. As with El Greco, the focus of activity lay in arms, torso and head. There was less emphasis on legs: the characters, more or less glued to the stage, danced on the spot. Such intense use of movement and mime is of course the opposite of a *tableau vivant*, which is static. But the idea that one could dance while remaining in one place was so novel that many of the spectators were disconcerted. To help them get round this problem Börlin, by a subtle psychological manoeuvre, called the work 'mimed scenes'. And, in point of fact, several critics seemed to be relieved, presumably relying on the rationale: 'Ah! Since he doesn't insist on calling it ballet, we can go ahead and judge this production in terms of what it seems to be.'

The argument remained secondary, and in watching the production, the audience would scarcely have been able to grasp its meaning. It was the dynamic of the ballet that was the essential thing: El Greco's baroque passion expressed through ash grey and indigo, sulphur yellow and watery green, pink and rust; human beings, activated, as it were, by an invisible scourge, breaking loose, appealing in the secret language of their muteness, convulsing under the effect of a profound inner anguish; human beings from another world crossing the centuries to encounter contemporary Expressionism and its need to give free rein to the passions and torments of our age.

Having first arranged the entire choreography without music, Börlin asked Inghelbrecht to compose the score. This old-fashioned method of working (it was current in the nineteenth century and had long since been abandoned) turned out to be appropriate thanks to Inghelbrecht's ability to free himself from the influence of his teacher Debussy and engage in the new movement. Börlin, capable of reading the most complicated score with ease, watched the creation of the music, step by step.

Inghelbrecht was one of the most highly regarded conductors in France, his reputation deriving above all from the symphonies he conducted, played by the full symphony orchestra of the Théâtre des Champs-Élysées, on those days when the ballet company was not performing. He was a great asset to the Ballets Suédois and also introduced the new young composers of the day to Börlin and de Maré.

El Greco was thus the second large Expressionist ballet, following closely on the heels of *Maison de fous*, on which it threw a new light and whose reputation it helped to establish. Börlin, in the principal role, was much applauded: he was 'the very incarnation of the naked young man with his half-crazed eyes and ascetic face, swarthy but pale, his close-cropped skull and puny beard, in whom El Greco's entire art is summed up and condensed', according to *Paris-Journal*, which also noted 'the ever-changing facial expressions and the perpetual mobility of the arms' exhibited by Börlin as well as by his partner Jolanda Figoni. In *Excelsior*, Reynaldo Hahn stressed that Börlin 'has also sought to render the passionate feeling and, as it were, the ecstatic frenzy of the master of Toledo. . . . He has succeeded in re-creating the same atmosphere of delirium.' 'The ballet's structural composition is perfect from every point of view', Pierre Scize summed up, adding: 'and, above all, one recognizes that this effort is primarily intellectual'.

DERVICHES
(DERVISHES)

An interlude between the two substantial works of the evening consisted of Börlin's solo *Derviches* (Dervishes), taken from his recital programme but now enlarged through the addition of a further four dancers.

The dancing dervishes of the Near East had fascinated travellers, particularly the English, and are described in many of their books. Rudolf von Laban noted two things (which also struck Börlin, independently but somewhat later) in these religious rituals: that the dance concentrated on the upper part of the body while movements retained an intimate contact with the earth – thanks to the dancers' relaxed plié position – and that the choreography and the music seemed to function independently of one another. Both these phenomena had links with the new concept of modern dance, and Laban amalgamated the dervish dance with the modern dancers' spiritual inheritance.

LES VIERGES FOLLES
(THE FOOLISH VIRGINS)

Despite the success of *El Greco*, *Les Vierges folles* (The Foolish Virgins) struck Antoine Banès of *Le Figaro* as 'the chief attraction of the evening'. It was an entirely Swedish ballet, inspired by eighteenth-century naïve painting, in which a number of characters from biblical parables were depicted dressed in the costumes of the age – the only ones known to those uneducated peasant painters. The Swedish artist Einar Nerman had created a décor and costumes of a highly refined naïve stylization, and young Kurt Atterberg, who was to number among Sweden's top composers, had written a score which received the praise of the music critics.

The clear, uncomplicated theme of the ballet was that of the parable of the wise and foolish virgins. It was an exquisitely elegant little piece, subtly choreographed by Börlin, who punctuated it with irony, mischievousness and humour. The public was highly entertained. 'The audience's laughter was more joyful and more ingenuous than I've ever heard', reported Paul Lombard in *L'Homme libéré*. 'Jean Börlin seems to become progressively more and more Parisian', wrote Raymond Charpentier in *Comœdia*. Could one wish for greater praise?

Les Vierges folles, performed 375 times in five seasons, was to be the Ballets Suédois' staple resource.

By simply introducing a traditional pas de deux between *El Greco* and *Les Vierges folles* (each the sincere expression of his choreographic intentions), Börlin was indulging himself in a manner that bordered on the impertinent. Jenny Hasselquist was a classical ballerina – even though she possessed an unusually broad repertoire, extending to the dramatic – and she had not yet had the opportunity to show Paris her purely academic dancing abilities – any more than the other dancers in the company, including Börlin himself, all of whom had an excellent classical technique.

De Maré got Eugène Bigot, the assistant conductor, to orchestrate a few pieces by Chopin, and Börlin created a choreography in the style of Fokine's *Les Sylphides*, in other words, using nuances, a flexibility and arm work that were more supple than in the classicism of the turn of the century, but which demanded of the dancer the same technical virtuosity in point work. He 'shows us a new side to the talent of these excellent dancers', wrote Raoul Brunel in *L'Aurore*. Börlin 'demonstrated a most remarkable suppleness and virtuosity' and Hasselquist 'executed points I didn't know she was capable of', noted Georges Boyer in *Le Petit-Journal*. 'An utterly Pavlovian grace and finesse', wrote Reynaldo Hahn in *Excelsior*, thus forging a neologism. Börlin, on the other hand, was severely criticized, in de Maré's place, for the orchestration of Chopin's beautiful piano music: 'Even given the best of transcriptions, it amounts to a trivialization' was an opinion shared by a whole string of critics, who employed numerous arguments to back their case; it 'reminds one of the nocturnal hum of a fairground'.

The music of a classical ballet was viewed at the time with much more seriousness than it is today, modern spectators tending to regard it rather as an accompaniment, sometimes simply as performing the function of a metronome. But, in the twenties, music and choreography were supposed to display a correspondence, an internal harmony, which created an essential unity between them. The music was preferably to be composed specially to be danced; and if the choreographer chose an existing work, he was supposed to conform closely to it, indeed to submit to it entirely, while interpreting the music. Isadora Duncan made movements evolve from music, while Fokine argued in favour of a coordinated creation in which composer

Les Ballets
Suédois de Rolf de
Maré ont promené à travers
le Monde les noms des plus
grands auteurs, des peintres les
plus modernes, des musiciens les
plus hardis. ● ▬▬▬▬▬▬
Les Ballets Suédois ont sauté à pieds
joints par=dessus les lieux communs
chorégraphiques. Ils s'en portent
fort bien. Ils veulent du nouveau.
▬▬▬▬▬● Le Ballet moderne,
c'est la Poésie, la Peinture, la
Musique autant que la Danse :
Synthèse de la Vie
Intellectuelle d'au=
● Les jourd'hui. ●
Ballets Sué= ●
dois méprisent
tous les préjugés,
ils vivent dans
l'espace et non
● Pour pas dans le
les Ballets ● temps. ●
Suédois, le but
est toujours le
● point de dé=
● Les Bal- ● part. ●
lets Suédois ne se
réclament de personne,
ne suivent personne. Ils
ont l'amour du len-
● demain. ● Les ●
Ballets Suédois
provoquent des enthou-
siasmes et des colères :
c'est qu'ils vi-
● vent. ●
● Et
demain les
Ballets Suédois
iront encore
plus en a-
● vant. ●

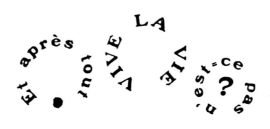

and choreographer worked side by side, although, for practical reasons, he rarely succeeded in putting this principle into action. And yet, Fokine's precept was probably more diligently followed by the Ballets Suédois than by any other company.

Börlin and de Maré were in tacit agreement with the critics regarding the orchestration of Chopin's music. Piano music used as an accompaniment to a ballet in a large theatre was out of the question, and yet the company's excellent classical dancers also had the right to show what, by dint of such hard work, they had spent half their young lives learning: classical dance in its pure form. As a result, Börlin expanded his pas de deux, which became a long, purely classical suite entitled *Chopiniana*. The beautiful piece of work was to enjoy a huge success with a wide public. It was performed two hundred and eighty-five times, but only on tour: de Maré and Börlin had too great a respect for French taste ever to put it on again in Paris.

The press, won over by the two great creations of the evening, *El Greco* and *Les Vierges folles*, and impressed by the Swedes' performances, stressed that in three weeks – between 25 October and 18 November – Börlin had put on nine world premières, each one different from the others: on the part of a single choreographer, that was a veritable test of strength. In each ballet, Börlin himself danced in a principal role, mastering the broadest repertoire of steps yet seen (discounting the totally exceptional Nijinsky), from pure classical ballet to modern free expression.

Between 18 and 20 November, in the space of three days, from Friday to Sunday morning, the Ballets Suédois were re-evaluated, now to be praised to the skies. Landret, in *La Rampe*, summed up the situation thus: 'It has to be said that no spectacle ever aroused so much loathing as the productions staged by the Ballets Suédois. All the regular critics of the new gathered together to slate this young company which, in the very opinion of painters and musicians, brings us the first fruits of a modern choreographic art.' Even *Maison de fous*, recently the victim of invectives, was now totally reappraised. 'This work is indeed conceived in the new spirit . . . purely representative of a Northern, thinking art. The music, the décors and the costumes frame this admirable choreography with a happy personal note . . . a spectacle possessing a precious unity.'

That same day, *Le Journal du peuple* wrote of *Maison de fous*: 'This piece is entirely descriptive of our age; it corresponds to this moment of victory, as the bourgeois life-style crumbles around us. . . . *Maison de fous* will be of great use to future historians and philosophers.' The writer also pulled Parisian society to pieces – 'that royal republic' – with its economic policies and its reactionary attitude, 'that Dadaist diplomacy . . . is it not a *Maison de fous*? Jean Börlin deserves great success.' It was probably the first time that a contemporary ballet could be interpreted as theatre of protest, carrying a social critique and contemporary political significance. In this respect, it is interesting to note the coincidence that the first fully fledged work in that vein, Jooss's *Green Table*, was to be launched and encouraged by Rolf de Maré twelve years later.

But let us get back to Landret, no less indignant regarding the lack of understanding with which the Ballets Suédois had been received, but for his own reasons: 'These are rare artists you see before you', he continued in *La Rampe*, 'since they possess the very precious gift of being able to adopt several new guises in the course of one and the same evening. . . . It is regrettable that by criticizing the Swedes, we have also been criticizing the art of our country, since Debussy and Bonnard, Ravel and Steinlen, Inghelbrecht and Laprade were all caught up in our reproaches. Börlin must be very proud to have found himself placed in such company and can be confident of the future which awaits him. . . . Paris will be surprised when it suddenly discovers him.' And that was precisely what the Parisian critics did. The daily papers were virtually unanimous: 'A month ago, we were criticizing the Ballets Suédois. Yesterday, nothing but praise and compliments were to be heard', *Comœdia* noted. 'The new programme . . . is simply admirable', went on *L'Avenir*. Until then, the critics had all made constant reference to the Ballets Russes; now, only one voice was heard to mention them: 'Thanks to this production, the Ballets Suédois definitively rank alongside, and not behind, the Ballets Russes' was the conclusion which Cœuroy drew in *L'Ère nouvelle* (21 November 1920).

1921

DECEMBER 1920 TO JUNE 1921
TOURS IN ENGLAND,
SPAIN AND BELGIUM

After fifty-odd performances in Paris, the Ballets Suédois went on tour. In the meantime, Rolf de Maré left the stage at the Champs-Élysées to Diaghilev's Ballets Russes, publishing their programme in a luxurious special edition of *La Danse*, the review which he had founded.

Diaghilev put on ten different ballets, only one of them a new creation: *Le Sacre du printemps* (The Rite of Spring), choreographed by Massine to replace the original choreography by Nijinsky. Four were masterpieces by Fokine, dating from before the war: *Les Sylphides*, *Polovtsian Dances*, *Sheherazade* and *Petrushka*. Five were by Massine: *Les Femmes de bonne humeur* (The Good-Humoured Ladies), *Contes Russes* and *Parade* (1917), *Le Tricorne* (The Three-Cornered Hat, 1919), and *Pulcinella* (première, 1920). Börlin's *tour de force* – nine new creations in the space of little more than a month – appeared now in an even more remarkable light, compared with the lack of novelty in the Ballets Russes' programme. The comparison was in fact unfair, Diaghilev being handicapped at the time by financial difficulties. It was an injustice which embittered him and, above all, his circle of friends, who did their best to belittle the Swedes.

The Ballets Suédois left for London at the beginning of December 1920 and continued to perform there until 21 January. At that time, England had not as yet formed its own ballet companies, although ballets, and great soloists like Adeline Genée, were attached to music hall. Interest in ballet was aroused by the tours of the Ballets Russes and above all by Pavlova, who made London the base of her travel worldwide.

Nearly all the English write-ups about the Ballets Suédois begin with nostalgic praise of the Russians: 'The Swedish Ballet has been a disappointment to most of us. We had hoped it would be something to take the place of the Ballets Russes during the too long absences of the latter from London' (Ernest Newman, *Manchester Guardian*, 16 December); 'The Swedish Ballet is, alas!, one of those entertainments which necessarily suffer from comparison' (*Tatler*, 30 December).

The remainder of the many short write-ups are mostly summaries of the ballets' libretti. Evaluations are brief, spanning a gamut from the friendly via the indulgent to the negative: 'This is a highly competent troupe, presenting material that is novel, arresting' (R.K.R., *Yorkshire Post*); 'an altogether fresh aspect of the dancer's art' (*Morning Post*); 'Quite a successful start' (*Westminster Gazette*); 'the public which likes the one [the Ballets Russes] will feel a good deal to attract it in the other [the Ballets Suédois]' (*Daily News*); 'Primitive effort with little real dancing' (*Daily Express*) (all dated 9 December); 'in these ballets of the modern school, the individual sinks more and more to a detail in a composition' (*The Nation and the Athenaeum*, 17 December).

Adeline Genée, London's leading prima ballerina, had the last word in an interview about the Ballets Suédois given to the *Observer* (9 January 1921): 'After all, if the art of dancing is to be taken seriously, technique must be the principal feature in the ballet. You might as well give performances of an opera and let the singers speak their words, as to produce a ballet and give hardly any exhibition of technique.'

One ballet stands out as receiving only words of praise: *El Greco*. 'The most original and distinctive thing in yesterday's program . . . which was very warmly received', commented the *Daily News* (9 December); and the *Daily Mirror* (29 December): '*El Greco* is a masterwork for which they will long be remembered.'

It took *The Madhouse* to arouse really strong feelings, however, not least as it was thrust on an unsuspecting public on New Year's Eve: 'In it the Swedish Ballet leaves nothing undone that stagecraft can suggest to curdle the blood in the veins of the beholder. There will be interest in seeing how London likes dumb nightmare' (*Daily Mail*). It was unanimously rejected – 'an appalling ballet', 'Grand Guignol thrill', 'gloomy and terrifying', 'particularly disliked' – and quickly removed from the playbill. *The Madhouse* had only been performed a couple of times, but it had left its mark.

LES BALLETS SUEDOIS. LES JE DOIS D'AVOIR DIRIGÉ EN LES D'ŒUVRES QUI ME SONT CHÈRES TANT AUXQUELS V.GOLSCHMANN JEAN BORLIN ROLF DE MARÉ ONT MONTÉ LES PREMIERS QUE JE N'OUBLIE PAS ET BALLET DE DARIUS MILHAUD BOIS ET JEAN EN 1921 UN BALLET DE R.DESORMIÈRE QUE JE N'OUBLIE PAS

touchagues

The next time the Ballets Suédois visited England, in October 1922, the fatal *Madhouse* – 'one of the ghastliest themes to which the delicate and lively art of the dance has ever been adapted' (*Evening News*, 11 October 1922) – turned out to have been remembered better than *El Greco*. Not that Rolf de Maré offered the English such fare again, giving them instead sedate programmes to pleasant music – Börlin's variety of *Chopiniana*, *The Toy Shop* to Debussy, and a divertissement – with the result that, on this occasion at least, the Ballets Suédois received 'a cordial welcome' (*News of the World*, 15 October).

The first tour took the Ballets Suédois to a dozen Spanish towns, including, of course, Madrid and Barcelona, which were the centres of fashion. Börlin enjoyed himself in Spain, whose dance he had studied in depth with a legendary teacher: José Otero. The latter was to forge other links with Sweden, moreover. In 1922, at Börlin's request, he was hired by the Stockholm Opera to help with a new staging of *Carmen* (1 November 1922), in which the prima ballerina, Ebon Strandin, above all danced, and to some extent sang, in the title role.

If one examines the Swedes' day-to-day programme, one wonders how they managed to cope with the great physical demands made on them by month-long tours, involving a performance of three or four ballets almost every evening, exercises every morning, and rehearsals throughout the day. In an interview, one of the girls dared to express a few timid complaints: she had seen absolutely nothing of all the exciting places they had been to, other than the route between theatre and hotel, always situated close by; and the train journeys – aeroplanes did not yet exist – sometimes took place the very same night immediately following a performance.

There were about thirty dancers, each of whom had a part in most ballets. Börlin himself danced three principal roles every evening. In his ballets, the participants were often all soloists, with the result that it was particularly difficult to replace someone in the event of illness. Yet, in five years, the Ballets Suédois were to cancel one, and only one, out of nearly a thousand performances on account of illness.

The administrative and technical personnel comprised around twenty people on average. The musical section had two or three conductors. One of these always went ahead of the company, in order to rehearse with the orchestra (preferably of between eighty and a hundred musicians) in the next town to be visited. He led a final rehearsal on the day of the performance, but in the evening the principal conductor took over. The company also had a pianist to accompany training and rehearsals and sometimes brought along a first violin to ensure a high quality.

The secretary, wardrobe mistress, stage hands and lighting technicians made up the remainder of the staff. Rolf de Maré did the lighting himself. The company carried with it about forty heavy, cumbersome projectors, since few theatres were perma-

nently equipped to allow for the creation of those subtle lighting effects in which the Ballets excelled and which amazed the contemporary public. With the help of Henri Prieur, his close friend and stage director, a war hero (awarded the Legion of Honour), de Maré invented a number of lighting devices which were subsequently copied by theatres visited by the Ballets Suédois.

The company carried with it ten tons of luggage. The technically most complicated ballet, *L'Homme et son désir* (Man and his Desire), took up a whole railway carriage.

All things considered, this itinerant ballet company (like its only contemporary of similar stature, the Ballets Russes) was a weighty machine, and one which tested Rolf de Maré's organizational skills to an extent of which the public remained quite unaware. There was nothing surprising in the fact that this man, by nature so calm, an enigma in the eyes of the critics, was enraged to hear the press refer to him as a wealthy patron amusing himself by maintaining a ballet company for want of anything better to do.

LA BOÎTE À JOUJOUX
(THE TOY SHOP)

After London, and before Spain, Rolf de Maré put on fifteen performances in Paris, during which Börlin had the opportunity to stage a new creation, *La Boîte à joujoux* (The Toy Shop; 15 February 1921).

Börlin's choice was determined by Debussy's superb score written in 1913 for a libretto and stage set – the first unequivocally Cubist ballet scenography – created by André Hellé. Because of the war, this ballet was not performed until December 1918, six months after Debussy's death, at the Théâtre du Vaudeville. Choreographed by Robert Quinault, a relatively unprestigious ballet director from the Opéra, it was only given a few times. The conductor was none other than Inghelbrecht. Like all admirers of Debussy, he regretted that this important piece of music was no longer being played, so he persuaded Börlin to read the score. Börlin took to it right away and created a choreography using angular movements adapted to Hellé's Cubist dolls, which he endowed with psychological characteristics and a mischievous sense of humour. The result was an original, light and graceful work, which would always be very popular with the public.

Performed no fewer than two hundred and eighty times, this was to be the only ballet, along with *Les Vierges folles*, which remained in the Ballets Suédois' permanent repertoire throughout their five-year career. It was to play an important role in making Debussy's work known to a wider public, above all thanks to the company's tours abroad. French intellectuals were grateful for this, as the contemporary press testifies.

6 JUNE
L'HOMME ET SON DÉSIR
(MAN AND HIS DESIRE)

The Ballets Suédois returned to Paris on 3 June, to take up their place once more in 'their' Théâtre des Champs-Élysées.

The première of *L'Homme et son désir* (Man and his Desire; Monday, 6 June 1921), a ballet by the poet and diplomat Paul Claudel, took the form of a gala in aid of war victims, under the patronage and in the presence of Princess Charles of Sweden. Everybody who was anybody in Paris was present; every last seat was taken.

The curtain went up on a set that was extremely complicated from a technical point of view. A vast arrangement divided the stage into four large planes, each the height of a man, and superimposed in storeys one on top of another, tiered like a staircase. The dancing took place on each of these four stages simultaneously, each group of movements inscribing itself like a musical note on a stave.

This unusual stage set – unique, in dance at least – evoked the stained-glass windows of a cathedral, or Italian painting prior to the introduction of perspective. For all its ultra-modern design, involving a touch of Cubism, it created the effect, in fact, of a medieval mystery play.

L'Homme et son désir represents a newly emerging tendency: the quest for a deeper dimension in dance. Indian dance, with its Bharata Natyam, had been steeped in this further dimension for thousands of years; Japan's medieval dance drama, the No, likewise. But European ballet was accustomed to depend for its libretti on anecdotal stories frequently concocted by not very literate ballet masters or hack writers.

L'Homme et son désir is a monumental poetic work of great richness, expressed through the medium of dance. Instead of using words, Claudel elected to transcribe his poem into movement: never had ballet received a finer gift nor such a declaration of confidence from a great poet.

It was Nijinsky who had been Claudel's inspiration. As French ambassador, newly installed in Rio de Janeiro in 1917, Claudel had attended a performance given by the Russian dancer. 'I have never had much feeling for the conventional art of ballet as practised, sometimes to absurd perfection, on many a subsidized stage, or by the sinister Pavlova. . . . Hence, I was one of those people who have never liked any dance other than that of the East . . . ', Claudel confided (*Mes idées sur le théâtre* [My Ideas about the Theatre]), making an apparent reference to the Bharata Natyam. He added: 'Nijinsky offered something else . . . the great human creature in its lyrical state . . . a grandeur and a dignity that were indescribable.' He invited Nijinsky to stay with him and was fascinated by the way the dancer moved, even offstage: 'He walked in the way that tigers do. . . . Even when he was relaxing, he seemed to be dancing imperceptibly.'

In the weeks that followed, Claudel nursed the idea of composing a ballet instead of writing a cycle of poems. A twenty-five-year-old composer, Darius Milhaud, had been awarded a scholarship to stay at the embassy and it was with him and with the painter Andrée Parr, married to an English diplomat, that Claudel discussed his ballet during the course of long walks in the tropical forest. Andrée Parr and Claudel together elaborated the scenography. Claudel himself selected the colours for the immense 'tapestry' which was to function as both a backdrop and a platform for the ballet. The arrangement in layered planes was also his idea: it evoked a page of an illuminated manuscript or a medieval simultaneous stage, the planes being superimposed rather than juxtaposed.

Andrée Parr executed collage-style sketches of costumes. In accordance with Claudel's instructions, the strange-shaped silhouettes cut out of coloured Bristol board sometimes had the head of a diver (or an astronaut), and the dancers resembled birds.

The orchestra was to be located on the stage, or rather on the stages. This notion enchanted Milhaud, who was already bubbling over with impressions and new ideas derived from popular Brazilian music, carnival melodies, tangos and machiches. In these syncopated rhythms, there was an 'imperceptible suspension, a nonchalant out-breath, a slight pause, which it was very difficult for me to capture'. He wrote the score for a highly original orchestra, comprising five strings only (a first and a second violin, a cello, a viola and a double bass), two harps, four wind instruments including a trumpet, and eighteen percussion instruments (kettledrum, drum, triangle, cymbal, etc.). To this he added a vocal quartet. The interest of the arrangement lay mainly in the combination of voices, strings and wind instruments. The nocturnal sounds (or racket, according to certain critics) of the forest were discreetly conveyed by the percussion instruments – never more than thirty bars at any one time.

Thus, the material for the ballet was at last more or less complete before a choreographer had even been brought in – a total departure from conventional methods. Nijinsky, unwitting inspiration for the project, was by now 'absent' in fact: since his performance at Rio, the great artist had been displaying symptoms of the mental illness which would finally – and soon – destroy him.

On his return to Paris in 1919, Claudel approached J. Rouché, director of the Opéra, to whom Milhaud played his score on the piano, without success. During the winter of 1920, Milhaud tried to interest Diaghilev in the project. Diaghilev liked young composers like Auric and Poulenc, but he had little time for Milhaud, who was perfectly aware of this fact. Nevertheless he got himself an audition with the great Russian.

'So, I played my score in an atmosphere heavy with frosty scepticism', Milhaud recounts in his memoirs. 'A conversation in

Les Ballets Suédois

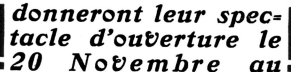 donneront leur spec= tacle d'ouverture le 20 Novembre au

Théâtre des Champs=Élysées

Les Ballets Suédois sont les seuls qui "OSENT"

Les Ballets Suédois sont les seuls re- présentatifs de la vie contemporaine

Les Ballets Suédois sont les seuls qui soient vraiment contre l'acadé misme.

CONTRE TOUS LES ACADÉMISMES

Les Ballets Suédois sont les seuls qui puissent plaire au public internatio- nal parce que Rolf de Maré ne pense qu'au plai- sir de l'évolution.

Les Ballets Suédois ne cherchent pas à être anciens, ne cherchent pas à être modernes ; ils sont en dehors des absurdités que l'on nous mont sous prétexte d'ART THÉA- TRAL ; ils vont propager la RÉ- VOLUTION par un mouvement d'où les conven- tions sont chaque jour détruites pour y être remplacées par l'invention.

VIVE LA VIE

Russian between Diaghilev and Massine broke the glacial silence that followed the audition.' The result: point-blank rejection.

Since his friend Honegger had just received a commission from Börlin (*Skating Rink*), Milhaud asked for an audience with Rolf de Maré.

'As soon as I had played *L'Homme et son désir* to him, he agreed to stage it, despite the unorthodox arrangement – singers, the orchestra of soloists and the numerous percussion instruments. Thanks to his generosity, the Brazilian collaboration could come into effect.' De Maré also engaged Andrée Parr.

Shortly before the première, Claudel was obliged to accompany Prince Hirohito, future emperor of Japan, on an official visit to Paris, and although he had little free time he would 'suddenly appear on the stage at the Théâtre des Champs-Élysées, dressed in a tall hat and a frock coat, and interrupt the rehearsal at the most unexpected moments, in order to point out some choreographic movements to Börlin'.

Börlin was never prone to take offence in matters relating to his prestige as a choreographer and he submitted patiently to Claudel's corrections. The same could not be said of the conductor Inghelbrecht who, when Milhaud gently requested of him 'some modification regarding nuance', replied violently: 'You have no say here.' But Inghelbrecht was, without doubt, a great conductor, and Milhaud was not worried, knowing that one of his friends was a flautist in the Ballets Suédois' orchestra and supported his point of view regarding the ballet's interpretation. This was Roger Désormière, later to be Diaghilev's regular conductor.

Börlin, of course, composed the choreography on his own, before the author's arrival. Claudel conceded on the day of the première that 'Jean Börlin's choreography is admirable and marvellously well adapted to my thinking' (*Comœdia*, 6 June 1920). The affinities between these two men could not have been greater: Claudel's conception of dance harmonized perfectly with Börlin's, and they shared their common experiences of Hellerau-Laxenburg (the institution founded by Jacques-Dalcroze in 1911), where Claudel saw *L'Annonce faite à Marie* (The Annunciation) staged in precisely the way he could have wished it to be. Jacques-Dalcroze's ideas regarding 'total theatre', which comprised sounds, dance and poetry, permeated Claudel's thinking, and were also fundamental to Börlin's philosophy.

Börlin himself danced in the principal role of the Man, which kept him on stage without a break for the entire duration of the ballet. His task lay in visualizing the complex and essential inner experiences of a human being during his life on earth: 'born' at the beginning of the ballet, by the end he had grown into a mature man. He reflected the external events which he encountered over the course of time, and his register of experiences and reactions increased in richness and subtlety as his transformation progressed. Employing formidable physical agility, an extraordinary sensitivity and depth of emotion, and highly expressive arm movements, at once precise and discreet, Börlin displayed the developing and changing feelings of the Man. The audience was fascinated, breathless with emotion, in the face of this new and total mutability of form, this unprecedented language of movement, created to express an inner reality – like a soul laid bare. Börlin's performance in *L'Homme et son désir* marked the summit of his career as a dancer. Inspired by Claudel, his inventiveness blossomed with wonderfully expressive nuances, which he controlled by virtue of his technical precision and his intuition.

The critics could not find enough words with which to praise this ballet: 'As for Börlin, he choreographed and danced it as no one else could possibly have done. Thanks to him, we have a new art form' (*Paris musical*, 1 July); 'The thought finds its exact and thrilling expression in the scenic realization: this can be said to be a work of genius' (Maurice Boucher, in *Le Monde musical*); 'When he was imagining scenes for it, several years ago, in Brazil, Claudel knew nothing of Börlin's existence, yet only Börlin could one day undertake to represent those scenes' (E. Marsan, in *Paris-Journal*, 12 June); 'It reflects the idea that the essential aim of dance, as of the other arts, is expression, and that this marvellous human body in its entirety, and not the face alone, is capable of rendering the soul visible, in its state of dancing, decision, and soaring flight' (*L'Intransigeant*, 9 June).

Börlin's costume, or rather his seeming lack of costume, provoked a variety of reactions. The poet's wish, to represent 'man in his nakedness', had to be respected – something that could scarcely embarrass Börlin, whose 'nakedness' the press had already remarked upon in relation to *El Greco*, where he wore only a short loin cloth. For the role of the Man, he wore as slight a costume, his whole body was smeared with shiny yellowish make-up which reflected the moonlight, and a pair of briefs served as a fig-leaf. From the auditorium this gave the required effect of a sculptural nudity. (The majority of photographs are deceptive, though, since Börlin was in the habit of putting on a pair of trunks for the photographers.) While Paris had found it perfectly acceptable that even 'serious' female modern dancers could perform completely naked, people were shocked to see a man apparently do the same for the first time. Antoine Banès summed up the situation thus: 'To be publicly nude for thirty-five minutes and avoid looking ridiculous truly requires a great deal of talent. Jean Börlin did not look ridiculous.'

Milhaud alone was slated by the critics, who attacked him violently for his 'cacophony'. It turned out that he had recently entitled an article of music criticism 'Down with Wagner', and the belligerent Wagnerians whom he had offended seized this opportunity to exact revenge.

Overall, *L'Homme et son désir* was nevertheless a resounding success. Despite the technical complexity of the scenic construction, which was extremely costly to transport, Rolf de

Maré was to keep the ballet on the company's repertoire for four years, taking it on their tours abroad.

In the summer of 1923, Claudel staged another version entitled *La Femme et son ombre* (The Woman and her Shadow) at the Imperial Theatre in Tokyo, where he was then ambassador. The scenic arrangement and content were similar, but the music, choreography and dancers were all Japanese.

L'Homme et son désir occupies an important place in the philosophy of Paul Claudel. The work opened up new perspectives for the development of dance: Claudel and Börlin had wedded poetry to dance, and this marriage was to be fêted over and over again in the modern dance of the twentieth century.

18 JUNE
LES MARIÉS
DE LA TOUR EIFFEL
(THE NEWLYWEDS ON
THE EIFFEL TOWER)

Following close on the heels of Claudel, Jean Cocteau was to be the third great writer to become caught up with the Ballets Suédois, whose ambition was to become the poets' ballet company.

Cocteau, whose influence permeated every field of artistic activity, was at the centre of the avant-garde movement which exploded on Paris. Rolf de Maré met him at the home of Nils Dardel, who, along with his wife, the writer Thora Dardel (an intimate friend of Raymond Radiguet and daughter of Baron Axel Klinckowström, one of the most versatile intellectuals in Sweden), formed the pivot of the Swedish artistic circle.

Perfectly cut out to head the French avant-garde movement, the Ballets Suédois suited the Cocteau of the twenties down to the ground. He and Rolf de Maré formed a close friendship, which was to last for life (they were born, and died, at more or less the same time). Börlin, for his part, was fascinated by Cocteau, whose lightning-quick intelligence was so different from his own more meditative bent. They shared a sense of humour and a total irreverence, and had fun staging their ballet together. But Cocteau also had a profoundly serious streak: he said of himself that he had one foot in life and one in the grave. Börlin, whose time was in reality running out, already aware of the shadow hovering over him, contributed to the project with his playfulness and imagination.

There was something new in the air, a reaction against naturalism, the supremacy of the word, the interminable and ingenious chatter which dominated the theatre. Cocteau sought a more genuine simplicity, a simplicity that was closer to reality, and in that way faithful to the reaction expressed by the new type of dancing: its aim was to transform the classical dancer's body, bound as the latter was by an aestheticism whose artificial technical virtuosity had become an end in itself. 'Free dance' depended, on the contrary, on man's natural movement as an expression of his inner truth.

Like Apollinaire, Cocteau was conscious of the limitations of spoken theatre. In life, movements, gestures, body language and facial expression play a far greater part in communication than 'naturalist' spoken theatre grants them. Circus, cabaret, variety, and fairground shows, which were still flourishing in the country, were all fresh sources for an anti-literary theatre. Their excesses and caricatures were, paradoxically, often closer to truth than was realism, according to Cocteau.

With *Parade*, in 1917, Cocteau made a first tentative attempt at creating alternative theatre. The production, choreographed by Massine, consisted of a sequence of solo items, conceived in the manner of variety shows and vaguely interlinked by the appearance of three 'animated structures': Cubist sculptures created by Picasso and inspired by his painting. The irreverence of the piece aroused the enthusiasm of the younger generation of artists, who saw their painting embodied in theatre for the first time.

The next attempt, in 1920, was a farce entitled *Le Boeuf sur le toit* or *The Nothing Doing Bar*, performed by the Fratellini brothers, the famous clowns from the Medrano circus, in which the slow, heavy movements of the choreography, or rather pantomime, conceived and arranged by Cocteau, contrasted with Milhaud's lively, spirited melodies, inspired by the Rio Carnival.

Here and there, the influence of Charlie Chaplin, silent cinema, and burlesque comedy, was noted, but the piece undoubtedly comprised too many separate elements for a central theme to be singled out. Neither of these experimental productions used language.

Cocteau was now ready to concentrate on a finished, definitive work, based on a written text: a ballet embracing speech and dance. He read it to Rolf de Maré, at the home of the painter Jean Hugo, and de Maré immediately saw how well it suited the purposes of the Ballets Suédois.

However, to de Maré's bitter disappointment, Cocteau did not want to involve Picasso in the project. As a long-time collector, de Maré greatly admired Picasso's work, frequently visited the artist in his studio, and had struck up a friendship with him. But, according to Cocteau, the remarkable 'animated structures' of *Parade* were too powerful and engrossed too much of the audience's attention, distracting it from what was most important: his own attempt to create total theatre. Cocteau maintained that, ideally, a ballet ought to be conceived by a single creator, who would combine the tasks of choreographer, librettist, composer, scenographer and dancer. In the twenties, this was the practice among modern Central European dance-soloists (although they were often not the authors of the musical accompaniment).

At the same time, Cocteau boosted the team-work on the ballet with a circle of friends. This circle existed thanks to the groundwork he had provided with his brief aesthetic treatise *Le Coq et l'Arlequin* (The Cockerel and the Harlequin), in which he attacked serious music 'to which one listens with one's head in one's hands', and pleaded in favour of Stravinsky, Satie and Auric. From that moment on, Cocteau was established as the standard-bearer of post-war music, both by the critics and by the young musicians whom Henri Collet (*Comœdia*, 20 January 1920) baptized 'Les Six': Auric, Durey, Honegger, Milhaud, Poulenc and Tailleferre. This name was adopted by the musical world, and the Six subsequently gave a joint concert, thus in fact sanctioning their existence as a group, which comprised in reality six musically very different individuals. The only unifying factor was their joint adoration of Satie. For several years, the Six assembled every Saturday evening at Milhaud's home to have cocktails and, later, to go and dine, always at the same bistro. These 'Saturday dinners' attracted sympathizers, musicians and painters such as Marie Laurencin, Irène Lagut, Valentine Gross, Jean Hugo and Fauconnet, and writers such as Lucien Daudet, Cocteau and his friend Radiguet. The latter introduced Thora and Nils Dardel, who in turn invited Börlin and de Maré. After dinner, the group would go to the fair at Montmartre, to the music hall or the Medrano circus to see the Fratellini brothers, and finally back to Milhaud's flat to play their latest compositions, read their latest poems, and enter into lengthy discussions.

Such an environment gave rise to an abundance of new ideas and artistic collaborations, and bonds of friendship were formed in this highly stimulating atmosphere, one that was perfectly suited to fostering the new creative impulses in Paris.

Rolf de Maré wanted Auric to compose the music for *Les Mariés de la tour Eiffel* (The Newlyweds on the Eiffel Tower), but there was too little time. So Cocteau suggested that the Six each write a part of the score. All but Durey accepted. Auric composed the overture, *Le 14-Juillet* (The 14th of July), and the *Ritournelles de Liaison* (connecting music between the different scenes); Milhaud wrote the *Marche Nuptiale* (Wedding March) and *Sortie de la Noce* (Wedding Procession); Poulenc, the *Discours du Général* (General's Speech) and *Baigneuse de Trouville* (Trouville Bathing Girl), with a slow waltz; Tailleferre, the *Valse des Dépêches* (Telegrams' Waltz) and a Quadrille; and Honegger, finally, composed a Funeral March. This was to be the one and only orchestral work produced collectively by the Six and represented the high point of the group's career. Henceforth, they were to give a commemorative concert every ten years, but otherwise their joint musical activities ceased.

Cocteau turned his attention next to the set and costume design. His first plan was to have Irène Lagut, Auric's girlfriend, design the costumes under his supervision, but he disliked her sketches and entrusted the work instead to Jean Hugo, great grandson of the celebrated Victor Hugo. This angered Auric, and the collaboration of the Six was in danger. Since Cocteau was still unable to get to grips with the décor, despite help from Hugo, he changed his mind and got Lagut to design the backdrop, while Hugo, assisted by his fiancée, Valentine Gross, took care of the costumes. Auric immediately agreed once more to compose his share of the music, and the group was back in business.

The characters in the ballet were highly stylized – stereotyped and grotesque. So much so, in fact, that the dancers themselves were unrecognizable. To go with Hugo's sketches, Cocteau did a number of transparent line drawings showing how each dancer was to be contained within his or her costume. The costumes themselves were created over a wire frame to carry the thick padding, while a mask concealed the dancer's face.

Cocteau maintained that a masked face was much more expressive in the footlights than a real one – a long-standing fad of Rolf de Maré's – and some of the women's masks in *Les Mariés de la tour Eiffel* were reminiscent of the Japanese No, much loved by de Maré.

The dancers' movements were inevitably hampered by the sheath-like costumes enveloping all but their arms and, at best, their legs. Only a few could still dance quite freely, and on points: the Trouville Bathing Girl and the Telegrams, represented by a group, like a corps de ballet – a discreet parody of classical ballet which went more or less unnoticed by the public but nevertheless gave Börlin a secret pleasure.

One evening, after the curtain had been lowered and costumes removed, Börlin's fellow dancers were to discover that it was Börlin himself who had danced the Bathing Girl, a virtuoso role normally assumed by Carina Ari. His mastery of points was such that no one had known the difference. Point work is of course never part of a male dancer's training, but Börlin had learnt it 'in order to understand my ballerinas better when I make steps for them'.

Börlin devoted his great inventiveness to giving an intense vivacity to the scenic action at all times. Cocteau, entranced by the way in which Börlin had understood his intentions and realized them to perfection, rendered warm homage to the choreographer. However, in 1948, when he published *Les Mariés* in a Gallimard volume of his complete theatrical works, he referred to 'choreography by Jean Cocteau', while praising Börlin in his preface for 'his modesty'! Börlin was long since dead, but his modesty had indeed been so great, and his devotion to Cocteau so sincere, that he would in any case most probably not have claimed his due.

This work, which Cocteau rightly considered to be one of the most important he had written, represented as crucial a moment in the development of theatre as in that of dance.

The dialogue was spoken by two actors (Cocteau sometimes played one of the roles himself) who were each concealed behind a screen on either side of the stage and spoke into the horn of a

Francis Poulenc

Georges Auric

Irène Lagut

Darius Milhaud

Germaine Tailleferre

giant gramophone. They introduced new arrivals, uselessly explaining what they did, commenting on events sometimes in the manner of a public speaker, sometimes as mouthpiece of the dancers. More often than not, the text was deliberately artless, imitating the language of children, devoid of those witticisms which Cocteau produced elsewhere with consummate ease. The tone was banal and everyday, 'like at a bourgeois breakfast, or in a railway carriage'. This seemingly light text at times appeared to have been improvised, like a string of associated ideas bordering on the surreal.

Anyone who has been to a ballet accompanied by a highly expressive musical score knows just how difficult it is to concentrate on both auditory and visual impressions at once. The case was similar with *Les Mariés de la tour Eiffel*. For the spectator wishing to listen to the text as well as observe the action, the ballet was difficult to follow, and tiring. Of course, the majority of spectators, for whom what they saw was more important than what they heard, viewed the actual spectacle as a highly entertaining piece of pleasantry – the poetic gravity of the whole resided, meanwhile, in the text, whose underlying tragedy was characteristic of all Cocteau's work. The ballet was like a dance on the crest of despair.

The plot is perfectly comprehensible, and even exaggeratedly so thanks to the 'explanations' offered by the gramophones, which echo the action of the characters.

In his memoirs (*Notes sans musique* [Notes without Music], 1949), Darius Milhaud summarizes the actions thus: 'A young newlywed couple, accompanied by their parents and an old friend, a general, turn up on the first platform of the Eiffel Tower to celebrate their wedding. They all sit down to a banquet, in the course of which the old General mimes a speech. The wedding party is being photographed; but each time the fateful words "watch the dicky-bird" are spoken, some unexpected character pops up from nowhere. It's the Trouville Bathing Girl, or the Telegrams (since the Eiffel Tower is the Telegraph Lady now that her aerial has been installed), and finally a Lion appears and gobbles up the General. But that's only the start of things going wrong for this unfortunate wedding party, which ends up being utterly wrecked by the Child to Come, like in fairground games. It interested and amused us all to take part in a production which brought together so many diverse elements, and where the fantasy was worthy of the Dadaist movement, then at its very peak.'

'Certain types of impudence are only sanctioned by the spirit of buffoonery', noted Cocteau, to whom Börlin had spoken of a sort of revue, or 'Spex' as it was called, popular in Swedish university circles since the end of the nineteenth century. This type of highly intellectual entertainment was staged collectively by the students who, through this foolery, were able to give their learned professors a few gentle kicks and the bourgeoisie a drubbing, while themselves remaining out of range, behind the grotesque quips and clownish antics. Thanks to Börlin, *Les Mariés de la tour Eiffel* took on the appearance of one of these student 'Spex'.

The press preview took place on 18 June 1921. The public greeted *Les Mariés* with enthusiasm, and if the French middle classes felt touched on the raw by it, they did not show it. As ever with the Ballets Suédois' press previews, in reality premières, Rolf de Maré assembled a curiously mixed audience: Paul Claudel, the Duchesse de Rohan, the Princesse Murat, Rouché, director of the Opéra, Georges Casella, Alfred Cortot, Maurice Ravel, Roger Cousin, André Warnod, Robert de Rothschild and his wife, and Rachilde, to mention only a handful of the important people present. The 'Cubists' sat together *en masse*, the entire group of the Six was there, and the Dadaists, sensing competition (Cocteau's supernaturalism anticipated Surrealism), came armed with whistles.

The critics were positive overall, though far from unanimous. A few years later, Cocteau said that they had been negative, but what one reads in the newspapers of the time hardly justifies this remark: the articles give accounts rather than judgments.

'The intention of the work is satirical', wrote *Paris-Journal* (20 June), 'with an underlay of sadness, as is natural: the sadness of an urban Sunday in the wrought-iron age as felt by sensitive hearts.' Cocteau's dialogues were popular and even quoted in the papers. The public, enchanted, thoroughly enjoyed itself.

Echoing the words of André Gide (in his preface to *Paludes*, [Marshlands]), Cocteau said that 'God's part' in *Les Mariés* was an important one, as if his own creation seemed to him independently to have acquired a symbolic significance deeper than anything he had foreseen. Shortly before his death, he went to the Dance Museum in Stockholm to study the original documents and see the text of the first version in order to get an idea of the modifications he had made to his piece in the course of rehearsals. Many things turned out to be different from the way he remembered them and he acknowledged, with some emotion, that *Les Mariés* had been one of his most important works. Moreover, he resolved there and then to restage the work, but he died before he had had time to do so.

Of all the extraordinary ballets in the Ballets Suédois' repertoire, *Les Mariés* alone has given rise to numerous in-depth analyses, particularly in recent years. Among them: Kerstin Höglund, *Jean Cocteau, un précurseur de l'absurdisme* (university thesis, Stockholm, 1985); Martin Esslin, *The Theatre of the Absurd* (London, 1980); Otto Wirtz, *Das poetologische Theater Jean Cocteau* (Geneva, 1972); Milorad, a psychoanalytical study in *Cahiers Jean Cocteau*, and Erik Aschengren, *Cocteau et la danse* (doctoral dissertation, Copenhagen, 1986). The latter has overlooked Börlin's quality as a choreographer and an important innovator. But the same is true of all other dance historians to this day – with one great exception: C.W. Beaumont.

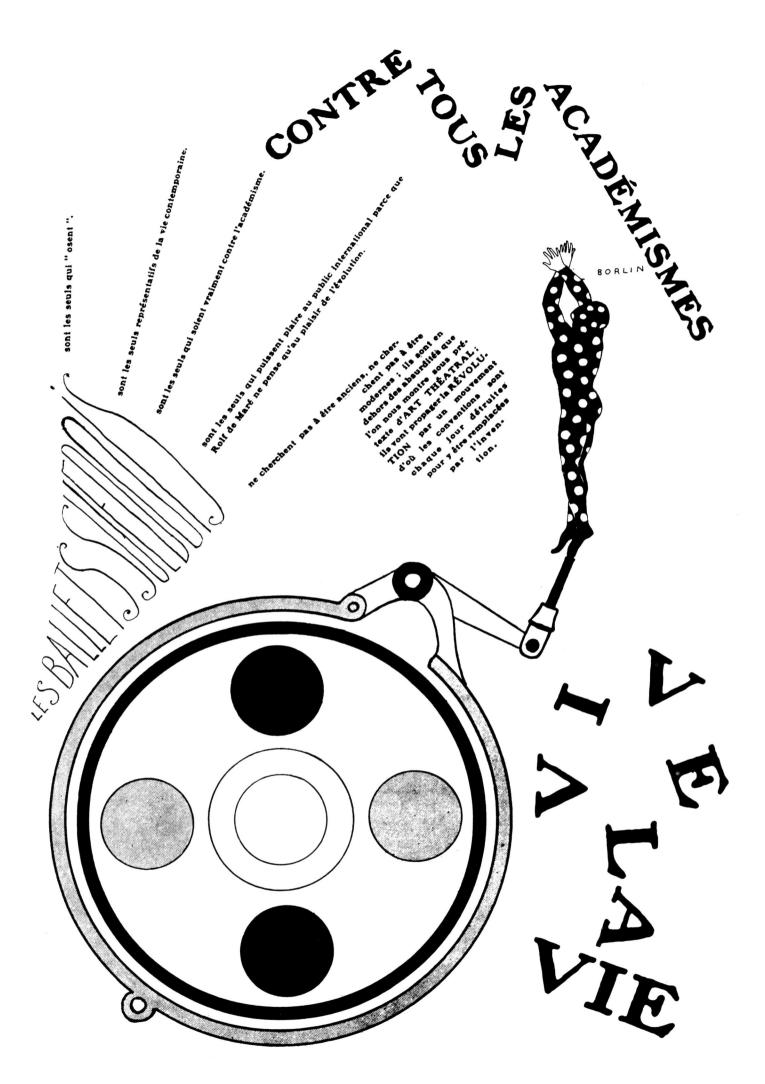

CONTRE TOUS LES ACADÉMISMES

sont les seuls qui "osent".

sont les seuls représentatifs de la vie contemporaine.

sont les seuls qui soient vraiment contre l'académisme.

sont les seuls qui puissent plaire au public International parce que
Rolf de Maré ne pense qu'au plaisir de l'évolution.

ne cherchent pas à être anciens, ne cherchent pas à être
modernes : ils sont en
dehors des absurdités que
l'on nous montre sous prétexte d'ART THÉÂTRAL :
ils vont propager la RÉVOLU-
TION par un mouvement
d'où les conventions sont
chaque jour détruites
pour y être remplacées
par l'inven-
tion.

BORLIN

LES BALLETS SUÉDOIS

VE
VI A LA
VIE

The Ballets Suédois' first season ended on 26 June. In a single year, Börlin had produced twelve ballets, half of his entire oeuvre, the majority of them important, complex and very different from one another, and almost all of them innovative. The Ballets Suédois had won respect and esteem and assumed a place in French cultural life. They were accepted. Rolf de Maré was pleased to grant his company a long holiday.

20 NOVEMBER
DANSGILLE OR
DANSES VILLAGEOISES
(VILLAGE DANCES)

The autumn of 1921 began with a grand provincial tour, from the beginning of November to 30 December, for which Börlin created a new ballet, *Dansgille*, an entertainment comprising folk-dances subtly adapted from Swedish folklore. Each item consisted of an authentic dance, characteristic of a region of Sweden, and involving only the original steps and figures.

This sequence of old village dances had a certain anthropological interest thanks to its relative authenticity. However, it was above all by its 'exoticism', its unsophisticated depiction of the charm of a foreign rural and ancestral culture, that *Dansgille* captured the public imagination and remained a popular item in the company's repertoire, being performed no fewer than 242 times.

The conductor, Bigot, arranged the simple country music for a large orchestra. The décor comprised a backdrop representing an old Swedish naïve painting (the original of which is hanging in Stockholm's Nordic Museum), while the costumes were the genuine folk costumes from each respective dance region. The various items were interchangeable, as was the order of presentation, and depended on the availability of the dancers and the time each one needed to change or rest in view of the other demands that were made on them. This adaptability was, of course, valuable when it came to planning each evening's programme. In other respects, however, this was a relatively insignificant item in the repertoire.

1 9 2 2

SKATING RINK

9 January 1922 marked the start of the Ballets Suédois' new season at the Théâtre des Champs-Élysées, and on 20 January the company presented an important international première, that of *Skating Rink*.

This was once again a poetic ballet, inspired by a 'danced poem' by the Futurist Riciotto Canudo, which was published in *Le Mercure de France* in 1920. The setting was a roller-skating rink, a sort of modern sports hall, popular at the time, where participants did artistic roller-skating to music on a wooden or asphalt floor. This form of amusement, particularly favoured where the climate excluded the possibility of ice-skating, was to be included in 1924, moreover, as a discipline in the European sporting championships.

Canudo turned this rink into a miniature image of the world, endowed with symbolism. In it he expressed 'one of life's major, elemental forms of anguish. That is, sensual longing, which thrusts living beings towards and counter to one another and creates collisions, unions, all the harmonies and all the disharmonies of love and hate.' In a dream-like atmosphere, an anonymous and homogeneous crowd hovers at the edges of the rink. A man detaches himself from the crowd: this is the Poet, or Fool, 'the individual who is, in himself, the sum total of every desire and every possibility, manifesting them in the guise of quiet elegance and feline suppleness'. A current of sensuality runs through the group, the women instantly attentive to the Poet, the men forming the negative, hostile pole and throwing themselves on the women in order to seize hold of and reclaim them. The couple at the centre of the rink indulge in love play as if they were alone, while a second man, 'trembling with desire for revenge', tries in vain to force himself upon them and disrupt their moment of intimacy. Finally, the woman faints under the effect of an excess of pleasure; her lover picks her up and disappears with his prize, while the crowd resumes its incessant circling.

The visual conception of *Skating Rink*, over and beyond the scenography proper, owed much to Fernand Léger. He was fascinated by the working-class public of the popular dance halls, which attracted such original types (although the Paris roughs had more or less disappeared by now), and he was to invite Börlin and Rolf de Maré to accompany him there, together with Thora and Nils Dardel. Léger and Dardel had probably known one another since before the war; in any case, in the Ballets Suédois' time, they were friends and remained so for life. Léger and de Maré also got on very well, drawn to one another by a certain reserve they had in common.

Léger had the opportunity to admire the exquisite collection of kachina dolls that de Maré had assembled during his visits to North American Indian tribes in the decade between 1910 and 1920. And henceforth, the typical colours of the Indians' ritual dance costumes, as painted on these wooden figurines, were to be the characteristic colours of Léger's painting.

Cubism had made its entrance on the ballet stage with Picasso's *Parade* and Hellé's *Boîte à joujoux*. With the sets for *Skating Rink*, it burst forth in brilliant, irresistibly eye-catching colours: the colours of Léger. At the beginning of the ballet, the tone was set by a front curtain. This went up to reveal a group of stylized characters against a slightly concave backdrop, on which were painted brilliantly coloured abstract figures rising high above the heads of the dancers. The costumes, designed at the same time as the choreography, formed a kaleidoscopic sequence of images which changed according to the evolutions of the dance. The finished effect was that of a big abstract tableau, whose lower section was engaged in a constant process of transformation. The ballet seemed to exist on two planes at once: the dramatic action, on the one hand, and the play of colours, on the other, both produced by the movements of the dancers and precisely calculated within the choreographic framework. Léger developed his work literally step by step in association with Börlin. This unprecedented interaction between colour and form announced future trends in ballet and was to reach a total integration in the work of Alwin Nikolais, a generation later.

In calling upon the services of great artists, the Russians had made painting an important element in the multiple art of ballet – something that was already true in Saint Petersburg, before Diaghilev's time, thanks to the work of Korovin and Golovin. In Paris, the Ballets Russes were to continue in this vein by drawing, in particular, on the scenographic genius of Léon Bakst. De Maré, who was a collector, and Diaghilev, who had been responsible for organizing exhibitions, were both art lovers, and both attached great importance to scenography. But it was the Swedes who were to take this dimension to the limit in creating, with *Skating Rink*, an enormous mobile painting.

The work was short and concentrated. The message was clearly conveyed by means of dance alone: no mime was involved, and no ornamentation through virtuoso dance. This severe discipline was characteristic of the choreography of Börlin, breaking with his classical past.

Stylistically, the choreography of *Skating Rink* illustrated Börlin's method for developing a new, modern and free type of dancing: the steps were slow, gliding, and never lifted far off the ground. The body's centre of gravity was low, and movements had an earthward tendency. A long way from Fokine and closer to Wigman (though in *Skating Rink* without Expressionism), the overall style was based on an abstract and ascetic modernism.

Börlin and Léger were to be somewhat surprised on receiving Honegger's score, composed without reference to them. It was not what they had been expecting, being above all an illustration of Canudo's libretto, punctuated with leitmotivs conceived in a Wagnerian spirit. It was to require all Börlin's profound musical knowledge to build a bridge between Léger and Canudo.

The audience greeted *Skating Rink* with a mixture of boos, shouts of protest and enthusiastic applause. The critics expressed themselves in a moderate, but rather negative, fashion. Long articles discussed the pros and cons of the piece. In *Le Figaro* (22 January 1922), Antoine Banès, who found that the libretto was incomprehensible and the sets 'according to the Cubist rites enacted by Fernand Léger, vie with one another in sheer lunacy', reserved a begrudging word of praise for the 'energetic director of the Théâtre des Champs-Élysées' (such compliments being addressed, as usual, to Hébertot, since few people knew that it was in reality Rolf de Maré who took all the decisions): 'An irresistible sympathy draws him towards the famous Six. He wants the whole world, like him, to adore these revolutionaries. . . . And perhaps he's right. Who knows?' The violent feelings which were shaking the contemporary musical world to the core were perfectly illustrated by what Banès then went on to say: 'I'm following their evolution with pleasure, always ready to defend their lucid moments even though, every day, hundreds of anonymous letters abusing them come flooding my doorstep from the four corners of the world.' That was what a critic got for not having fairly and squarely slated the avant-gardists – but what invectives were not raining down on the interested parties themselves!

In *Excelsior* (22 January), Émile Vuillermoz, himself a composer, took up the defence of Honegger's music: 'Everything about it is animated by a feverish movement and a heady glissade. It is hot and teeming like the tableau it describes: it speeds along like the skaters' roller skates on the cement floor, it is lit by the arc lamps and muffled by the cigarette smoke.' Léger,

on the other hand, he tore to pieces, the artist's Cubism being diametrically opposed to Honegger's music: 'There is a total incompatibility of mood between this music and these canvases . . . which are plastered, moreover, with blinding colours which, depending on your visual training, either delight you or fill you with horror.' But he approved in principal the initiative of the ballet's creators: 'An experimental laboratory is indispensable to the progress of art. When one finds a director or a patron disinterested enough to endow Paris with such a laboratory, it is perfectly absurd to try and discourage them.'

Something that needed saying, since we imagine too readily that the fantastic decade of the twenties was a godsend for avant-garde artists and that fame depended at that time simply on inventing something new. In reality, conservatism was well and truly established and innovators had to struggle hard to impose their views – contrary to today's spirit, today's readiness to greet favourably any new idea.

Börlin, who danced as usual in the principal role, was almost unanimously spared by the critics; he even received a few words of praise: 'new movements which will, I believe, mark a high point in the evolution of modern ballet' (Pierre Bénard, in *Bonsoir*, 21 January); 'He saved the piece; better still, gave it character, beauty, a real originality' (Dominique Sordet, in *L'Écho national*, 22 January); 'Jean Börlin is one of the most beautiful actors I know; likeable, graceful . . .' (*L'Université de Paris*, unsigned).

JANUARY 1922 TO MAY 1923
THE BALLETS ABROAD

The day after their Paris season ended, on 29 January 1922, the Ballets Suédois left for a long tour of Central Europe. In Berlin, where they performed from 1 to 15 February, their success was such that they were obliged to return there for a whole month, after going to Vienna and Budapest. This second visit to Berlin was followed by appearances in several large German towns, in particular Cologne and Hamburg, and then in Stockholm during the second half of May.

Their Central European tour was crucially important from the point of view of the influence that the Ballets Suédois were to exert on the evolution of dance. Börlin's choreographic innovations were to clear the way for modern dance in the countries of Central Europe: a dance liberated from the aesthetic of classical ballet. Börlin went in fact far further than Fokine. Indeed, he should be viewed, historically, as occupying a place in the field of what came to be known as 'modern dance' or 'free dance' rather than in that of ballet.

The Ballets Suédois' reception in Central Europe was attentive and serious. Intellectuals published long articles analysing their works in elaborate detail. Important above all was the very particular enthusiasm that the company generated among fellow dancers wherever they went. The most eminent personalities of modern dance later bore witness to the trouble they took in order to attend performances by the Ballets Suédois, some going so far as to follow the company from town to town in order to see the same programmes again and again.

Modern dancers were having great difficulties, both practical and economic, to gain recognition. Their public was limited, although comprising a large section of the intellectual élite. Dancers were generally forced to perform solo, executing their own choreography and appearing alone on stage for an entire evening in a sequence of several short compositions. There was a limit to the number of these 'danced soirées' that an individual dancer could afford in the course of a year. It was also necessary to renew one's repertoire constantly, since it was often only possible – and sometimes even then with difficulty – to fill an auditorium for one single performance in the same town.

For such dancers, the discovery of the Ballets Suédois was a revelation, a dream come true: here was an important company, employing magnificent stage sets and a complete symphony orchestra – like the Russians, but with a repertoire of avant-garde works which were radically innovative and sometimes more advanced than the boldest modern experiments performed by the solo artists themselves. They greeted Börlin as a kindred soul, and the company was set up as an example in attempts to win over the direction of various opera houses: it was time for modern dance to be performed on the large, official stages of the national theatres. Gradually, several modern choreographers were to be appointed as ballet directors in a number of different Central European opera houses, whose outdated classical ballets they replaced with artistic free dance.

The Ballets Suédois' performances were above all to produce positive results on the choreographic level. The young Börlin had been influenced by modernists like Wigman and now, not yet thirty, he had reached his artistic maturity and become a front-line choreographer. Wigman, seven years his senior, had just succeeded in making her breakthrough as a solo choreographer around 1919. Klamt, Gert, Trümpy and Kieselhausen were of the same generation as Wigman. All the others destined for fame – Jooss, Palucca, Kreutzberg, Georgi, Schoop, Impekoven, Skoronel, Swaine, Chladek, etc. – were at present no more than adolescents, while Laban had just published his first book (which Börlin had, of course, read), *Die Welt des Tänzers* (The World of the Dancer; 1920). The Ballets Suédois' arrival marked the beginning of the supremacy of modern dance in Central Europe, which took off somewhat later in the United States.

Clearly, there were almost no qualified dance critics around, classical ballet being, as we have noted, a dying art, Diaghilev having faded from the scene, and modern dancers being known only to a restricted circle of connoisseurs. Critiques of the Ballets Suédois thus appear perplexed in the face of so much that was new. Arthur Michel (*Vossische Zeitung*, 15 April 1921) stressed

that Börlin's aim was to extend the domain of ballet by introducing into it a new way of looking at things. One paper found Börlin's imagination mind-boggling, another remarked that the Swedes' method of working with the whole body was a far cry from classical technique – a perfectly correct observation. One of the most lucid critiques (appearing in *Stettins Ostsee-Zeitung* and signed Dr P.L.) distinguished in Börlin's work a number of different styles, 'which could be called Expressionism, Cubism and Futurism', and considered 'the creator of this new style of dance, Jean Börlin, a genius'. In spring 1922, the famous magazine *Der Querschnitt* devoted several positive articles to different aspects of the Ballets Suédois. In Vienna, where the Wiesenthal sisters had specialized in the waltz, and where Rosalia Chladek was to make a name for herself, as also in Budapest, where Valeria Dienes created her great danced dramas (1924 and after), the Ballets Suédois excited the same kind of admiration they had won in Germany.

Next to Börlin it was Carina Ari who enjoyed the greatest personal success during the tour. The newspapers showered her with praise for her temperament, her range of dramatic expression and her irresistible sense of humour.

On 16 May 1922, the company arrived in Stockholm – for the one and only time that the Swedish dancers were to perform in their native city. For Rolf de Maré, the visit was tantamount to hurling himself into the lions' den. The Royal Opera had still not forgiven him for having filched its best dancers, and the administration launched a smear campaign against de Maré and Börlin in the right-wing newspapers which, in its viciousness and its falsehoods, remains unrivalled in the history of the Swedish press. De Maré had a certain unconscious tendency to rub people up the wrong way, the other side of his absolute honesty being a lack of flexibility and diplomacy, or, quite simply, of tact.

A Swedish journalist in Paris, David Sprengel, applying for a post as head of publicity at the Théâtre des Champs-Élysées, had been scornfully and insultingly rejected by de Maré, who shuddered at the mere idea of having recourse to one's own publicity agent. The incident inspired an insane hatred in the volatile Sprengel who, on marrying one of Sweden's foremost writers the following year, came into contact with such circles as would give him scope for revenge. He wrote a series of articles, constructed around a core of utterly false accusations regarding the Ballets Suédois and their director, and published them in the Swedish press which, at that time, was scarcely *au fait* with events taking place in far-off Paris. The Ballets Suédois were apparently a total fiasco, Börlin was said to unleash nothing but laughter and booing from his audiences, and de Maré was depicted as an extravagant fool, despised by the whole of Paris. The management of the Royal Opera continued discreetly to feed public opinion with such injurious rumours, with the result that Rolf de Maré's reputation was marred right up until the fifties.

The Ballets Suédois' two weeks' worth of performances in Stockholm were to change public opinion in favour of Börlin, who was rehabilitated both as a choreographer and as a dancer. The ballets favourably impressed a number of important people, among them the art historian Gotthard Johansson and the composer Vilhelm Petersson-Berger, who published passionately enthusiastic critiques of their work. Petersson-Berger emphasized that Börlin possessed exceptional choreographic gifts and he invited the 'representatives of the Opera present in the audience to reflect on this fact, which has been so brilliantly borne out'.

The Royal Opera gradually had to yield to this reversal of opinion and soon after invited Börlin to create a ballet, *Bergakungen* (The King of the Mountain), in a décor designed by Prince Eugene, the king's brother (première 7 February 1923). The banality of the libretto and the management's reluctance to allot sufficient rehearsal time were part of the reason for its meagre success. Börlin also staged at the Opera *Marchand d'oiseux* (The Snare) and *Les Vierges folles* (8 September 1923), two of the 'easiest' of all his works in the Ballets Suédois' repertoire.

After a few months' holiday and rehearsal time, the Ballets Suédois toured the French provinces, travelling subsequently to Switzerland, then to Scandinavia once more – performing in Copenhagen and Oslo, and other towns, but avoiding Stockholm. Afterwards they went to London and toured England for more than a month, then spent February to April 1923 in Italy.

De Maré selected a cautious programme for London, including *Chopiniana, El Greco*, a divertissement comprising eight items and *La Boîte à joujoux*: it was both long and insipid. Such a programme was in stark contrast to the undaunted temerity de Maré had shown in Paris. But his great German tour had cost him dear: he had signed contracts in marks with the German theatres well in advance of the tour, but as the money started coming in, the German currency was devalued. Since the dancers' salaries and other regular outgoings were guaranteed in Swedish kroner, the budget deficit had become very worrying and de Maré needed to make a profit in England in order to get back on course.

The English public was unpredictable, but the company's takings were good this time, both in London and in the provinces. Diaghilev, by contrast, had ruined himself the previous year with a sumptuous production of *The Sleeping Beauty*, British enthusiasm for the Russians having now cooled for no apparent reason.

The critics showered the Ballets with praises. This dancing 'is totally different from Russian dramatic dancing. Just go and see *The Foolish Virgins*, a perfect jewel of a ballet', ran an unsigned article; and Julia Chatterton, writing in *Musical Standard* (18 November), commented: 'in the working up of the subject there is to be felt a subtle rhythmic influence which at once places this particular ballet on a level with the highest form of the art'. Every aspect of the Ballets was admired and each soloist praised. People marvelled at Börlin's dervish dance, at the Swedish folk scenes which formed part of the divertissement, and even at *Chopiniana*, despite the fact that Jenny Hasselquist – the only dancer to have enjoyed success during the first London tour – had by now left the company, reckoning that in her capacity as classical ballerina the Ballets Suédois were not her vehicle.

'Judging him [Börlin] by this pantomime alone . . . we place him, of all the choreographs whose work has been seen over here, next to the supreme pedestal which is Fokine's. Indeed, in a sense, *El Greco* makes an advance on Fokine's work', commented *The Nation and the Athenaeum* (28 October). Only Kineton Parkes, who had seen all the Ballets Suédois' Paris productions, regretted, in a long and well-informed article, that the Swedes' programme did not include *Le Tombeau de Couperin, Skating Rink, Les Mariés de la tour Eiffel*, or *L'Homme et son désir*: 'Nothing comparable has been shown in England, but what we have seen nevertheless bears the stamp of a great artist – Jean Börlin.' Parkes's conclusion is interesting: 'Behind Rolf de Maré marches a little army of artists – choreographer, designers, painters, musicians, composers and sculptors – many of whom accompany their director on his trips to the capitals of Europe, gradually founding a reputation comparable to that of the Ballets Russes, the sole difference being that the Ballets Suédois possess a total homogeneity.'

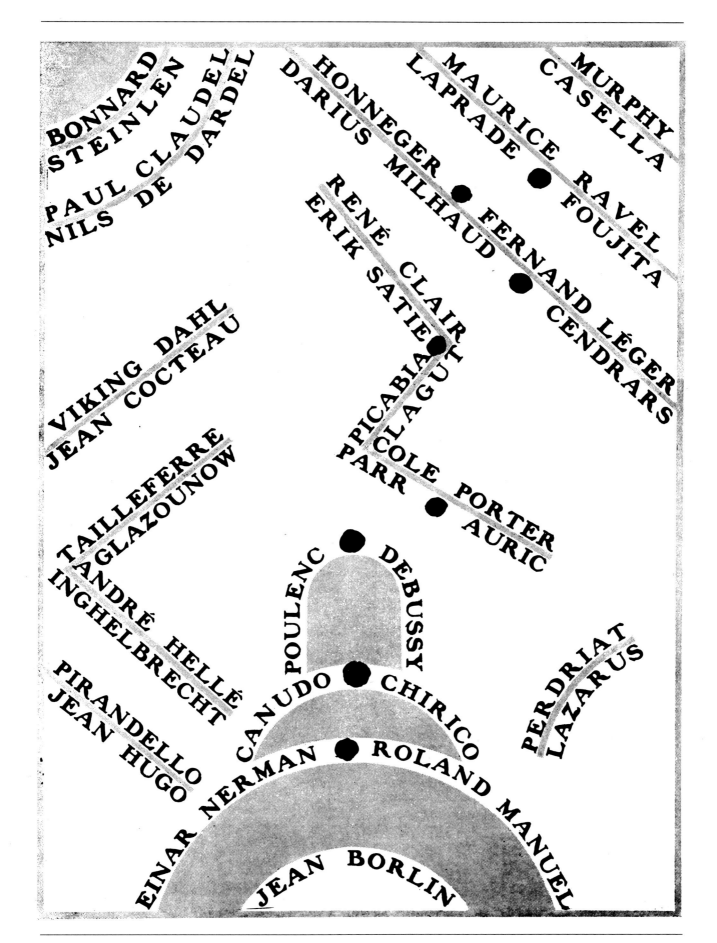

OFFERLUNDEN
(SACRED GROVE)

In May 1923, the Ballets Suédois returned to Paris, after an absence of more than a year. On 25 May, Börlin was ready to present two new ballets, *Offerlunden* (Sacred Grove) and *Marchand d'oiseaux* (The Snare).

While he was in Stockholm on his own (choreographing *Bergakungen* at the Opera), to the delight of his family Börlin agreed to choreograph a score by a relative of his, Algot Haquinius, a well-known pianist and teacher. The action of the resulting ballet, *Offerlunden*, centred round a sacrificial Viking site and unfolded in décors created by the painter Gunnar Hallström.

Börlin found the whole project, and particularly the old-fashioned theme, fairly uninspiring, and on seeing the ballet, Rolf de Maré (just returned to Paris after lengthy travels abroad, preparatory to further tours) decided to discontinue it. It was to be performed only five times.

MARCHAND D'OISEAUX
(THE SNARE)

The other ballet, *Marchand d'oiseaux* (The Snare), also created during Rolf de Maré's absence, gave Börlin in the principal role scope above all to express his charming sense of humour. *Marchand d'oiseaux* was a light work which contrasted with the generally aggressive and innovative spirit of the Ballets Suédois.

The moral of the libretto is a simple one. Two sisters, one proud, the other gentle and unassuming, are courted by two suitors. The proud sister thinks she has made a good catch by attracting a rich and powerful man, while the gentle sister dearly loves a poor man (Börlin, the bird seller). In the end, the situations turn out to be the reverse.

The music was composed by Germaine Tailleferre, one of the Six who had already had a hand in *Les Mariés de la tour Eiffel*. It was a choice that suited Rolf de Maré, who had a high regard for the Six, even though he was not involved in the creation of this particular ballet. '*Marchand d'oiseaux* is Germaine Tailleferre's most important work to date', André Messager said in *Le Figaro* (28 May 1923). The music, at once fresh and highly complex, was written in a Futurist spirit.

The visual conception and scenery were the work of Hélène Perdriat, wife of a Norwegian painter, Thorvald Hellesen, whom Börlin had met at the home of Nils and Thora Dardel. The sets glittered with strong and daring colours, the costumes had an utterly Parisian elegance, and the overall effect was consciously and wholeheartedly naïve, superficial and frivolous.

'Charming, quite charming, and deliberately so', declared Marcel Achard in *Le Peuple* (29 May). 'Quick, let us smile at *Marchand d'oiseaux*, at its fresh, acid décor, its ironic costumes. . . . A scenario? You want a scenario? Why?', asked Colette (27 May).

People were not accustomed to enjoying themselves in such a carefree fashion at the Ballets Suédois' performances. This and their few other relatively unambitious creations were to make the company truly popular and attract 'no longer just the élite or the snobs, but the general Paris public. That's real success', as Georges Auric concluded at the end of a long article.

Marchand d'oiseaux was performed twenty-eight evenings in succession, then a further sixty-five times during the following years.

Meanwhile, Rolf de Maré began making preparations for a tour of the United States, while projects for two new works which were to tie in with the Ballets Suédois' ambitions were already well under way. The première of *La Création du monde* (The Creation of the World) took place after the summer vacation, on 25 October 1923.

25 OCTOBER
LA CRÉATION DU MONDE
(THE CREATION OF THE WORLD)

Anthologie nègre (Negro Anthology), published in Paris in 1921, was an account of the myths and legends of Africa by the writer Blaise Cendrars, based on his own intensive studies. The author recorded ancient theories regarding the creation of the world, which differed from the Judaeo-Christian ones, although they all shared certain philosophical traits. This genesis of the black races inspired Cendrars to create a wordless scenic narrative which he proposed to de Maré as an idea for a ballet. De Maré was instantly fascinated by the possibilities such a scenario offered. 'This *Anthology* has a highly poetic quality', wrote Gilbert Seldes in *Vanity Fair* (December 1923), after attending rehearsals for the ballet. 'What we have here is, not a single poem, but rather a collection of poetic elements.'

The score was entrusted to Darius Milhaud, on whom the strange sonorous universe of the tropical forest and the African sounds of Brazilian music had left their mark.

In his Paris recital in 1920, Börlin had performed one of his first compositions, *Sculpture nègre*, a Cubist solo of great originality. For *La Création du monde*, he also studied some documentary films of the dances of black Africa by Rolf de Maré. As a result, this was the first European ballet in which the choreography was essentially derived from African dance.

'The purest movement we know is probably mechanical movement, hence that of *Skating Rink*', Karl Einstein had written in *Der Querschnitt* in the spring of 1922. Léger was to develop his ideas on the aesthetic of the machine in an article published in the same review the following year and dedicated to Mayakovsky: 'Modern man lives increasingly in a preponderant geometrical order.' Léger was planning a work of art conceived on the basis of geometric motifs in movement.

Léger himself painted the vast front curtain for *La Création du monde*. Offering a sort of prelude to the action, it rose slowly to reveal a stage plunged in darkness. At the back was a Cubist image, beneath which a shapeless mass could be discerned. Three enormous figures emerged, eight metres tall: the gods of creation, according to the legend. The figures began to move and, gradually, the whole tableau changed. From above, from below, and from either side, new pictorial elements joined in, came and then went, while the central mass 'boiled' like the lava in a crater, and weird, mysterious giants shuffled around on crutches, trees began to grow, a leaf turned into a huge insect, soon to be accompanied by the colourful shapes of various animals: reptiles, flying birds (carried by ballerinas on their points), and, finally, monkeys. The ballet's originality lay in the fact that all these figures represented the elements of a gigantic tableau, in constant movement and manifesting a kaleidoscope of varying designs and shifting colour constellations.

The gods united and glimpses of human forms could be seen emerging: a large unfinished leg, a back, a torso – until, finally, a couple appeared, the preliminary outlines of Adam and Eve, sculpted in muscular volumes, their tiny heads devoid of distinct features (the head of the costume was placed on top of a long neck which reached above the dancer's own head).

The first humans performed a fertility rite, a solemn, hieratic ceremony. Negroid figures, male and female, came to join them,

forming a large mobile chorus which took over the entire stage. Gradually, the action began to fade out, the décor reverted to its original simplicity, the vast stylized image of nature returned to rest, and characters and scenic elements quitted the stage, leaving the primal couple clinging together tenderly.

It should be stressed that the dancers blended completely with the mobile scenery and, dancing as they did on a shallow stage, seemed to move in a two-dimensional universe, like a painted picture. The performers were totally disguised by their costumes representing birds, insects or divinities, which had nothing in common with the human form but developed as free creations of the painter. Léger's basic principle was that the performer's face should be hidden behind a mask, to fix and neutralize its expression.

Milhaud's music added a further dimension to the visual action, which it supplemented. The score seemed appropriate, although the dancers' steps were not in time with the music but deliberately followed their own rhythm, sometimes in counterpoint fashion.

La Création du monde introduced several new – and lasting – ideas, such as:

the invention of movement in art or of art in movement (seven years before Léger's meeting with Calder, whose subsequent mobiles were defined as 'plastic forms in motion');

blues and off-beat elements heralding concert jazz and offering early strains of Concretism;

a totally abstract choreography, involving pure forms of movement, freed even of the limitations of the human body, as later found, for example, in the work of Maya Dehren and Alwin Nikolais and in video art;

music and choreography unfolding side by side as equal and autonomous entities whose respective contributions are essential but independent of one another – a technique opening up a host of new possibilities, to be rediscovered by John Cage and Merce Cunningham some thirty years later, and widely employed in modern dance.

It was perhaps the most innovative of all the Ballets Suédois' productions, crammed with fresh initiatives.

In the circle which gravitated around Rolf de Maré numerous theories were being elaborated, which were put to the test, in concrete form, on stage. It is difficult to establish *a posteriori* who contributed the most in the course of these interminable discussions and who had such and such an idea first. Cocteau, as we know, was to see his wishes fulfilled with *Les Mariés de la tour Eiffel* and subsequently participated less in such gatherings. Dardel, with his original and irreverent brainwaves, was always present at them. Satie and de Maré were closely attuned.

Börlin and Léger got on well and Mme Jeanne Léger was especially attached to the young choreographer, whom she took under her wing. Picabia added spice to the discussions. Milhaud contributed his own ideas and also acted as a channel for those of Claudel, by whom he had been profoundly influenced. Others participated in a more sporadic fashion.

The only one among them to record in writing the conclusions of this intense intellectual exchange was Léger, who spoke the least and listened the most attentively. Léger's 'ideas on theatre', published the year after *La Création du monde*, reflect the thoughts which were aired and the opinions and objectives elaborated in the Ballets Suédois' intimate circle. Léger was a theoretician who had a gift for summing up and expressing with clarity both his own and other people's thoughts.

The friendship Léger felt for de Maré, and perhaps still more for Börlin, underlined the artist's attraction to the theatre, an attraction which became evident in his painting. Léger was to look at the city with new eyes, discovering in it parallels with a theatrical spectacle. He and Börlin adopted the habit of going for long walks across Paris, enthusiastically discussing and analysing what they saw. In writing about painting in 1924, Léger crystallized theories that had been 'tried and tested' by the Ballets Suédois.

'To have to talk about spectacle is to imagine the world in all its daily visual manifestations (it has become one of the fundamental needs of existence). It dominates all contemporary life', Léger noted (*Functions of Painting*). Börlin, too, we may remember, sought in various ways to manifest a sense of the theatricality of life: that of the common people in contemporary Spain (*Iberia*), Italian body language (*La Jarre*, The Jar), a crowd as abstraction (*Skating Rink*).

According to Léger, the actor had to be absorbed into a scenic landscape in which the sets were mobile. The dancers and scenic elements were to be integrated by means of a mechanical choreography, giving the stage a physical and dynamic homogeneity. In evoking a production conceived in perfect accordance with his principles, what Léger was in fact describing was *La Création du monde*: the stage is shallow to create the impression that the action takes place in a two-dimensional universe, as though in a picture; the background is composed of mobile paintings which form part of the action, and the human components blend with, indeed vanish in, a variety of mobile sets, merely functioning as the motive force behind them.

In *Parade*, Picasso had suggested to Massine the notion of introducing a couple of compères who would wander around with a Cubist sculpture enveloping the upper part of their bodies, while their own legs were visible beneath. In his solo composition predating the Ballets Suédois, *Sculpture nègre*, Börlin had created, unaided, the first totally Cubist actor, a dancer transformed into a moving African sculpture. In *Les Mariés de la tour*

Eiffel, the actors had been entirely enclosed in constructions which represented caricatural types and lacked any physical resemblance to the performers. But it was in *La Création du monde*, with its insects, birds, and divinities devoid of human characteristics, its pure painterly creations, that this idea – the mechanical transformation of human reality – was given full expression.

The sets could equally well have been moved around by machinery, if sufficiently sophisticated robots had existed for the purpose: the fact that they were shifted by invisible dancers was merely a practical solution. *La Création du monde* was 'mechanical theatre', involving an unprecedented range of movements, whose wealth and variety remained unrivalled until the emergence of Alwin Nikolais, creator of abstract ballet in the purest sense of the term.

It is interesting to recall, too, the similar experiments that were taking place in Stuttgart, under the aegis of Oskar Schlemmer (particularly after 1922, when he became director of the Bauhaus theatre), as well as the dancing figures of the Italian painter Fortunato Depero.

As we have seen, one detail that Léger stressed in his theories was that the human face should be concealed, either by a mask or by make-up, which would fix and neutralize its expression. In this, he was reiterating one of Börlin's favourite arguments – inspired perhaps by the powerful impression that No theatre had exerted on Rolf de Maré in Japan, long before the inception of the Ballets Suédois. De Maré had often remarked that, thanks to the slight and subtle movements of the actors' heads, No masks acquire a more delicately nuanced, varying expression than any human face ever does. As was pointed out earlier, certain masks in *Les Mariés* resembled those of No theatre, and the stylized make-up in *Skating Rink* echoed the same principle.

In discussing Léger's ideas on theatre, art historians customarily recall the inspiration the artist drew from circus tradition – being, perhaps, more familiar with the latter than with dance. That Léger was profoundly influenced, from the start of his artistic career and for many years to come, by his encounters with the Ballets Suédois' leading lights, and his collaboration with them, merits far greater attention.

Léger was to speak out, the year after *La Création du monde*, and congratulate de Maré, once more the butt of attacks, for having been the first in France to dare stage a production involving nothing but machinery and light, and in which not a single human figure was visible on stage. In gently mocking terms, he also rendered homage to Börlin and to the rest of the company: the dancers had been reduced to moving stage sets around, and were far from pleased; they had become no more than objects in a collective and anonymous game, with no scope for expressing their own personality.

Reading the reviews devoted to *La Création du monde*, sixty years on, one is surprised by their scornful tone and unrelenting hostility: 'A semi-symphonic, semi-choreographic feast offered up by astute organizers to their benevolent snobbery' (Gustave Lamageuille, in *La Revue mondiale*, 15 November 1923); 'De Maré's dancers . . . too readily imagine that they are revealing to us the embryonic music and choreography of the future . . .' (*Feuilleton de temps*, 14 November); 'The feeling one gets listening to Darius Milhaud's latest productions is rage. . . . Going back to tom-toms, xylophones, bellowing brass and noise is not progress' (Pierre de Lapommeraye, in *Le Ménestrel*, 2 November); 'The painter has got out his antiquated glad rags, though one might have thought they had been put away for good' (Marcel Atais, in *L'Action française*, 6 November). In *Comœdia* (28 October), André Levinson, a very conservative young Russian language professor, passed the following judgment on *La Création du monde*: 'What an aberration, taking on living dancers to imitate the formulas of exotic sculptors by contorting themselves. No one can ever create a work for dancers by translating the conventions peculiar to the plastic arts by means of saltatory movement . . . the glamour of Negro sculpture, exalted to the skies by some great modern artists and adopted by the snobs.' Levinson's books on contemporary ballet exerted a strong influence on later historians, and his persistent scorn for the Ballets Suédois was largely responsible for the fact that their contribution to ballet has been so much neglected and undervalued by posterity – right up to the present day.

WITHIN THE QUOTA

The other ballet first staged by Börlin on 25 October 1923 was initially called *Landed* during the rehearsals. *Within the Quota*, the title finally selected, was an allusion to the United States' immigrant quota. Specially created in view of the company's impending American tour, the ballet told the story of a Swedish peasant boy who sailed to New York to make his fortune (Sweden was still poor and young unemployed Swedes were emigrating *en masse* to America).

The story-line provided an ironic treatment of the naïve peasant theme, but it was above all a satire ridiculing the 'American way of life': an entertaining piece of theatre with a wickedly cutting edge. One may wonder whether it was expedient for a company invited to visit a country to be criticizing its host from the outset. In fact, Rolf de Maré felt great warmth for America, retaining happy youthful memories of travelling across the entire country, playing at being a cowboy on a farm and living with Navajo and Hopi tribes; but tact was not his strong point and sentimentality scarcely in his nature.

However that may be, the libretto and also the scenography were the work of an authentic American, Gerald Murphy, the wealthy heir of a famous family of leather industrialists who had settled in the United States three generations earlier. Like many

Americans of his age, Murphy had made a home for himself in Paris. He was primarily a painter, long neglected, but rediscovered today as an interesting independent American artist of the twenties. The credit for being the first to discover his talent belongs to Rolf de Maré, who was also the first to recognize that of a young American playboy in Paris, Cole Porter, whose fame with the American press resided principally in his marriage to a high-society Southern belle, Linda Lee Thomas. *Within the Quota* was Porter's first important commission, predating by five years the wide acclaim he was to win in 1928. His gifts were perfectly suited to this witty jazz score which recalled themes borrowed from the rich resources of black rhythms.

La Revue de France described this first true jazz ballet in the following terms: 'Backdrop: an immense page from an American newspaper, as though projected on to a screen, presenting sensational pieces of news carefully selected to create an American atmosphere: *Unknown banker buys Atlantic*, etc. To one side of the stage a cameraman is filming. American characters take it in turns to come and say, without resorting to words, merely through their American dress and their American mime: "America is the country of contrasts." The wide-eyed immigrant, encumbered with cases, sees the whole New York carnival passing before him: the millionairess swathed in pearls, pursued by the social reformer; the Negro dressed in old rose, with his ragtime music and his bottle of whisky, fleeing from the clutches of the income-tax collector; the hip-swaying *femme fatale* lectured by the gloomy Quaker; the cowboy brandishing his revolvers; and, just when the unfortunate immigrant seems to have given up all attempts to get acclimatized in the New World, the blonde film star, Sweetheart-of-the-World. Frenetic finale: the characters "revolve" jerkily, as in an old movie. When the spectators start clapping, the cameraman swivels his apparatus towards the audience: the "revolutions" continue. A thoroughly enjoyable show, full of irony, laughter and movement.'

This lively and amusing ballet was greeted with enthusiasm by the Paris public, and the press reported laughter and applause.

In the programme, *Within the Quota* was described as a 'ballet-sketch'. The original intention had been to call it a 'ballet-cine-sketch': not only were the roles borrowed from the world of cinema, but the form of the ballet itself also borrowed from screen technique. The shallow stage space appeared flat, tending to create a two-dimensional effect, and short sequences rapidly succeeded one another, with linked cuts or dissolves, reminiscent of film montage. Here was yet another ballet involving the invention of a totally new form.

The evening's programme also included two purely musical sections, one of them devoted to Satie (two *Gymnopédies*, *Rêverie de Pantagruel*, *Marche de cocagne*, *Jeux de Gargantua* and *Danses du piège de Méduse*), as well as two choral pieces by

Charles Koechlin, who had orchestrated Cole Porter's score for *Within the Quota*.

The second musical section introduced the Arcueil school, four young admirers of Satie: Henri Sauguet, Roger Désormière, Maxime Jacob and Henri Cliquet-Pleyel. These young composers were mercilessly slated by the critics, and a few additional barbs were aimed at Rolf de Maré himself for having had the insolence to introduce Paris to such insipid talent.

Due to shortage of time, this programme comprising *La Création du monde*, *Within the Quota* and the concert was only presented three times at the Théâtre des Champs-Élysées prior to the company's departure for the United States; but Rolf de Maré had been eager for his beloved Paris to have, as always, first bite at the cherry.

NEW WORLD TOUR

On 3 November 1923, Rolf de Maré set sail for New York from Cherbourg, accompanied by Murphy and the conductor Golsch-mann, who was due to begin rehearsals with the orchestra. Cole Porter left the same day from Le Havre, followed a week later by Börlin and the rest of the company. When they left to make their conquest of the New World, the Ballets Suédois had eight hundred and fifty European performances to their credit.

Jenny Hasselquist had left the company in 1921, and Carina Ari in the spring of 1923. The principal roles had been taken over by Irma Calson and Margit Wahlander, classical ballerinas who had succeeded in adapting their technique to Börlin's style. Other important solo dancers were Jolanda Figoni, Dagmar Forslin and Greta Lundberg. These last, however, handed in their resignation just before the United States tour, and Ebon Strandin, prima ballerina with the Stockholm Opera, then joined the company, along with a number of other dancers.

The contract for this tour had been made with the impresario Richard Herndon and his associate Florence Ziegfeld. It was subsequently revealed that Ziegfeld had had no part in the drafting of the contract and that Herndon had overlooked the stage dimensions prescribed by de Maré. At the time, there were only four or five theatres in New York large enough to accommodate the Ballets Suédois' stage sets.

Herndon had promised the company the Metropolitan Opera, but having failed to obtain it, had hired the Ambassador Theater for six weeks and fixed the date of the première for 19 November. To his consternation, however, de Maré discovered that the Ambassador's stage was too small. Inevitably, finding a larger theatre that was free at the eleventh hour was practically impossible. By good fortune, however, he succeeded in obtaining the Century Theater, whose reputation was equally good, but whose stage was barely adequate, and whose technical equip-ment, particularly with regard to lighting, was poor. The theatre

was not free until 26 November and the company remained idle for a week. Moreover, the Century was only available for one week, during which the company was to give nine performances with additional matinées on the Wednesday, Thursday and Saturday, an exhausting programme for the dancers. Following this week in New York, two weeks of performances had to be organized in an improvised fashion in Philadelphia and Wash-ington, before the company returned once more to the Century for a further spell.

Such uncertainty prior to the première, whose importance in a city like New York needs no stressing, was extremely detrimental. Press communiqués had to be sent out to encourage the public, geared up for the 19th, to be patient, and to announce, moreover, a two-week break right in the middle of the run. The damage was irreparable.

The company's second season, which began on Christmas Night, failed to attract the interest of the public or the press and had to be cut short by two weeks, following which the company was obliged to tour twenty-six provincial towns. To crown their misfortune, the second New York period coincided with a large motorcar exhibition which lured a great many people away from the Broadway theatres.

In the general course of things, competition was fierce in New York, whose density of theatres was unparalleled in Europe. During the Ballets Suédois' New York period, three productions of *Hamlet* were running, with a choice between John Barrymore, Walter Hampden and Sir John Martin Harvey; ten other plays by British authors such as George Bernard Shaw, John Galsworthy and Somerset Maugham; five French plays; and two in Spanish, including one by Molnár; also on offer were Scandinavian and classical dramas starring Eleonora Duse, and productions by companies visiting New York, such as the Moscow Art Theatre and Paris's Grand-Guignol.

The Americans were less used to ballet than the Europeans. Diaghilev failed to draw a full house during his first tour in 1914 and did little better in 1920. A handful of Russian émigrés, including Adolph Bolm and Pavley-Oukrainsky, founded com-panies that were more or less short-lived. Only Anna Pavlova succeeded in filling the theatres wherever she went, her conservative and romantic repertoire, quite as much as her brilliant technique, corresponding perfectly to public taste. In the free modern style, American pioneers like Ruth St Denis, with her Oriental-style dancing, and Ted Shawn had their following; Isadora Duncan, better understood in Europe, met a fair amount of resistance on returning to her native country.

Fokine, Bolm and other Russians opened schools to train young Americans, but 'no native talent in this limited time has had a chance to become fully developed', declared a correspon-dent for *Dancing Times* (April 1924).

Rolf de Maré was eager to start the tour with some of his most advanced works: *L'Homme et son désir*, *Les Mariés de la tour*

Eiffel, Skating Rink, and *Les Vierges folles*. Although it had been included in the original schedule, *La Création du monde* could not possibly be staged in the available theatres and had to be omitted.

It turned out to be rough fare, indigestible for a public unaccustomed to such things. The critics split into two camps: one went in for subtle analyses, calmer and more objective than many of those that had been published in Paris; the other either claimed point blank not to understand a thing or jeered.

But praise prevailed in the end: 'The Swedish Ballet represents a definite breaking off from what may be called the Romantic Period of the ballet, as exemplified and brought to its perfection by the Russian Ballet. . . . M. De Maré has made the bold decision – a decision which may revolutionize choreography – to attempt to express the modern world in terms of itself' (*New York Tribune*, 18 November). The *New York Times* (6 December) spoke of an 'extraordinary event in New York's most international season', and the *Washington Times* (6 December) went still further: 'An absolutely unprecedented experience in the theatre . . . remarkable choreography, which is really the synthesis of the ultramodern tendencies in music, art and the dance. . . . The outstanding thing about Le Ballet [*sic*] Suédois is that it undertakes to unify modern tendencies in the arts for the first time, just as Wagner combined those of his less hectic time.'

As so often before, journalists queried the Ballets Suédois' links with Sweden. Certainly, the dancers and the directors were Swedish, but 'The Ballets Suédois is distinctly Parisian in flavour. . . . French composers of the most advanced school have their first adequate American hearing in this program. . . . The names of Auric, Milhaud and Honegger are prominent, on the scenic side of the production, the outstanding artist is Fernand Léger, who outpaints the Russians in modernity' (*State Journal*, Columbia, 2 December).

The dancers all received their share of praise and the American critics understood better than their opposite numbers in France that the new choreography demanded a different type of execution from what they had become accustomed to in classical dance. On 26 November, Leonard Liebling wrote in the *New York American*: 'the Russe style is much simpler than the Suédois. There is less actual dancing to the latter and a great deal more pantomiming. The "bite" of the stories is sharper. The humour verges on the bitterly ironical.'

The reception by the press was overly respectful and positive, though no critic appreciated all four works in a programme. One found a particular ballet excellent, another hated it but praised a different one. 'Only one of the four ballets . . . came easily within our comprehension', confessed Burnes Mantle in the *New York News* (26 November). 'To some of it we responded instantly, some of it we respected, although we may not have understood perfectly. With some of it, however, we

found ourself [*sic*] in instant and violent disagreement' (*New York World*, 9 December). 'New York never heard a greater hub-bub of discussion than was evoked by this modern music, these new art formulas, this new school of expression – amusing, stimulating and very wonderful' (*Times of St Louis*, 1 December).

Among the reporters who poked fun at the Ballets there was Alexander Woolcott of the *New York Herald* (26 November), who saw Jean Börlin in *L'Homme et son désir* 'writhe for fifteen minutes in a talented manner – wearing the while no more protective covering than what seemed to be a thin and insufficient coating of butter'. In *Les Mariés de la tour Eiffel*, he noted, 'sundry of the new composers take several tunes and twist them till they howl'.

Unlike the French, the Americans did not appreciate being 'bowled over'. Another of these witty critics wrote: 'Nothing behind the footlights was more interesting than the collective expression of the observers in front of them. The audience, in bewilderment, figuratively clapped its collective hand to its collective head and then pinched itself to make sure that what it saw it was really seeing. . . . When the audience had partly recovered from its pained surprise it sat up and took notice. It did partly recover, it is true, but it is doubtful whether it will ever be quite the same audience again.'

The review in *Variety* (6 December) echoed the sentiments of the spectator in a matter-of-fact way: 'Pretty tiresome stuff this Swedish Ballet. Over two and a half hours of different varieties of ballet terpsichore is too consistent a diet for any playgoer . . .'. (But this critic liked neither *La Chauve-Souris* nor the Moscow Art Theatre, so the Ballets Suédois were in good company at least.)

A few days later, *Les Mariés de la tour Eiffel* was replaced by *Within the Quota*. This ballet was unanimously acclaimed and the remarks made by *Musical Courier* (13 December) reflected the opinion of the entire press: 'this was the best thing the company showed. It was bright, witty, finely danced and pantomimed.' The ballet was greeted as typically American thanks to its rapid rhythm, its jazz music and, of course, its allusions to the cinema greats, as also its humour. The fact that it thereby mocked its host country was in no way taken amiss, except by the Swedish immigrants, who expressed in their journal (published in Swedish) their indignation that a Swede should have been depicted as a country bumpkin.

After nine performances in one week, the Ballets Suédois left for Philadelphia and Washington. In the capital they had to make do with its smallest theatre and consequently abandon the idea of staging any of their most important ballets. An operetta, *La Chauve-Souris* (The Bat), being performed simultaneously by a Paris company in one of Washington's largest theatres, was entirely sold out, whereas the Ballets Suédois did not even manage to fill their tiny auditorium. The *Washington News* provided the explanation: the two performances were equally interesting, it said, but the price of tickets for the Ballets Suédois was more than double that for *La Chauve-Souris*, that is, eight dollars against three dollars and thirty cents. The Ballets Suédois' impresario, the incredibly blinkered Mr Herndon, had tried to compensate for the small number of seats by fixing a far higher ticket price than anything the public was used to.

Rolf de Maré was seriously worried. He had hoped to make a name for his ballet company in the United States and establish a second arena there. He was acquainted with a number of interesting, as yet little-known, American artists and composers and calculated that there might be scope for a large permanent ballet company in the United States. He had envisaged settling there for six months of the year, while remaining the other six in Paris.

In anticipation of the company's return to New York, he decided to compromise on the repertoire in order to give the public more of what it liked – something he had never done in Paris. On 25 December, he opened the season with the company's easiest ballets: *Marchand d'oiseaux*, *Nuit de Saint-Jean*, a lengthy divertissement and, of course, *Within the Quota*, which had rapidly become very popular; later on, he also restaged *La Boîte à joujoux*.

This lighter programme was greeted with enthusiasm. One of its readers, Ray Jamieson, wrote to the *New York Times* (26 December): 'The new numbers are so pleasing, so charming, so beautiful, the dancing so skillful and graceful, the composition of the ballets so original and unique, that at the finish of the program I found myself filled with unlimited enthusiasm for the Swedish Ballet.' But the writer admits that 'on tour its success was but mild. America was not yet ready for the modernists.'

One consequence, at least, of the Ballets Suédois' tour was that it gave rise to a lively debate on the future of this art form: 'Why Can't We Have a True American Ballet?', one headline read, spread across five columns of the *New York Herald* (20 January). All the papers agreed that ballet would be the great art of the future in the United States. And how right they were!

The lengthy provincial tour, taking in twenty-six towns, required a tremendous effort on the part of the dancers. They were generally well received and their takings were now more satisfactory, thanks to the price of seats being dropped to a reasonable level. But the theatres were often poorly equipped and the journeys were tiring. The company's dancers were no doubt more used to touring than many others (with the exception of Pavlova's), but their journeys across Europe had been, above all, more tranquil affairs and their ballets were complicated to execute, particularly with regard to technical requirements and lighting. The tour ended at Allentown on 1 March 1924, and Rolf de Maré granted the weary company a long holiday (with full salaries paid, as always), so that the dancers would have time to return to their families in Sweden.

On his return to Paris, Rolf de Maré began legal proceedings against the American organizers of the tour for alleged malpractice. The case dragged on, and in the end de Maré decided that, being a foreigner, it was hopeless for him to continue fighting with cavilling American lawyers and he gave up. Until that point, the Ballets Suédois had more or less managed to cover their expenses, except during the period of inflation on their German tour. The sums lost in the United States made serious inroads into de Maré's resources. He was well off, it is true, but not as rich as was generally believed. He began quietly selling pieces from his immense art collection, which comprised works by all the great contemporaries, only keeping the paintings to which he was most attached: works by Dardel, Picasso, Braque, Bonnard, Laurencin and Léger. At that time, a Gauguin, Monet, Kandinsky or Miró did not fetch the astronomical sums they go for today, but the sheer number of works sold brought in enough money for de Maré to continue to maintain his company.

1924

Caught up in the task of devising new programmes and preparing the choreography for them, Börlin took no holiday: no fewer than five works had to be created for the autumn of 1924. Diaghilev, far more cautious, continued to stage retrospective performances of Fokine's masterpieces from the years 1909 and 1910, putting on fewer new creations. In contrast, de Maré, like Börlin, was impatient to create and innovate. And yet the fate of *La Création du monde* remains hard to explain: this ballet, perhaps the Ballets Suédois' greatest masterpiece, was only performed three times prior to the American tour and, due to the American theatres' lack of technical equipment, not at all during the tour itself; the fact that it was then only given nine more times in Paris, and was thus performed only twelve times in all, seems incomprehensible. But a similar fate had previously befallen an even more important work, Nijinsky's *Sacre du printemps*.

The première of the 1924/25 season took place on 19 November and comprised four new ballets: *Le Roseau* (The Reed), *Le Porcher* (The Swineherd), *Le Tournoi singulier* (The Curious Tournament) and *La Jarre* (The Jar). The Ballets Suédois were also in the middle of preparations for another major ballet, *Relâche* (Cancelled) – unaware that it was in fact to be their last.

LE ROSEAU (THE REED)

Le Roseau (The Reed) was based on an old Persian legend: while listening to the sound of a flute, a young man is smitten with love. But another melody brings him a divine revelation and he recognizes that his longing is spiritual in origin. He renounces earthly love in order to devote himself to prayer. Medieval Persian miniatures provided the inspiration for some very beautiful costumes and, to go with Daniel Lazarus's polytonal music, Börlin created a sensual choreography based on Indian body movement.

LA JARRE (THE JAR)

La Jarre (The Jar) was based on a libretto by Luigi Pirandello, with music composed by Alfredo Casella, and sets and costumes created by Giorgio de Chirico. De Maré and Börlin went to see the collaborators in Italy in order to coordinate the work, and Börlin took advantage of the trip to refresh his knowledge of Italian folk dancing. Their aim was to create a vast realist depiction of the life of the common people – like de Maré's earlier ambition with regard to Spain (*Iberia*) and Sweden (*Nuit de Saint-Jean*).

The ballet opens with a festival in a Sicilian village. A gigantic oil jar has cracked, and the humpbacked potter, come to mend it, is obliged to get inside for the purpose. Once he has finished the job, his hump prevents him from getting out again. The jar has to be broken a second time to free him, and his release gives rise to much hilarity. This rustic farce, full of abrupt reversals with their roots in the *commedia dell'arte*, provided the pretext for lively, large-scale danced scenes in the Sicilian tradition.

'An ingenious pretext', wrote Georges Auric in *La Revue française* (14 December 1924), 'for a succession of scenes that are by turns playful, solemn, tumultuous, ironic, joyful, and even poetic and moving, as in the delightful Nocturne which divides the action into two.' With regard to Casella, *Le Figaro* observed that he 'behaves rather like a magician. . . . He lines up so many orchestral combinations, almost all of them performed at breathtaking speed, that one finds one ends up dazed, but very agreeably impressed, without being able to assess the true value of the music.'

'De Chirico's scenery in *La Jarre* is worthy of the artist', wrote Paul Husson in the review *Montparnasse*. 'The almost unreal whiteness of the stone, as if transfigured into something human . . . the costumes, harmonizing with the décor, are happy splashes of colour in the overall picture, musical notes depending for their quality on day- or night-time lighting effects.'

LE PORCHER
(THE SWINEHERD)

Le Porcher (The Swineherd), which appeared in the same programme, was a light entertainment based on Hans Andersen's fairy-tale about the princess and the swineherd, and accompanied by tunes from old Swedish songs. The ballet's naïve style recalled that of *Les Vierges folles*, though *Le Porcher* lacked the coherence and rigorous formal construction of the other work.

Börlin incorporated into it a major classical solo, for no other purpose, apparently, than that of showing off his technical expertise. He was tired of seeing his abilities called into question by various critics and, in particular, by the fanatical Levinson, who loathed anything that smacked of modernism. And for the first and only time, Levinson expressed himself in complimentary terms: 'Börlin has given himself over to a great variation of glissades and leaps with impressive diagonal descents; and this, while doubling his cabrioles and skilfully executing certain flying entrechats cinq, or even entrechats sept, if I observed correctly.'

LE TOURNOI SINGULIER
(THE CURIOUS TOURNAMENT)

Le Tournoi singulier (The Curious Tournament), initially entitled *Golf Links* during the rehearsals, borrowed its theme from the work of a great Renaissance poet, Louise Labé, precursor of Ronsard. The story was inspired by a classical myth: Love, wounded by Folly, goes blind, and to punish Folly, Venus condemns her to remain an eternal companion to Love.

The action was transposed to a modern golf course, and it was in teaching him how to play the game that Folly wounded Love in the eye with a badly hit ball. Foujita's scenery blended stylistic components from Japan and Europe: a combination of disparate elements prefiguring Surrealism. Accompanied by Roland-Manuel's highly elaborate, at once archaistic and discreetly modernistic musical score, *Le Tournoi singulier* was a work of great eccentricity.

The four new ballets of 19 November 1924 had definite qualities, without being – with the exception of *La Jarre* – important works. The public enjoyed them for their thematic diversity and contrast, heightened by the inclusion of *La Création du monde* in the same evening's programme. Jane Catulle-Mendès wrote in *Presse et Patrie* (23 November 1924): 'However vigorously the tendencies of Rolf de Maré's productions may continue to be discussed, there is no denying that they are governed by a harmonious and precise artistic purpose. In this way, we enjoy a variety of pleasures, interlinked by a sort of single inspiration whereby the different aspects of the same

orientation may be demonstrated. That excess should be the norm in these works comes as no surprise to anyone.... Horrors! Futurism has almost reached its classic hour.'

4 DECEMBER
RELÂCHE (CANCELLED)

The plan for *Relâche* (Cancelled) originated in the winter of 1923 and was devised by Blaise Cendrars, author of *La Création du monde*. Rolf de Maré asked Erik Satie to compose the music, and Francis Picabia, who was passionate about the project, to create the sets.

Cendrars's original idea was gradually eroded as Picabia began to develop his own. And since the writer had gone off travelling in Argentina, *Relâche* was to become rather more Picabia's work (with assistance from Börlin and Satie) than Cendrars's.

Picabia had been a member of the Dadaist movement, but had just broken his ties with it, on the grounds that it was too exclusively literary. The Dadaists did not like the Ballets Suédois, their ideological rivals, and disliked them all the more after Picabia switched his allegiance. The bizarre situation thus arose in which two similar tendencies, each as radical as the other, came into conflict, while the same public admired and respected the ultra-innovative quality of both.

Picabia launched the first attack in *Paris-Journal* (27 June 1924): 'Erik Satie is in my opinion the most interesting of contemporary French musicians, and if I am collaborating with him on this ballet, which is called *Relâche*, it is because I see him as such, and as the youngest, and more alive than many young men who strut through life like so many Montgolfiers', and so on – all of it directed against his opponents, the Dadaists. A week later, on learning that René Clair was in the process of making a film, written by Picabia, for the Ballets Suédois, René Faucher wrote in *Candide cinématographique*: 'I know that one ought not to judge a work in advance. But I am inclined to think, nevertheless, that all that Picabia has done up to now, up to Dadaism's latest lucky windfalls, has struck us as the fruit of the most sinister brainwashing, or of a brain atrophied by the emanations of a genius no doubt too great for it.' Rolf de Maré was interviewed in *L'Ère nouvelle* (26 October): 'And what about Picabia's famous ballet?', asked Raymond Godin. '*Relâche* will not mean *relâche* [cancelled] for the public, you can be sure of that', replied de Maré (unwisely, as we shall see . . .). 'The sets? – They are perhaps not sets, just as the music will and yet will not be music, just as it will be a ballet while not being a ballet. . . . That's life as Picabia sees it.'

Even the title of *Relâche* was provocative, giving Rolf de Maré the opportunity to create a play on words: '*Relâche n'est pas relâche, mais "Relâche"'* (*Relâche* is not *relâche* [cancelled] but '*Relâche*' [break, relaxation]).

On 27 November 1924, all of fashionable Paris flocked to the Théâtre des Champs-Élysées, as it always did for the Ballets Suédois' premières: 'Avenue Montaigne was black with tail coats, the pearls and the diamonds shone, and an agreeable bottle-neck of luxury cars, added to the barbarous clamour of horns, gave the overall scene a distinctly Cubist feel' (*La France*, 29 November 1924). And yet, there were no lights at the Théâtre des Champs-Élysées and ushers, posted outside, invited those arriving to stay in their cars. There was . . . *relâche*, no performance!

The guests wondered for a moment if a practical joke had been played on them, but were finally convinced by Picabia and de Maré's detailed explanations: Börlin was ill, with a fever of 104°; de Maré had decided to cancel the performance, but it had been too late to inform the public through the media.

Börlin was finally able to dance on 4 December and fashionable Paris once more donned its evening dresses and its dinner-jackets and returned to see this 'instantaneous ballet', vividly described by Jane Catulle-Mendès in *Presse et Patrie* (6 December): 'In a profession of faith recorded in the programme, Francis Picabia announces an "art representing its time with all the possibilities of that time" and assures us that: "Henceforth, theatre will be able to unite everything, without boring the public; nothing in theatre is definitive: it is a marvellous, dazzlingly bright slate, capable of constant and multiple renewal." Has he, with *Relâche*, fulfilled the promise embodied in these fine words? Yes . . . in these frenetic and baroque excesses, there is an art that is at once wild and deliberate, and a sort of stormy harmony. . . . These furious notions have one happy consequence at least, which is that they upset the routine of the theatre, they make it impossible. They have prompted us to breathe new life into, and to synthesize, the dusty and amorphous art of staging which previously ground along in its antiquated way. They perform an important service. . . . There is [newness] in this enormous farce, governed by a sort of rhythm relating to cosmogony and ataxia and, all in all, fairly representative of this age of ours which Francis Picabia is seeking to render instantaneous. . . . First of all, we have some cinema – very funny, thanks to the opposition of slow and super-fast motion – in which we see two men, one moving in a methodical fashion, the other frantically, shooting a cannonball at us: a symbol that is not difficult to interpret. Then, the curtain rises on a strange, glittering décor, clearly intended to symbolize the wings of a theatre by presenting a magnified image of the lighting panel, seen in terms of enormous coloured discs. The backdrop is made up of several hundred motorcar headlights – a salute to Balla! – directed towards the auditorium. When these are lit, the spectators, blinded, can no longer see what is happening on stage. A fireman wanders around, and since we

are in the realm of paradox – which frequently assumes the appearance of reality – he lights a cigarette and smokes it. A woman wearing diamonds, no doubt the star dancer come to rehearse, arrives via the auditorium. She practises a few steps, sits down, and smokes a cigarette, too. Enter five slender gentlemen in black evening dress. The woman and the puppet-men play games. She half undresses and walks over their bent backs as if they were a bridge. Finally, one of them carries her off. *Entr'acte*. A highly bizarre sequence of film acts as a filler here, pushing to the limit the "chases" typical of American cinema; it's a sort of convulsive bacchanal, giving frantic expression to the current material and moral disorder. The story? It has the incoherence of those we are habitually being shown. It's a form of idiocy to which a stick of dynamite has been added: dazzlingly inventive. A sportsman is trying to shoot an egg balancing on a jet of water. He succeeds. A pigeon flies out and settles on the sportsman's cap, which is decorated with a pheasant's feather. Another marksman aims his gun at the pigeon, and kills the man instead. Funeral: the hearse drawn by a camel; macabre, far-fetched jokes. The hearse unhitches itself from the camel and clears off, accelerating as it goes. Family and friends in pursuit. A topsy-turvy landscape, upside-down sky, rooftops sticking their chimney-pots into the ground, all hell let loose. Finally, the hearse tips out the coffin, from which steps, not a corpse, but an urbane gentleman wreathed in smiles [Jean Börlin]. Clearly, there is a philosophy to be uncovered in this intentional hysteron proteron. But let us not dwell on it. *Second act*. Another sort of backdrop. Zig-zag, snake-like arrows, groups of broken lines, parallel slanting lines, verticals, ellipses, polygons, notices, advertisements, provocative spiralling and whorled maxims, the whole' Futurist excess. Re-enter men in evening dress and lady with diamonds, brought in on a wheel-barrow and accompanied by a nurse. None the worse for this, she begins to interact once more with the puppets in black, etc. While they continue their antics, the fireman, as a true brother of the Danaides, repeatedly pours water from one bucket into another. What is meant by this? With regard to the fireman, the sense is clear. As his name indicates, he personifies the stagnancy of obsolete traditions. [The secondary meaning of *pompier* (fire-man) is 'conventionalist; uninspired, traditional person'.] As for the rest, we are told that it signifies the "Dog's tail". Better not to enquire further. The music of Erik Satie, the great patron of the noisy young school, is based on themes from children's round games, in which I thought I recognized, among others, *À mon beau château, ma tante Tirelirelire*, and uses rhythms imitating modern machinery. All the cinematographic comings and goings follow the triple time of a locomotive engine puffing out steam at full pelt, repeated to the point at which it produces a kind of oppression. First Erik Satie was cheered, the audience clamouring for him to be hauled back on stage; then Picabia, who came out, bowing, in a motorcar, with Erik Satie at his side, and the latter's many followers applauded him a second time. For hardly anyone was shocked, or jeered . . . there wasn't a hint of a whistle. Was Francis Picabia – who claimed: "I prefer to hear them shouting than clapping" – not going to be disappointed by his success? Jean Börlin – a little thinner, it seemed – gave of his customary grace and alluring, thoughtful artistry. Mlle Edith Bonsdorff provides a very effective partner for him.'

De Maré and Börlin could draw comfort from the fact that people generally were enthusiastic, and the Dadaists so taken aback as to have forgotten to use their whistles. They had won the day without compromising their beliefs and had presented a work that was totally different from anything previously staged.

Relâche was a forerunner of much later trends. The formula was adopted again in around 1950 by John Cage, Merce Cunningham and Robert Rauschenberg, fervent admirers of Satie and of all that he stood for, and 'dance-less' ballet is an accepted phenomenon today – thanks to the work of Pina Bausch. Happenings in a way also originate with *Relâche*, their apparently absurd and disconnected events reflecting, in a minutely calculated, rigorous but irregular form, a language of oneiric and hermetic symbols which is open to valid interpretation by each individual spectator. James Joyce's *Finnegans Wake* (1939) and certain types of modern art carry similar implications. And let us not forget the significance of Satie's 'furniture music' (of which *Relâche* was the most potent manifestation) for musical trends up until the sixties, given the success of 'Muzak'. *Relâche* contains so many innovative ideas that it can still function today as a source of inspiration.

Conservative critics had a whale of a time slating the ballet. Jean Gandrey-Rety, writing in *Comœdia* (6 December), piled on the invectives: 'You are the worst of conventionalists [the double meaning of *pompier* ('fireman', 'conventionalist') is lost in translation], conventionalists busy pumping the void, pundits of the abstruse, academicians of the ugly . . . all the banalities of the most run-of-the-mill advertising, all the rituals of the most current third-rate acting. And our dear composer – the greatest in the world, don't you know! – comes to take his bow, awkward, shy, as overcome with emotion as a young girl', and so on – two columns' worth in this vein.

André Levinson also published one of his vituperative articles in *Comœdia*: 'There is nothing more paltry than the evolutions of a corps de ballet made up of fops in evening dress. . . . The laborious and awkward inconsistency of their exercises. . . . The film *Entr'acte*: all the comical effects of its shooting, all the tricks of the lens, all the changes in speed, unprecedented short cuts, contradictory superimpositions, all the successive trick pictures current in the cinema have been applied by René Clair. Clair preaches incoherence, the untampered development of the image, the surprise of chance juxtapositions . . . .'

The composer Georges Auric, who collaborated on *Les Mariés de la tour Eiffel*, affirmed that Satie's work 'is a miserable pastiche, lacking any lustre or warmth, and in which everything is false, awkward and outdated. An orchestration of exceptional poverty adds to our embarrassment . . .'.

Roland-Manuel, who had composed the music of the Ballets' *Le Tournoi singulier* (premièred only a few weeks earlier), published a crushing three-column critique in *L'Éclair* (9 December): 'Picabia and Satie impose on us the games of a fantasy without imagination, the insults of a vulgarity without spirit, which are truly unbearable. Erik Satie's music . . . an imitation of the most shameless caterwauling. . .'.

The once friendly circle of collaborators had by now disintegrated: some of them had developed a violent mutual dislike and felt no qualms about viciously attacking the others' work. Georges Pioch, writing in *Partisans* (January 1925), commented: 'The right to senility is in the nature of things and, hence, indefeasible. Erik Satie's glory lies in having made use of that right to an extent that defies all competition . . .' (Satie was fifty-eight). *Le Monde musical* (December 1924) simplified matters: '*Relâche* can't be discussed, recounted, or analysed. *Relâche* isn't anything at all.'

Even a critic generally as serene and elegant as Émile Vuillermoz adopted a scornful tone: 'The indefatigable Rolf de Maré . . . has resumed with touching application his role of Bolshevik by persuasion . . . and has requested Picabia, Erik Satie, Fernand Léger, Blaise Cendrars, Darius Milhaud and their like to continue the sequence of their dreary excercises as *agents provocateurs*' (*Candide*, 27 November). He concluded by warmly praising the ballet *La Jarre*: 'While congratulating Rolf de Maré for presenting us with a work of such high calibre, let us hope that he may at last understand that such works represent more decisive, more courageous, and indeed more daring, annexations in the domain of art than the back-room farces which amuse fashionable Montparnasse but which exert no real influence on the musical history of our time.'

It is strange to see a great critic, as Vuillermoz, during the course of his lengthy career, certainly was, erring so seriously with regard to a work of such historical importance: *La Jarre* may indeed have been a good ballet, but it was not epoch-making like *Relâche*, and Casella may have been a good composer, but he came nowhere near Satie. The difference is so clear to us all today that it is hard to understand how a critic of Vuillermoz's calibre could have been quite so badly mistaken.

Vuillermoz was eventually to change his mind. When, twenty-five years later, Rolf de Maré suggested that he might like to write a book about Börlin, he agreed enthusiastically. With hindsight, he regarded the Ballets Suédois in quite a different light, recognizing that they represented one of the most important artistic events he had witnessed. (He died, unfortunately, before he had had time to write the book.)

René Clair and his film *Entr'acte* were a little more warmly received. The film has the advantage of living on after the ballet

finished running, and *Entr'acte* is today a classic of cinema history, repeatedly shown throughout the world, particularly now that the sound-track of Satie's music has been added.

It is perhaps surprising that de Maré, like Diaghilev, never filmed his ballets. And yet de Maré was a great film buff, had even created several full-length films himself, and was to go on to produce documentaries. In an interview given to *Scénario* (1 March 1921), he explained why he had not had any films made of the Ballets Suédois: 'It seems to me that there is too big a gap between dance and screen. We are faced with a question of rhythm and timing which is difficult to sort out. It would require the reel to be run by an invisible conductor.' (The only dance by Börlin to be filmed was *Dervishes*, where the absence of music was not felt to be important.)

So the difficulty, according to de Maré, resided in the fact that the film was silent and that an exact correspondence between the dancing and the music was practically impossible to achieve when one had, on the one hand, a mechanically run film and, on the other, an orchestra physically present in the auditorium. Satie resolved this problem in relation to the film *Entr'acte* by writing music which did not need to synchronize with the performers' movements, but offered, on the contrary, an independent, parallel commentary on those movements: it consisted of 'ritornellos', and the manner in which this repetitive music seemed to alter in tone according to the influence exerted on it by the images was simply miraculous.

There was something extraordinary, something unprecedented, about the passion and genuine hatred which *Relâche* provoked among the critics of its time. Scarcely equal to their task, these same critics were to be condemned by posterity, which recognizes in *Relâche* a masterpiece of modern ballet.

END OF THE ADVENTURE

One final show, in which the company presented its latest 'inventions', formed part of a gala evening given on New Year's Eve. The show, on a smaller scale than usual but employing the services of important artistes, finished with a dinner in the theatre. The programme opened with *Relâche*, followed by a new cine-sketch written by Picabia, with sets by René Clair. The production included Marcel Levesque in the role of the Thief, Marcel Duchamp as the Naked Man, Man Ray as the Chatterbox, Jean Börlin as the Agent, Francine Picabia as the Naked Woman, along with Edith Bonsdorff and many others.

Paul Achard published an interview with Picabia in *Paris-Midi* that same day:

'Yes, my dear, I, Picabia, have written a revue, or more precisely, a sketch, in order to end the year on a happy note, or at least to go some way towards it. ... The point of departure is this: up until now the cinema has followed the theatre's lead, whereas I have tried to do the opposite by bringing to the stage the living method and rhythm of the cinema.'

'Will there be a theme?'

'Yes, a little story, beribboned, though, with a mass of coloured details. I'm re-creating, in this way, a picture by Cranach, the only painter I can bear at the moment. We see this evocation of Adam and Eve appearing in the midst of a kitchen. The characters will be entirely naked: I'd rather tell you that straight away, so that there's no misunderstanding. Marcel Duchamp and Francine Picabia, one of my spiritual children, will bring this charming canvas to life.'

A separate entertainment followed, including: classical dance by Mlle Jasmine; two songs by Satie (*Daphénéo* and *La Statue de bronze*), interpreted by the singer Maurizi from Stockholm's Royal Opera; the enigmatic dancer Caryathis performing *La Belle Excentrique*, to music by Satie, in a costume and mask by Cocteau; the singers Marguerite Carré and Yvonne George; and finally 'New York's latest jazz band', the Georgians. Rolf de Maré knew better than most how to organize a gala performance in order to produce both a memorable entertainment and a great artistic event.

However, just at that time, major personal worries were compounding the various anxieties attaching to his situation as an artistic mentor. These had developed as a consequence of the total confidence de Maré had invested in Jacques Hébertot, a person for whom he felt great affection and whom he considered his closest friend. Having come to seek his fortune in Stockholm, this young journalist had been appointed administrative director of the Théâtre des Champs-Élysées by de Maré. All the important activities relating to the theatre – the choice of guest performers (including the Ballets Russes) during the Ballets Suédois' tours, the management of the Comédie des Champs-Élysées (the second auditorium), as well as of the Studio (the third and smallest auditorium, constructed by Rolf de Maré as an experimental stage) – were undertaken in the name of Jacques Hébertot; and it was he who was praised by the press for initiatives stemming in reality from Rolf de Maré, who was, by nature, perfectly happy for his best friend to receive the benefit of such praises.

On his return from his American tour in the autumn of 1924 – a tour marked by significant financial losses – Rolf de Maré found himself suddenly confronted with an extremely unpleasant discovery: part of the theatre's takings failed to show up on its books, a number of tickets having been clandestinely printed twice over. Clearly, free of the controls which the management should have been imposing, several people – responsible for the ticket office and the theatre doors – had to be implicated in this operation, which had been going on for some considerable length of time. De Maré had a stormy interview with Hébertot, but did not take the matter to court, with the result that the guilty parties were never exposed and Jacques Hébertot's role was never clarified. The latter left his job and de Maré, deeply hurt by the affair, refused ever to see him again.

It was a personal catastrophe for Rolf de Maré. Finding another director was not a problem: André Daven, whom he took on, was to prove very efficient. But some of his joy in creating had gone. As for Börlin, he had given too much of himself not to be showing signs of weariness. In four years, he had created twenty-four ballets, and in five, had given around nine hundred performances, having himself danced three principal roles in each; and the lengthy tours, especially the American one, had drained him. Rolf de Maré refused to replace this unique performer and faultless collaborator. Alone in the face of these problems, he had numerous ideas for new creations, but after *Relâche*, they all seemed like retrogression or stagnation. As far as he was concerned, the most important steps towards a new art had already been taken. Repetition was not in his nature. Nor was consolidation: he wanted to be an explorer, a discoverer.

In 1925, the Ballets Suédois began a lengthy tour of Belgium and France, visiting thirty-five towns, where, because of their technical complexity, the Ballets' most important works could not be given.

On 17 March 1925, following a lack-lustre performance at Épernay, Rolf de Maré announced to his associates his decision to disband the company: the Ballets Suédois had come to the end of their life. Following the break-up, Börlin continued to give occasional performances, in particular at the Théâtre des Champs-Élysées in a concert programme with Irma Calson and Inger Friis. He was warmly praised by the press, which was perhaps suffering from a guilty conscience over its earlier failure to offer his talent sufficient encouragement. He also played the principal role in a film by René Clair, *Le Voyage imaginaire* (The Imaginary Journey), which premièred in the autumn of 1925.

Börlin had a Swedish girlfriend called Hermine Jourde, who had made a fortune by setting up a perfumery in Paris. She was slightly older than Börlin and lavished maternal care on her lover. Her two young daughters from an earlier marriage, Miarka and Zita Fiori (who sometimes called themselves Fjord), studied under Börlin and were to be his last partners. Performing as a threesome, they put on programmes composed of extracts from the great Swedish ballets, along with a number of new creations which were acclaimed by the press. Zita was to continue her career as a modern solo dancer, faithful to the choreographic style she had learnt from Börlin.

During a tour in Brazil, Börlin contracted hepatitis, which subsequently became chronic. Hermine Jourde and he decided to settle down in New York, where Hermine opened another branch of her Paris shop: the poor immigrant of *Within the Quota* thus returned for good to the American metropolis. It was there that he died, on 6 December 1930, at the age of thirty-seven.

The other members of the company dispersed, finding themselves new employment. The young ballerinas, with their attractive looks and excellent standard of dancing, continued to perform for a while in various different theatres before 'marrying well', as the saying went. Only Ebon Strandin returned to the Royal Opera in Stockholm. The two star dancers who had left the Ballets Suédois very early on were the only ones to pursue an international career. Jenny Hasselquist became a movie star in Germany and ended her days in Stockholm, where she set up a famous dance school. As for Carina Ari, she was to take charge of the ballet at the Opéra-Comique in Paris and create the choreography for several ballets at the Paris Opéra, where she partnered Serge Lifar in one of his masterpieces, *Le Cantique des cantiques* (The Song of Songs). Later on, she married the owner of Bols liqueurs, the Dutchman Jan de Moltzer. As a widow, she willed her immense fortune to a Swedish foundation which gives out annual bursaries to young dancers and financial assistance to former ones who have retired from the stage. The Carina Ari Gold Medal, which she designed herself, represents the most important annual dance prize in Sweden, awarded each year by Princess Christina to a laureate selected for merit in furthering the art of dance.

AFTER THE BALLETS SUÉDOIS

The agreement Rolf de Maré had drawn up with the Théâtre des Champs-Élysées remained valid for a further two years. In 1924, he ceded the management of the Comédie des Champs-Élysées (the theatre's medium-sized auditorium) to Louis Jouvet, the leading actor with the company which regularly performed there. The small Studio theatre was taken over the same year by Gaston Baty.

De Maré then proceeded to turn the main auditorium into an 'opera-music hall', a title intended to emphasize the quality of the theatre on offer there, which was diametrically opposed to the usual 'bawling' variety. Music hall had recently become very fashionable in Parisian avant-garde circles: the expression, perhaps, of a weariness with regard to the theatre, and of a need to root out established norms in order to make way for new forms of expression.

The stage of de Maré's opera-music hall was graced by the most extraordinary range of entertainments. Brief appearances by Pavlova alternated with those by Cécile Sorel. Jean Richepin, Maurice Rostand, Colette and Paul Fort came to read poetry there, rubbing shoulders with the best acrobats in the world. Escudero, the most famous Spanish dancer of the time, crossed paths with Artur Rubinstein at the piano and Loie Fuller enacting her scintillating abstract visions. And de Maré signed up a new arrival direct from America, the unknown Josephine Baker, who was to be the new darling of fashionable Paris, before being adopted as such by the entire world.

Another important discovery was that of a young French painter by the name of Paul Colin. It was from Colin that de Maré commissioned the sets for Josephine Baker's *Revue nègre*, as well as a large number of posters for each of the artistes performing in his opera-music hall; and Colin was subsequently regarded as the greatest poster designer of the century.

The opera-music hall at the Théâtre des Champs-Élysées was not destined to become permanent. In point of fact, the programmes devised by de Maré were ruinously expensive, even though the shows were regularly performed to a full house. These productions represented a gesture of thanks towards a public which had remained faithful to him during the difficult creative years, and Parisians were to remember his music hall as the most brilliant, the most lavish, entertainment they had ever known.

Rolf de Maré continued to work to promote dance. Establishing that no scientific research centre existed yet in this field, he founded in Paris, in 1932, the Archives Internationales de la Danse, which he rapidly built up into the largest dance library in the world. He took on Pierre Tugal as curator; and Paul Valéry, Rudolf von Laban, Serge Lifar, Mathilda Kschessinska and professors from the Sorbonne came to give lectures there. That same year, de Maré set up the first choreography competition, the prize for which was won by Kurt Jooss with his *Green Table*, the first political ballet.

De Maré also recognized that ancient dance traditions in the Third World were gradually being corrupted and would eventually disappear altogether. The very first dance research expedition – undertaken in order to salvage such traditions from total oblivion – took him to Indonesia, where he was to shoot twenty documentary films. Despite the asthma from which he had suffered since childhood, and an increasingly delicate state of health, he travelled throughout Africa, Asia and South America, taking with him an assistant and a trunkful of medication, and refusing to be dragged down by illness. The only fixed point of this existence was a coffee plantation which he bought and successfully managed in Kenya.

Closed during the war, the Archives Internationales de la Danse were in danger of being looted. Serge Lifar came to their rescue by naming himself as the temporary 'administrator' of the Archives and installing a German officer in the librarian's vacant apartment. Thanks to this initiative, the priceless collections remain, but the action was misinterpreted after the war, Lifar being quite unjustly branded as a collaborator, though Sweden was officially to express its gratitude to him for having acted in a loyal and selfless manner.

In 1950, Rolf de Maré decided that the Archives were by now too important a collection to remain in the hands of a private individual and he donated them to the Bibliothèque Nationale, which installed the vast collection of specialized literature, engravings and documents in the Bibliothèque de l'Opéra.

The documents relating to the Ballets Suédois, and in particular the four hundred and fifty gouaches and original drawings attached to them, appeared to excite no public interest at all. The Ballets Suédois had sunk into oblivion, as if they had never existed. In works on the history of ballet, a few lines at most were devoted to the company. The only book dealing with the Ballets was published by de Maré himself in 1932, but the editing unfortunately left much to be desired and anyway few copies were sold. The bulk of the edition, kept in the basement of the Archives, was accidentally destroyed during the war. The current work, published more than half a century later, constitutes the first study on the history of the company.

The heritage left by the Ballets Suédois, together with the important Indonesian material de Maré had collected during his research trip, was successively offered to Paris, London and Copenhagen as the basis for a museum devoted to the art of dance – but in vain. Nobody in a position to decide such a matter considered a museum for the art of dance worthwhile. In 1952, an international dance museum (the Dansmuseet) was finally set up in Stockholm, and in 1969, the Swedish government decided to grant it public, State-subsidized status. Substantial additions have been made to its collections over the course of time, and in 1982, the UNESCO collection of dance films and videos was officially opened at the museum as a repository and research centre by the director general of UNESCO and Sweden's minister of culture.

On the death of Rolf de Maré, in 1964, the Dance Museum became the residuary legatee of his fortune, which amounted to the equivalent of some hundred thousand pounds. During his lifetime, de Maré had hardly ever had more money than that at his disposal.

Legend would attribute to Rolf de Maré the prodigality of a patron. But this patron was, in reality, both an enterprising and far-sighted man of the theatre, and a relentless worker. He was a visionary, who could discern today the ideas of tomorrow; who knew how to safeguard creative artists, and, calling on the services of the most innovative among them, offered his contemporaries a little of that future which so beguiled him.

BENGT HÄGER

ROLF DE MARÉ

'I WAS DIRECTOR OF
THE BALLETS SUÉDOIS'

'I have never understood how anyone could say that my aim was to compete with the Russian ballets. On the contrary, I readily acknowledged the merits of such works; and yet it seemed to me that ballet was open to a different interpretation from theirs and that dance had something more to offer. . . .

'I had watched Jean Börlin for a long time, and had numerous conversations with him – and consultations with Fokine – and I saw that the only person in the whole of Scandinavia who could carry out my ideas, and really inject life into them, was this young man with no reputation and not much of an artistic past. And I was right.

'Let me simply quote Michel Fokine. After Jean Börlin's death, the man who so brilliantly choreographed *La Mort du cygne* (danced by the unforgettable Pavlova) said: "Börlin was the one who resembled me most. He corresponded to my ideal of a dancer." . . .

'Jean Börlin was the life force of the Ballets Suédois. An excellent musician, who could read the most difficult scores with ease, an artist through and through, he was also an unusually modest person. . . . Jean Börlin had made his début in Paris, performing a solo dance recital that was organized by M. Jacques Hébertot. It seemed to me that Hébertot was just the man to recruit the dancers I needed; and he did in fact make a first-class job of it. Since our Opera did not employ many men, however, we had to look further afield for our male dancers and hire a number of Danes. . . .

'Once the company was assembled, we needed a stage in Paris (since Paris was to be our centre) – a large theatre where the company could move freely and give a full season's performances, together with a studio, for research purposes. The Théâtre des Champs-Élysées happened to be free and I bought the lease, appointing M. Hébertot as administrative director, in whose name the lease was signed. Broadening the range of his activities, Hébertot also founded a publishing house, a venture in which I participated as a sleeping partner. As a result of disagreements, we parted company in 1924, and I took over as sole director of the Théâtre des Champs-Élysées, setting up the Opéra-Music Hall, which continued until the day I sold the lease.

'I was perfectly aware of my lack of experience and – despite my desire for innovation – to begin with called on the services of recognized musicians and painters, ones who were nevertheless said to be "progressive". Together we produced a few "inoffensive ballets" – with the exception, that is, of *Maison de fous* and *El Greco*. The former could perhaps be described as eccentric, while *El Greco* was actually more than just a ballet. After several months of methodical, hard work, the achievements of the company were unanimously acknowledged by the press and Jean Börlin and I felt that the moment had now come when we

could afford to be a little more adventurous. This was the era of *Les Mariés de la tour Eiffel*, *Skating Rink* and *La Création du monde*: ballets which provoked a variety of reactions but which I think I can safely say were forerunners in the field of dance. . . .

'At this point I feel I must say a few words about the reception we got from certain critics. They were the bane of my life! Really great artists like Ysaye never read press cuttings referring to themselves. I knew that, but I was too young to be able to adopt quite such a carefree attitude. Every bad review – and God knows, there were enough of them! – caused my colleagues and me real suffering. At times we found ourselves confronted with utter incomprehension. . . .

'On our return from America, Börlin and I were faced with the task of shaping an ultra-modern ballet. *Relâche* was beyond us all, in fact. We were in an impasse. Up until this point, we had done our best to interpret modern life in terms of dance; we had endeavoured to breathe into it the very breath of modern life; but now we had reached a turning point: the new cadences had begun to jar on us. A number of writers, musicians and painters had nevertheless offered me some really interesting new ideas. . . . But I was doing battle now with the public, with the critics, and even with my own company. It was clear that the public would resent any more innovations and that we would be reduced to dancing before a restricted circle of friends, our numbers seriously depleted, since many members of the company had declared their firm intention of leaving if we continued along these lines. . . .

'Moreover, looking back over the ground we had covered, it seemed to me that we had produced something which had a clear beginning and end, and that it would be senseless to try and go any further.

'There had been some fierce battles, but perhaps we had succeeded in opening a path for others. Perhaps I could retire now, and wait for someone else to take up where I had left off.

'On the evening of 17 March 1925, after a dreary performance at Épernay, I announced my decision to the company.

'The Ballets Suédois had come to the end of the road. . . . When, later, I created the Opéra-Music Hall des Champs-Élysées, I introduced Paris to a number of dancers it scarcely knew: among them, Menzelli, Marie Valente, Grace Christie, Elsie Janis, Escudero, Harry Reso, together with some truly excellent ballet companies.

'*La Création du monde* had been a Negro ballet danced by Europeans. Josephine Baker, a dancer who, in a few years, was to become an international star, brought a new aspect of Negro art to my music hall. And in the wake of *Iberia* came a genuine Spanish zarzuela – the first time Paris had witnessed such a spectacle.

'Anna Pavlova did me the honour of agreeing to come and dance on my stage – the first time she had done so in a Paris music hall.

'Jean Richepin, Maurice Rostand, Colette and Paul Fort came and read their poems there. . . . In fact, some of the greatest artistes performed at my Opéra-Music Hall.'

ROLF DE MARÉ, LES BALLETS SUÉDOIS,
——— PARIS, 1932 ———

'The Ballets Suédois have demonstrated that a bold kind of theatre, unhampered by classical conventions, is both possible and acceptable to the public. It was a question of taking risks. Rolf de Maré knew that and he has pushed this venture to the limit, always adopting the most innovative projects, never trying to impose limits on them. It is regrettable that such an endeavour should have come to a halt just when it was about to be acknowledged worldwide.

'Jean Börlin was the driving force behind this brave company. So great was his talent, he always knew how to turn to account the at times irksome scenic requirements imposed by the new style of ballet.'

——— FERNAND LÉGER ———

'It is thanks to them [the Ballets Suédois] that I was able to put on *L'Homme et son désir* and *La Création du monde*; Honegger, his *Skating Rink*; and Tailleferre, *Marchand d'oiseaux*. But the Ballets' aim is to represent their age as broadly as possible. They draw upon the works of those who have gone before – *Jeux*, by Debussy, *Tombeau de Couperin*, by Ravel, *El Greco*, by Inghel-brecht – and those whose tendencies have little in common with my own (Roland-Manuel, Lazarus). Such eclecticism is to be admired.

'And finally, still in hot pursuit of innovation, M. de Maré was the first to introduce orchestral works by the Arcueil school (Désormière, Sauguet, Maxime Jacob) and to mount *Relâche*, the last work by our great Satie. In *Relâche*, we see film and theatre blended for the first time: an innovation introduced by René Clair's *Entr'acte*, for which Satie wrote a magnificently energetic and powerful piece of music.

'The Ballets Suédois have likewise introduced us to Swedish works, encouraging us to love their country's dances and folklore, and also demonstrating the artistic trends currently evolving in Sweden.'

——— DARIUS MILHAUD ———

'The originality and modernity of the Ballets Suédois are so clearly apparent to the intelligent and sensitive spectator that the critic can scarcely hope to do more than prepare him for what is to come by indicating the foundations and outlining in a sober

fashion the structure of this architectural marvel. These ballets are not based on chance discovery, nor are they inspired by the fashion of the day: they are the product of a series of experiments carried out by an opportunistic director. The aspirations of their creator, M. Rolf de Maré, derive from a precise notion of what theatre ought to be, and the Ballets Suédois differ from all other ballet companies in that they originate from an ideal. The ballet that we knew before the arrival of M. Rolf de Maré was materialistic in the sense in which it was almost exclusively decorative in intention – thus reflecting artistic demands of the time. Rolf de Maré and Jean Börlin have created, in contrast, a new art and a new aesthetic sensibility.

'Rolf de Maré could have entitled his venture "The Union of the Muses". He saw in ballet a unique opportunity to unite three aesthetic elements under the direction of a fourth, entrusted with the power to connect and unify them, for the purposes of creating a new entity. These elements – poetry, music and painting – united by the guiding element – choreography – produce here quintessential art. For the first time in the history of dance, choreography assumes a leading role in the creation of a ballet. For such a creation to be a success, it was essential that the choreographer possess not only technique and emotional familiarity with dance, but a superior sensibility, as much with regard to the art of poetry, painting, sculpture and music. These qualities, which we may call, collectively, cultural imagination, are qualities that belong to Jean Börlin. Combined with his belief in the aesthetic principles upon which the Ballets Suédois were founded, they were a major reason for the successful realization of de Maré's ideas.

'It was integral to this artistic schema that a choreography could not be applied to existing poems or music: sets, costumes, music and text had to be specially created. The essential characteristic of the Ballets Suédois is thus itself a rigorous unity, deriving from a special creative process. Not only that, but the stamp of modernity was clearly apparent in all of de Maré and Börlin's projects. They employed the most representative names and the most diverse tendencies in modern art, calling upon the services of the poets Claudel, Cendrars, Canudo and Cocteau; the painters Léger, Andrée Parr, Steinlen, Bonnard, Murphy, Irène Lagut, Hélène Perdriat, Nils Dardel and André Hellé, and the composers Debussy, Milhaud, Poulenc, Honegger, Germaine Tailleferre, Auric, Porter, Ravel, Alfvén and Atterberg.

'Since the dominant theme of Rolf de Maré's ballets is the spectacle itself, the plot or the story is subordinated to, and as far as possible absorbed into, the primary objective of 'plasticity'. It exists, but never ambiguously. On the contrary, it is openly recognized and given its due importance in, for instance, *Les Mariés de la tour Eiffel* and in *Within the Quota*, where it provides a thin and unobtrusive story-line for the choreography, as also in *Marchand d'oiseaux*. In the case of *L'Homme et son désir* and *Skating Rink*, two stories told musically and "pictorially" by the composer and the painter, the dynamic beauty and movements of the human body remain the crucial component.

'Ballets like *El Greco*, *Skating Rink* and *L'Homme et son désir* mesh with the very roots of human nature and are essentially human in subject matter. They owe their international success to the fact that, as vehicles for emotions common to all mankind, they affect the sensibilities of people throughout the world. And those ballets which are more properly spectacles to delight the eye and the mind (examples being *Les Vierges folles*, *Marchand d'oiseaux* and *Les Mariés de la tour Eiffel*) likewise share an ability to inspire pleasure in the spectator through their flights of fantasy and glittering variety.

'Here, then, we have the two aspects of Rolf de Maré's poetic creation: on the one hand, his works plumb the depths of the human soul, possessing, on the other, an imaginative fairy-tale quality that delights and satisfies the senses. Serious and joyful at the same time, they mark a new stage in the development of aesthetic creation.'

—— Maurice Raynal ——

'We are witnessing the gradual development in France of a type of theatre that is not ballet properly speaking and which finds its niche neither at the Opéra, nor at the Opéra-Comique, nor on any of our Boulevard stages.

'This new genre, more closely attuned to the modern spirit, and overlapping with music hall, is still an uncharted world, rich in discoveries.

'M. Rolf de Maré's enterprise and Jean Börlin's unstinting hard work have recently thrown open a door for explorers. Thanks to the Ballets Suédois, young artists will be able to undertake new projects in which fairy-tale, dance, acrobatics, pantomime, drama, satire, orchestra and speech all combine, reappearing in an unprecedented form; they will carry out, without "private resources", what official artists consider to be back-room farces and which are nonetheless the plastic expression of contemporary poetry.

'If they accomplish all they set out to do, Messieurs de Maré and Jean Börlin will render France the greatest service. They will deliver it from its labours. They will cure it of its hesitancy in breaking with routine, will neither seek out nor fear scandal, and will show us our astonished reflections in a mirror as clear as Northern ice.'

—— Jean Cocteau, in *La Danse*, 1921 ——

'M. Rolf de Maré owns an interesting collection of paintings which reflects the taste of the modern amateur. Old masters include El Greco first and foremost; more recent painters, Daumier, Courbet, Claude Monet, Seurat; and the current

generation, Picasso and the Cubists. Differing from those monied individuals who view art merely as an appendage to their wealth, fame and snobbery, he regards his collection in the manner of a true art lover, as someone who loves the very products of art and is thereby prompted to adopt a different, and far from banal, method of collecting. His love of the plastic arts led de Maré in the direction of the theatre. He was perceptive enough to see that decorative details sometimes occupy too conspicuous a place in modern art. The unilaterality of Cubism destroys the coherence of the image – a coherence without which we cannot conceive of evolution – but it breathes new life into the impoverished tradition of stage scenery. De Maré, like the Russians, has opened a valve for the new decorative trend in painting, and together with his collaborators, in particular Jean Börlin, has elicited from Bonnard, Léger and other French painters décors which far exceed the straightforward research approach that tends to mark the start of such experiments. The most daring experiment, in my opinion, is the stage setting mimicking the paintings of El Greco. I have to admit that I went along to this production with a slight shudder of anticipation, but was astounded at how tastefully and tactfully the dangers of such a realization had been avoided. Let us hope that the enterprise begun by this enlightened lover of the arts will acquire the breadth and depth necessary to serve both art and the common herd.'

—— Julius Meier-Graeffe ——

'M. Rolf de Maré's [Opéra-Music Hall] productions are always full of variety and fantasy. Artists from the most different genres rub shoulders on his stage. We have, first of all, a series of assorted acrobats.... Finally, the Champs-Élysées Girls show us Saint-Granier mounted on a pedestal.... The public is enthusing about the dancer Jean Börlin, happy to see him back in the theatre where, at the head of the Ballets Suédois, he has defended so many works of contemporary French music. He is making his début at the Music Hall, in the company of Mlles Irma Calson and Inger Friis, offering us a waltz and a merry dance by Schubert, classically choreographed, followed by Debussy's *Golliwog's Cake Walk*. The remainder of the programme is made up of "mementos of his earlier ballets": *Derviches* by Glazunov; *Moria Blues* by Roland-Manuel (extract from *Le Tournoi singulier*), and finally a number of delightful Swedish dances reminiscent of *Nuit de Saint-Jean*.

'During the interval, an excellent piece of Negro jazz music caused quite a stir, but it was only a pale prelude to what was to come in the second half.

'*At last, a genuine Negro revue in Paris!* Three years ago, when last in New York, I was fascinated by the splendours of jazz and used to go every evening to one of the Negro theatres, where operettas and revues, like *Shuttle Along* and *Lisa*, were being performed, or to the "Up Town" dance halls in the Negro quarter, such as the Capitol. . . . At last, M. de Maré has brought it to Paris. The show we have been waiting three years for. The *Revue nègre* is produced by Caroline Dudley. The staging is by Louis Douglas. . . .

'Every scene is a success, brimming with vitality. Louis Douglas sweeps triumphantly through several solo numbers, while Josephine Baker is hugely popular, and deservedly so. Her dynamic energy, her suppleness and irresistibly funny face are the unequivocal elements of the show's success.'

DARIUS MILHAUD, *MA VIE HEUREUSE*
——— PARIS, 1973 ———

CREAT

IONS

SCULPTURE NÈGRE

BALLET BY *JEAN BÖRLIN*. MUSIC BY *FRANCIS POULENC*.

COSTUME BY *PAUL COLIN*. CHOREOGRAPHY

BY *JEAN BÖRLIN*. PREMIÈRE 25 MARCH 1920.

Sculpture nègre was probably the most interesting composition in Börlin's first solo recital, given at the Comédie des Champs-Élysées. Dressed in a costume imitating a wooden African statuette (later echoed in *La Création du monde*), he danced this piece in a deliberately ponderous fashion.

'The body's flexible points all bend as if under the weight of an abominable compulsion. . . . It rose up, slowly and as if ossified by years of contemplative immobility. And what this god unveiled before our eyes was the primitive eurhythmics of the first beings: an extraordinary vision in three-dimensional form.'

——— Pierre Scize ———

JEUX

Danced Poem by *Claude Debussy*.

Scenery by *Pierre Bonnard*. Choreography by *Jean Börlin*.

Dresses Made by *Jeanne Lanvin*. Orchestra Conducted by *D. E. Inghelbrecht*.

First Young Woman *Jenny Hasselquist* / Second Young Woman *Carina Ari* / A Young Man *Jean Börlin* / Created by *Nijinsky* 15 May 1913. Première 25 October 1920.

The libretto refers to a tennis game between a young man and two young women, set against an atmospheric background that has a subtle, sensual and evanescent quality.

'*Jeux*, by Claude Debussy, was, in visual terms, by far the most perfect achievement of the evening. It would be unjust to compare Nijinsky's interpretation of this ballet with that given us yesterday by Jean Börlin. If my memory – which has had much to do since – serves me right, I recall that the famous Russian choreographer made of *Jeux* a vast and violent canvas on which charm was partially submerged beneath I know not what barbaric, oriental cruelty. The nocturnal setting contributed still further to this almost sadistic, at all events extremely voluptuous interpretation. The question is whether Debussy's score – which is full of that adorable effervescence of youth and at whose surface a kind of bubble of high spirits is continually bursting, a ripple of happy laughter continually flowing – did not suffer ill effects from so many complications. Whatever the answer to that, we must acknowledge that M. Jean Börlin devoted all his efforts to creating the restrained grace, the youthfulness, the bounding joy that mark his interpretation. All his attention went into giving the composer's rhythms heightened spontaneity. At moments, the two young women's flirtatious gestures, the languid disinterest of the handsome young man, the to-ings and fro-ings, the sulky looks and smiles equalled that quality of emotion inspired by a scene from Marivaux. Bonnard's décor would have gained from less precise lighting effects and also a smaller stage.'

 Pierre Scize

'The orchestra, too, succeeded in expressing all the fluid poetry of *Jeux*, a mannered and disturbing fantasy by Claude Debussy. Not long ago, it was interpreted by the brilliant Nijinsky. M. Jean Börlin's imagination does not soar like Nijinsky's; he has none of the latter's mysterious poetry. He gave us a very pretty picture of the adolescent's emotion. This is Fortunio, or Cherubino. He has nothing of the tempter about him, and the two young women who charm him and whom he attracts, and finally whisks away, are in no great danger. On the contrary, the trio's evolutions, set against a charming and nebulous landscape by Bonnard, are lithe and innocent.'

 Nozière

IBERIA

Spanish Scenes in Three Acts. Music by *Isaac Albéniz*.

Sets and Costumes by *Steinlen*. Choreography by *Jean Börlin*.

Orchestra Conducted by *D. E. Inghelbrecht*.

I – EL PUERTO / TWO YOUNG FRUIT SELLERS MARGARETA JOHANSON, ASTRID LINDGREN / YOUNG WOMEN, FISHERMEN, ETC. / DANCES CARINA ARI, HOLGER MEHNEN AND THE CORPS DE BALLET / II – EL ALBAICIN / FIVE YOUNG WOMEN CARINA ARI, MARGARETA JOHANSON, KLARA KJELLBLAD, MARGIT WÅHLANDER, ASTRID LINDGREN / A WOMAN HELGA DAHL / FOUR YOUNG MEN JEAN BÖRLIN, AXEL WITZANSKY, HOLGER MEHNEN, PAUL WITZANSKY / III – CORPUS CHRISTI IN SEVILLE / A CAFÉ SINGER CARINA ARI / A PROCESSION, THE CROWD, ETC. / DANCES MARGARETA JOHANSON, JEAN BÖRLIN AND THE CORPS DE BALLET. BETWEEN THE ACTS OF IBERIA, THE ORCHESTRA WILL PLAY IBERIA BY CLAUDE DEBUSSY: I PAR LES RUES ET PAR LES CHEMINS (AFTER THE 1ST ACT) II LES PARFUMS DE LA NUIT III LE MATIN D'UN JOUR DE FÊTE (AFTER THE 2ND ACT). PREMIÈRE 25 OCTOBER 1920.

'The admirable folk music of Spain, in which so much reverie blends with so much rhythm, is one of the richest in the world. This very richness seems to have been the cause for the slowness with which the "other" music has developed. A sort of embarrassment about enclosing so many fine improvisations in a formulaic framework stayed the hand of "professionals". For a long time, they contented themselves with writing those popular-style zarzuelas in which the sound of guitars rises up from the street to the stage, in virtually unaltered form. But the rough beauty of the old Moorish cantilenas remained unforgettable, while the fine

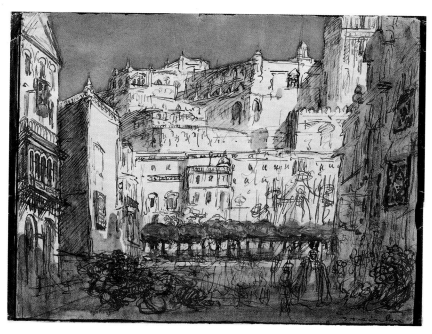

traditions of Escobado and Moralès, teachers of the great Victoria – all three of whom adorned the Spanish Renaissance – fell further into oblivion. There was no reason for things to change.... What more could one wish for in a country where the very stones in the road dazzle the eyes with a voluptuous light, and where the muleteers draw from the depths of their throats the sincerest strains of passion? Why should we be surprised by the decadence of the last century; why should we even call it that, since the music of the ordinary people retained its beauty? Wise and happy those countries which jealously guard this wild flower, sheltering it from administrative classicism.

'At about this time, that pleiad of composers came into being whose aim was to display the inestimable treasure that lay hidden in the songs of Old Spain. Among them, let us pick out the name of Isaac Albéniz. He was first of all an incomparable virtuoso, who was later to acquire a marvellous knowledge of the composer's

profession. While in no way resembling Liszt, he brings him to mind through the prolific abundance of his ideas. He was the first to turn to account the varied melancholy and the special humour of his native region (Catalonia). Few musical works are equal to *El Albaicin*, in the third *Iberia* movement, where we relive the atmosphere of those Spanish evenings heavy with the scent of carnations and the reek of *aguardiente*. . . . It is like the soft, plaintive notes of a guitar heard in the night, punctuated with sudden cries of alarm and convulsive bursts of sound. Without imitating popular themes precisely, this is the work of one who has heard such themes and slipped them into his music while blurring the dividing line between them. There are many other elements in these *Iberia* movements which show Albéniz giving of his best and carrying his eagerness to "write" to the point of exaggeration thanks to the rigorous self-imposed requirements which even led at one point to his "throwing the music out of the window".'

——— CLAUDE DEBUSSY ———

NUIT DE SAINT-JEAN

BALLET IN ONE ACT BY *JEAN BÖRLIN*. MUSIC BY *HUGO ALFVÉN*.

SETS AND COSTUMES BY *NILS DARDEL*. ORCHESTRA CONDUCTED BY

NILS GREVILLIUS, CONDUCTOR WITH STOCKHOLM'S ROYAL OPERA.

A Farmer's Daughter *Jenny Hasselquist* / A Young Peasant *Jean Börlin* / Peasant Men and Women / Dances *Jenny Hasselquist, Carina Ari* and *Jean Börlin* / Drinking Dance *Axel Witzansky, Paul Witzansky, Holger Mehnen, Kaj Smith, Kristian Dahl* and *Paul Eltorp* / Finale: Corps de Ballet. Première 25 October 1920.

Following a very old tradition, midsummer's night in Sweden is an annual occasion for great festivities: a typically Swedish national festival, which is celebrated up and down the country. Men and women, and boys and girls, gather round a flowering may tree, where they perform lively and very graceful dances and rounds to old local tunes. Between each round, the dancers gather together and touch glasses before drinking, according to an old Scandinavian custom. They only stop dancing with the arrival of the short-lived night: a gently nostalgic moment, which ends with the appearance of the rising sun. At which point the music starts up again, the dances and rounds recommence and the procession continues from village to village.

'One evening, on 25 November 1920, during a performance of *Nuit de Saint-Jean*, the dancers, Jean Börlin included, were not a little surprised to see some unknown person stepping up behind them. Bizarrely dressed in eighteen-thirties garb, with a green frock coat and a tall, broad-brimmed hat, he came and took his place at the table where the peasants pretend to be eating cake and drinking. But the dancers had more surprises in store for them. For here were the huge wooden goblets, normally empty, full that evening of excellent wine, and in place of the painted cardboard cake an enormous, mouth-watering brioche. And so they ate and drank in earnest, to the great astonishment of M. Rolf de Maré, watching this scene from the wings and not knowing what to think. At the moment when the peasants begin a hectic farandole round the midsummer's night tree, the gentleman in the green frock coat joined hands with the others and danced to his heart's content. The ballet came to a very lively end . . . at which point, to everyone's utter amazement, the frock-coated gentleman revealed his true identity: it was the great painter Steinlen, eager to make his début as a dancer. . . .'

——— Press Cutting ———

MAISON
DE FOUS

DRAMA BY *JEAN BÖRLIN*. MUSIC BY *VIKING DAHL*.

SETS AND COSTUMES BY *NILS DARDEL*. CHOREOGRAPHY BY

JEAN BÖRLIN. ORCHESTRA CONDUCTED BY *NILS GREVILLIUS*,

CONDUCTOR WITH STOCKHOLM'S ROYAL OPERA.

THE GIRL OF SOUND MIND *JENNY HASSELQUIST* / THE PRINCE *JEAN BÖRLIN* / THE SORCERESS *THORBORG STJERNER* / THE BLIND GIRL *JOLANDA FIGONI* / HER FRIEND *GRETA LUNDBERG* / THE WOMAN WITH THE MIRROR *CARINA ARI* / THE CLOWN *AXEL WITZANSKY* / THE WOMAN IN MOURNING *HELGA DAHL* / HER KNIGHT *KRISTIAN DAHL* / THE GIRL WHO CATCHES BUTTERFLIES *IRMA CALSON* / THE POET *HOLGER MEHNEN* / THE WOMAN WITH THE FAN *ASTRID LINDGREN* / THE HUNCHBACK *PAUL WITZANSKY* / TWO YOUNG GIRLS WHO PICK FLOWERS *DAGMAR FORSLIN, GRETA LUNDBERG* / THE VIOLINIST *KAJ SMITH* / THE HYSTERICAL WOMAN *KLARA KJELLBLAD* / THE WOMAN WITH THE BROOM *MARGIT WÅHLANDER* / A CHURLISH INDIVIDUAL *PAUL ELTORP* / FOUR LUNATICS *MARGARETA JOHANSON, NILS ÖSTMAN, BERTA KRANTZ, THERESE PETTERSON.* PREMIÈRE 8 NOVEMBER 1920.

The curtain rises on a group of lunatics. A young woman arrives in their midst and is surprised and horrified by the unexpected sight of this frenetically gesticulating crowd. Her fearful, hesitant looks attract the attention of the lunatics and their agitated gestures increase, contributing further to her horror. Mesmerized by the devilish procession, she feels madness overcoming her and tries in vain to resist its grip. Her mind wanders and she is no longer in control of her actions. Unwittingly, she begins to imitate the gestures of the mad people around her. They begin to circle faster and faster; she loses consciousness, then soon becomes delirious, falling prey, at last, to a form of dementia even more frenzied than their own. And the lunatics, themselves now horrified by her gestures, back away, shocked and trembling; in confusion, they search for a way out and flee, panic-stricken, leaving the girl alone with the prince. Each of them is the victim of overwhelming nervous obsessions. Suddenly, the prince is seized with the desire to strangle the young woman. She, having now recovered her senses, tries to flee, but in vain. She dies. A hideous sorceress, who had been crouching in the shadows, still as a statue, since the departure of the lunatics, raises her eyes to heaven, cackles, and spits in the young woman's face.

'M. Jean Börlin is the prince. He pirouettes with a cardboard crown on his head in a nightmare forest where he is encircled by the obsessed, a hideous figure grinning into a mirror, two girls with umbrellas gathering flowers, a mad widow, an hysterical woman, a sorceress, a clown, a bully, a hunchback, and many varieties of the hideous. It is the kind of dance one might have dreamt of in the influenza season, a very ghoulish thing. Innocence (Mlle Jenny Hasselquist) drifts into this forest, and she woos the prince with her whiteness and her grace. Strange, grotesque, and almost horrible, the performance makes more calls on the miming of the ballet than on their powers of dancing. But it is as interesting as it is gruesome, and it was received with considerable applause last night, most of which went to M. Börlin, Mlle Hasselquist, and the conductor.'

——— *THE TIMES* (UNSIGNED), 3.1.1921 ———

'*Maison de fous* – the new ballet which Jean Börlin presented to the public on 8 November 1920 – unleashed a welter of artistic passions and prompted the most violent discussions. This creation gave adversaries of Börlin's art scope at last to formulate a precise objection: reproaching the Ballets Suédois for not actually dancing, they claimed that these ballets were not in fact "ballet" at all. The critics split henceforth into two camps, fighting, on the one hand, for rhythm as accentuated by the dancers' bodies and movements, and, on the other, with Börlin, for that pictorial element which interprets modern dance in terms of attitudes and visual effects. On the evening of the première, a section of the house expressed their dislike of the work. Despite such reservations, however, it was soon generally agreed that the Swedish choreographer had once more succeeded in doing what he had set out to do, since here again the music, sets and costumes serving this choreography offered a piece of theatre that had perfect unity and a harmony which was both visually and aurally satisfying. The great interest of *Maison de fous* lay in an aspect utterly characteristic of Börlin's art: the combination of intense pictorial effects with the quest for innovation. The dancing in this ballet, into which Börlin had incorporated a choreography of the highest complexity, was without question one of his best creations. He had ensured that each dancer arranged their own steps individually, while collectively forming an irreproachable whole.'

——— PRESS CUTTING ———

LE TOMBEAU DE COUPERIN

Music by *Maurice Ravel*. Sets and Costumes by *Pierre Laprade*.

Choreography by *Jean Börlin*.

Orchestra Conducted by *D. E. Inghelbrecht*.

FORLANA *CARINA ARI, MARGARETA JOHANSON, MARGIT WÅHLANDER, DAGMAR FORSLIN, AXEL WITZANSKY, HOLGER MEHNEN, KAJ SMITH, PAUL WITZANSKY* / MINUET *JENNY HASSELQUIST, JEAN BÖRLIN* AND THE CORPS DE BALLET / RIGAUDON *JENNY HASSELQUIST, JEAN BÖRLIN* AND THE CORPS DE BALLET. PREMIÈRE 8 NOVEMBER 1920.

'*Le Tombeau de Couperin* is a delicious musical entertainment composed of a brisk, fast-moving introduction, nimbly and sharply executed, and full of charming coquetry, and of three dances, a forlana, a minuet and a rigaudon, traditional steps exquisitely dressed up in "modern" garb. There is nothing more slyly mischievous than the minuet, nor more impudent, more bold, more firmly planted on its two feet, than the robust rigaudon. These four pieces, so French in tone and flavour, were the delight of this Swedish evening. The audience applauded at length this lovely suite, which seemed all the lovelier after the lamentable *Maison de fous*. It is correct to say that M. Börlin has arranged for M. Ravel's music some very pleasing "figures", which were elegantly executed, in a very attractive setting. Though why, in a homage to Couperin, do we see *Directoire*, Louis XVI and Louis XV costumes, and nothing recalling that particular king during whose reign the great musician lived?'

——— REYNALDO HAHN ———

. . . After those dismal extravagances, M. Maurice Ravel's ballet is a welcome arrival. A short time before, this subtle musician had written a piano suite entitled *Le Tombeau de Couperin*. One might have expected this suite to be performed by the Ballets Russes. But, on the contrary, it was presented by the Ballets Suédois. The ballet, in a setting of gardens *à la française*, shows us a handful of gracious figures, dressed in *Directoire* style, who come and go, adopting precious, elegant and nonchalant poses. These are the "*incoyables*" (omitting the "r", as they themselves did [*incroyable* (literally, 'incredible', 'unbelievable') was used during the *Directoire* period to denote a beau or a belle]). They dance in groups of eight, four and two; and it is all very pleasing. The music is a delightful little thing: sharp and subtle, prettily poetic, witty, even mocking. Qualities, each of them, measured out by an artist of precise and unfailing skill.'

——— ADOLPHE BOSCHOT ———

'To accompany these three dance tunes, M. Jean Börlin has arranged three pretty dances, whose measured poses nevertheless struck me as a little exaggerated. But this is undoubtedly a national characteristic, since we see it in abundance in the folk-dances of *Nuit de Saint-Jean*. We cannot reproach these Swedish ballets for being Swedish. On the contrary, we should commend them for it, at this time in their lives when they are searching for an identity, in pursuit of what will later come to be recognized as their original character. . . . The costumes all seemed to me a little on the skimpy side, especially those of the ballerinas, whose clinging skirts make one long for panniers.'

——— LOUIS LALOY ———

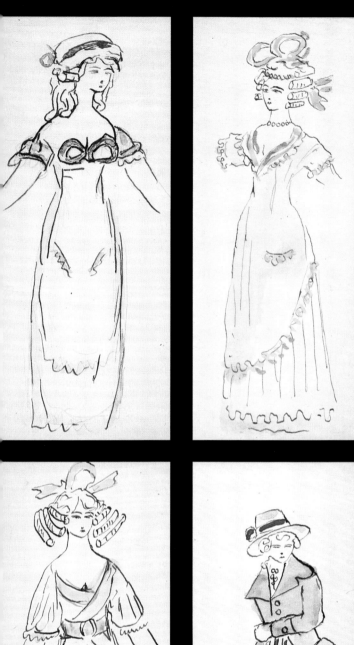

EL GRECO

Mimed Scenes by *Jean Börlin*. Music by *D. E. Inghelbrecht*.
Composition by *Jean Börlin*. Sets Based on the Paintings of El Greco
and Created by *Mouveau*. Costumes by *Jean Börlin*, Based on the
Paintings of El Greco. Orchestra Conducted by *D. E. Inghelbrecht*.

THE YOUNG CHRISTIAN WOMAN *JOLANDA FIGONI* / HER TWO MAIDS *THORBORG STJERNER, MARGARETA JOHANSON* / THE YOUNG MAN *JEAN BÖRLIN* / HIS BROTHER *NILS ÖSTMAN*. PREMIÈRE 18 NOVEMBER 1920.

Setting: a square in Toledo. The weather is wild: flashes of lightning zig-zag across a dark sky and thunder rumbles. The crowd, terrified, begs for divine mercy. But a young man in its midst calls one moment on heaven, the next on hell. A group of monks approaches and observes him in silence. At the far end of the square, a funeral procession passes by: the blasphemer's brother, killed by the lightning, is being carried to his resting place. A young Christian woman makes her way through the crowd, which, suddenly falling silent, draws back to let her pass. She approaches the young man and he repeats to her his sense of despair, and blasphemes again. She responds in a friendly fashion, trying to comfort and encourage him with her description of eternal life. But he rejects her claims. In her attempts to convince him, she becomes more and more insistent, answering all his denials with increasingly affirmative arguments. Her efforts are finally rewarded and, little by little, the young man regains his faith. The sky clears and the returning light transfigures the scene.

. . . In terms of striking visual effects, the most interesting ballet I have seen. A vision in which the old master's canvases come to life, his characters step out of their frames and mingle together in a hallucinatory Sabbath imbued with that atmosphere of pathos, at once pale and feverish, which we encounter in the works of El Greco.'

———— GOTTHARD JOHANSSON, IN *ARES*, NO. 18, 1922 ————

'The project is so daring that one tells oneself in advance "It will not work", sympathizing with the remark made by the German critic Meier-Graeffe, who said that he went along to the performance *mit einem leisen Schauder* (with a slight shudder). But like him, I was completely won over by the finesse and enthusiasm with which the experiment had been carried out. Naturally, we are not talking simply of a series of *tableaux vivants* based on El Greco's work, but of a fresh scenic fantasy in which anguish and terror, the mystery of death and, finally, transfiguration and ecstasy form a framework backed up by the music.'

———— AUGUST BRUNIUS, IN *GÖTEBORGS HANDELSTIDNING*, 18.5.1922 ————

'El Greco's paintings provide, as we know, the inspiration for this production. The backdrop is recognizable as *Toledo*, in the Havemeyer collection in New York, and *The Burial of the Count of Orgaz* (Toledo) may be guessed to have influenced the funeral composition. All the elements thus derive from El Greco. . . . In Jean Börlin's *El Greco*, the dynamism of the baroque has been allowed to break down the barriers within which pictorial art had confined it. It has been liberated and transformed into a mimicry of life. The stage is drowned in lightning flashes and rolls of thunder. The crowds, as if driven to and fro by some giant scourge, gesticulate and cry out, voiceless, writhing in impotence. The lees of the soul are stirred up and float to the surface.'

———— ANDREAS LINDBLOM, IN *DAGENS NYHETER*, 24.5.1922 ————

DERVICHES

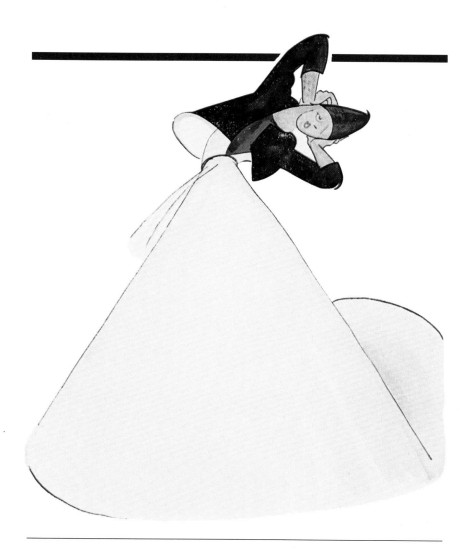

DANCING BY *JEAN BÖRLIN*. MUSIC BY *GLAZUNOV*.

SCENERY BY *MOUVEAU*. COSTUMES BY *JEAN BÖRLIN*.

ORCHESTRA CONDUCTED BY *D. E. INGHELBRECHT*.

DERVISHES *Jean Börlin, Holger Mehnen, Kaj Smith, Paul Eltorp, Nils Öst-man.* PREMIÈRE 18 NOVEMBER 1920.

This dance, which was directly inspired by Muslim traditions, was inserted between *El Greco* and *Les Vierges folles*. The ballet was very popular and was incorporated into the company's permanent repertoire. In a golden mosque, a group of dervishes is praying. They bend and rise up again slowly, like stems bearing heavy blooms, then begin to turn, swept along by the music, until they fall face down on the ground.

'*Derviches* is an interesting exercise, in which Jean Börlin gives free rein to his virtuosity. Moreover, we notice the expression of a kind of pain in this slender torso and this head tilted forward over the swirling flight of his long gown. Börlin's ecstatic and martyr-like dervish is truly in a state of trance. A whirling god possesses and drives him on. And when, at last, he falls, it is truly as if a flower had dropped its petals.'

——— PIERRE SCIZE ———

'*Derviches* is an exercise in rotation, the puerility of which provoked a few smiles in an otherwise good-natured audience.'

——— LOUIS LALOY ———

'Our next stop is Turkey. A pretext for a very lovely décor, simply done in grey and gold: a mosque door with lintel in a decorative surround, finely executed in a solid high-relief style. Against this serene and harmonious background, a number of Turkish soldiers, in their shirt-tails, solemnly ape the dances of the whirling dervishes.'

——— MAXIME DETHOMAS ———

'[*Dervishes* offers] a fine delineation of the soul of the dervish, tormented into extravagant and perverse attitudes of abasement before a God more cruel than the drifting sands in deserts scorched by eternal fire. Five religious devotees at prayer in an Arabian mosque are caught up by the terrible flames of religious exultation and twirled into an intoxicated dance which ends in prostrate oblivion.'

——— *MORNING POST*, 29.12.1920 ———

LES VIERGES FOLLES

BALLET PANTOMIME BY *KURT ATTERBERG* AND *EINAR NERMAN*. MUSIC
BASED ON SWEDISH MELODIES, BY *KURT ATTERBERG*. SETS AND COSTUMES
BY *EINAR NERMAN*. CHOREOGRAPHY BY *JEAN BÖRLIN*. ORCHESTRA
CONDUCTED BY *NILS GREVILLIUS*, CONDUCTOR WITH STOCKHOLM'S ROYAL OPERA.

THE BRIDE *JENNY HASSELQUIST* / THE BRIDEGROOM *JEAN BÖRLIN* / FIVE FOOLISH VIRGINS *CARINA ARI, KLARA KJELLBLAD, DAGMAR FORSLIN, BERTA KRANTZ, IRMA CALSON* / FIVE WISE VIRGINS *HELGA DAHL, MARGARETA JOHANSON, MARGIT WÄHLANDER, THORBORG STJERNER, GRETA LUNDBERG* / TWO ANGELS *ASTRID LINDGREN, JOLANDA FIGONI*. PREMIÈRE 18 NOVEMBER 1920.

'From the middle of the eighteenth until the final years of the last century, it was the custom among the peasants of Dalarna and Småland and other Swedish provinces to drape their houses with large pieces of cloth decorated by village craftsmen using motifs borrowed from the Scriptures. Of all these stories, treated in the naïve manner one might expect, it was the parable of the ten virgins, as told in the Gospel of St Matthew, which was widely preferred (a tapestry displaying this theme can be seen in the Nordic Museum). This is the popular theme on which the ballet *Les Vierges folles* is based. Costumes and stage sets have been created to match the tone of the village paintings, while the music draws its inspiration from old Swedish tunes. The beginning and end of the ballet are taken from an old hymn, popular in Dalarna for three centuries, and which relates, precisely, to the parable of the wise and the foolish virgins. This is how the first verse runs: "The kingdom of heaven will be like ten virgins. / Each of them different in character. / Five of them are a mirror of our idle nature, / Of our lifeless soul weighed down with sin. . . . / May God come to our aid, poor sinners we!" And here, as an offshoot to the story, is the charming construction given to the ballet by Jean Börlin. The bride steps forward, accompanied by the "wise virgins" and the "foolish virgins". The first of these are attentive to the light in their lamps, carefully protecting the flame, while the latter, the reckless virgins, are mindful only of the games and festivities. Their wise companions reproach them for their dangerous levity, but they refuse to listen, laugh and carry on as before. The young women are overcome with drowsiness and, one by one, they fall asleep, with the bride in their midst. The latter sees the bridegroom in a dream. The vision fades, and the bride wakes up, radiant and refreshed, and rouses her companions. But the foolish virgins are startled to find that they have no oil left in their lamps. They look anxiously at one another and try, in vain, to persuade the wise virgins to give them some of their oil; where, otherwise, will they find the precious fuel for their lamps, they wonder. Meanwhile the bride's dream has come true: the bridegroom has arrived. He has taken her hand and together they have stepped inside the church, with the wise virgins leading the way. And when the foolish virgins return, with the intention of following them into the church, the angels bar the entrance, and all they can do is stand by and watch the couple and the wedding procession leaving the church.'

———— *LA DANSE*, NOVEMBER 1920 ————

'It is important to point out that, in its conception as in its realization, each production marks an undeniable progression from the one before. (Excellent sign!) But it is unquestionably with *Les Vierges folles* that the Ballets Suédois have achieved mastery of the art, adding to the riches of modern ballet a charming and original work.'

———— *COMŒDIA* ————

NERMAN

LA BOÎTE À JOUJOUX

La Boîte à Joujoux

BALLET BY *ANDRÉ HELLÉ*. MUSIC BY *CLAUDE DEBUSSY*, ORCHESTRATED BY *ANDRÉ CAPLET*. SCENERY AND COSTUMES BY *ANDRÉ HELLÉ*. CHOREOGRAPHY AND STAGING BY *JEAN BÖRLIN*.

THE DOLL *JOLANDA FIGONI* / PULCINELLA *AXEL WITZANSKY* / THE SOLDIER *HOLGER MEHNEN* / THE HARLEQUIN *KAJ SMITH* / THE PIERROT *PAUL ELTORP* / THE SAILOR *PAUL WITZANSKY* / THE OTHER DOLL *ASTRID LINDGREN* / THE ENGLISH SOLDIER *IRMA CALSON* / THE GOLLIWOG *TOR STETTLER* / THE SHEPHERD *PAUL WITZANSKY* / THE SHEPHERDESS *KLARA KJELLBLAD*. PREMIÈRE 15 FEBRUARY 1921.

'This delightful ballet, which the Swedes staged during their last series of performances in Paris, is being given once again by M. Rolf de Maré's company. The public still remembers the brilliant and moreover well-deserved success this fresh, graceful and naïvely charming work enjoyed at the Théâtre des Champs-Élysées. André Hellé's droll inventiveness and bright colours and Debussy's engaging, delicately nuanced and sensitive music harmonized into a successful whole, which Jean Börlin's choreography completed by endowing it with kinetic life, while continuing to adhere most closely to the composer's musical intentions – though not without displaying the originality and sense of line which make of this young Swedish dancer an incomparable ballet master. The genesis of this ballet is not without interest. The original idea for it was a stage set executed in 1912 by André Hellé for one of the tableaux in the revue by Régis Gignoux and the late Charles Müller performed at the Théâtre des Arts. It was that same year that André Hellé composed a ballet, which he submitted in 1913 to Claude Debussy. The composer of the *Golliwog's Cake Walk* in his *Children's Corner* suite, enchanted by the originality of the subject matter and aware just how much scope it offered his lively musical talents, immediately agreed to write the music for it. And he set to work without delay.

'André Hellé has jealously guarded a few hastily scribbled notes written to him by the composer, who took an avid interest in their joint project, and whom the world was so soon to lose. We have the good fortune to be able to reproduce a few passages from them here. Debussy wrote: "*25 July 1913*. For my part, I have begun serious work on the drum. *29 July 1913*. One request, among others, is that you put the rose on the cover of the published score, in the middle: this rose is as important as all or any of the characters. I would even ask you to allot a place for it among the characters. *7 August 1913*. The first tableau is nearly finished, all the same." The score appeared in December 1913. M. Gheusi, then director of the Opéra-Comique, planned to put *La Boîte à joujoux* on there in 1914, but was prevented from doing so by the war. However, he kept the project in mind and in December 1918 staged the ballet, choreographed by Robert Quinault, at the Théâtre Lyrique du Vaudeville. Rolf de Maré's Ballets Suédois performed it again this year, and Jean Börlin's choreography turned it into a new creation, quite different from the first – with what success is already well known. But alas! Claude Debussy, whose death robbed French music of a composer at the height of his glory, was never to see his ballet performed in full. He had not even managed to complete the orchestration, which was finished off by M. André Caplet. But *La Boîte à joujoux* will continue to claim its place among the utterly engaging and infinitely nuanced works his genius created, works that are the expression of the loftiest musical feeling.'

——— F. D'HAUTRELIEU, IN *LA DANSE*, JUNE 1921 ———

'The new work in this programme was *La Boîte à joujoux*, written by Debussy to accompany André Hellé's luminous motifs, and deliciously orchestrated by M. Caplet in a diligently pious spirit. The Swedish company has given us a light and gracious interpretation of this child-like and charming masterpiece. Engrossed as children, we witnessed the love affair of the doll and the tin soldier, the rival moves by Pulcinella, the great battle between the puppets and the soldiers, all of which was presented to us in an amiably straight-faced fashion, and with a highly delicate sense of parody.'

——— PIERRE SCIZE ———

'*La Boîte à joujoux* benefits from an unparalleled interpretation. Each doll retains its own identity. Pulcinella is quite astonishing. It is as if we see his strings being pulled by a child's hand, so bizarrely does M. Axel Witzansky move. Mlle Yolanda Figoni as the doll displays the same degree of artistry. She has a style all her own in point work, at times appearing as if she were perched on stilts. Mlle Carina Ari as the shepherdess – a broken or badly made doll – limps endearingly. Each of the individuals who appear in the ballet of Debussy and M. André Hellé are virtuosos. They have produced a collective work that is truly admirable. Besides, this ballet is, quite simply, a little masterpiece.'

——— RAYMOND CHARPENTIER ———

L'HOMME
ET SON DÉSIR

Danced Poem by *Paul Claudel*. Music by *Darius Milhaud*.

Choreography by *Jean Börlin*. Sets and Costumes by *Andrée*

Parr, Executed by *Mouveau* and *Muelle*. Théâtre des Champs-

Élysées Orchestra, Conducted by *D. E. Inghelbrecht*.

MAN *JEAN BÖRLIN* / WOMAN *MARGARETA JOHANSON* / THE OTHER WOMAN
THORBORG STJERNER / THE PAN-PIPES *KAJ SMITH* / THE FIRST GOLDEN NOTE
CARINA ARI / THE MOON / THE SERVANT OF THE MOON / THE REFLECTION OF THE
MOON / THE REFLECTION OF THE SERVANT OF THE MOON / THE BLACK HOURS / THE
WHITE HOURS / THE BELLS, THE GOLDEN NOTES / THE CYMBALS. PREMIÈRE 6 JUNE
1921.

'The stage is divided into three levels, the middle one being the widest. On the far
edge of the third, *the hours* are to be seen, represented by a line of women walking
one behind the other. 1. A few bars to indicate that the drama is continuing in some
way. 2. Appearance of *the Moon*. – There will be two of them, one on level III, the
other on level I. These are *the Moon* and its reflection in water. Each of them holds
a small drum, with their hand outlined on its surface. They walk in opposite
directions, taking the entire duration of the drama to cross the stage in a very slow,
almost imperceptible movement. . . . With *the Moon* and *the hours*, who continue, on
their different levels and using their specialized motions, to process across the stage
for the entire duration of the action, we have the visual equivalent of the bass in
music. 3. *Man* asleep and the ghost of *dead woman*. – This ghost is double: one walks
in front as if to lead it, the other behind, pushing – alternately. . . . 4. *Man sleeping* on
his feet, wavering as if in a draught, and as if weightless. 5. All the forest inhabitants
which come to look at *man* while he's sleeping. Represented solely by rhythms and
movements. No costumes. . . . 6. Dance of passion. A back-and-forth movement,
increasingly eager, desperate, like an animal coming up against a wall and returning again and again to the same spot. Perhaps without moving the feet. . . .
7. Reappearance of *woman*, little by little drawing *man* closer by slowly revolving in
front of him on the stage and completely wrapping him round in her veil. . . . 8. *Moon
I* has disappeared first; now *Moon II* disappears in its turn. *The black hours* have
slipped away. We see the first *white hours* appearing.'

 PAUL CLAUDEL ———

'In reality, there are no new subjects. When a writer imagines he has found some,
they are generally mediocre and artificial. Poetry only ever goes over the same
themes, the same sentiments of the human heart, which are eternal and inex-
haustible, like nature. That is what is meant in my danced poem by the march of
the hours and of the Moon, which frames the human drama. There is nothing new
about the subject of this drama, any more than there is in the boldest tragedies. It is
the theme of man trapped in a passion, an idea, a desire, and vainly endeavouring to
escape, as though from a prison with invisible bars, until the point when a woman,
the image of both Death and Love, comes to claim him and take him with her off-
stage. You might say that just as *L'Annonce faite à Marie* tied in with medieval
mysteries, *L'Homme et son désir* continues the tradition of our old morality plays.'

——— PAUL CLAUDEL, IN *LES BALLETS SUÉDOIS*, PARIS, 1932 ———

'*L'Homme et son désir* is the fruit of a collaboration between three friends who –
each Sunday during the year 1917 – shared a picnic of ideas, music and drawings in
the sierra overlooking Rio de Janeiro. This little danced drama has grown out of the
atmosphere of the Brazilian forest in which we were in a sense submerged, as though
engulfed in a new kind of element. How strange it is, at night, when it begins to fill
with movement, sounds and glimmers of light! And it is precisely one such night
that our poem seeks to represent. We have not tried to reproduce the inextricable

matting of the forest flora photographically. We have simply thrown it down like a carpet of purple, green and blue, around the central blackness, on the four tiers of our stage. This stage is vertical, perpendicular as you look at it, like a painting on a wall, or a book while one is reading it. It is also, if you like, a page of music where each piece of action is written on a different stave.

'On the far edge, the hours of night file past, dressed all in black and wearing golden headdresses. Below is the Moon, led across the sky by a cloud, like a servant walking ahead of a great lady. Right at the bottom, in the waters of the vast primal swamp, the reflection of the Moon and of her servant follows the regular march of the celestial couple. The drama proper takes place on a platform midway between the sky and the water. And the main character is man, reclaimed by the primal forces, robbed by night and by sleep of his identity and all semblance of human form. He arrives led by two twin veiled figures who disorientate him by swivelling him around like the "seeker" in the children's game of hide-and-seek. One is image, the other desire, one memory, the other illusion. They play with him for a while, and then disappear. He remains standing there, with arms outstretched. He sleeps in the bright glow of the tropical moon like a drowned man deep under water. And all the animals of the eternal forest leave the orchestra one by one to come and watch him and to utter their own particular sound in his ears: the bells and the Pan-Pipes, the notes and the cymbals.

'Man begins to come alive in his dream. Now he is moving and dancing. And what he dances is the eternal dance of longing, desire and exile, the dance of captives and abandoned lovers, the dance that sends fever victims, tormented by insomnia, tramping back and forth across their verandah all night long, the dance of menagerie animals hurling themselves repeatedly against the impassable bars. Presently, it becomes an enervating perfume. The theme of obsession grows increasingly violent, frenetic, and then, in the depths of this solemn darkness that precedes the day, one of the women returns and circles, as if fascinated, round the man. Is she dead? Or alive? The sleeper seizes hold of the corner of her veil as she turns and uncoils herself while circling around him – until he himself is enveloped like a chrysalis and she is almost naked – and then, bound to man by a last fragment of material like the fabric of our dreams, woman places her hand over his face and together they disappear towards the edge of the stage. All that is left is the reflection, down below, of the Moon and her servant. The black hours have all filed past; the first white hours appear.'

——— Paul Claudel, Ballets Suédois Programme ———

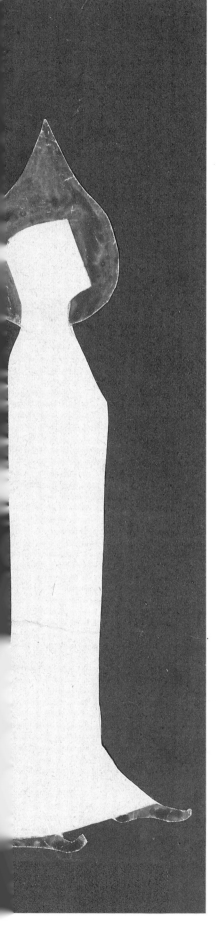

'On my return to Europe, my associates in the Six thought like me that this danced poem would be impossible to stage and that no theatre company would agree to my demands. Indeed, instead of using a normal symphony orchestra, I needed eleven soloists, seventeen additions to the percussion and a vocal quartet. Moreover, the stage's division into four levels meant that this work could not easily be taken to the provinces or abroad.'

——— DARIUS MILHAUD, IN *PARIS-JOURNAL*, 25.5.1923 ———

'The only thing I was anxious about was the percussion passages. They provoked no unfavourable reactions, however, since they were short and the intervening music immediately soothed the spectators' nerves; and then the vocal quartet acted as a sort of sedative.... The audience's reception was different each time, sometimes noisy, sometimes quietly thoughtful. These varied reactions had no influence whatsoever on de Maré, who kept my ballet in the repertoire regardless.'

——— DARIUS MILHAUD, *MA VIE HEUREUSE*, PARIS, 1973 ———

'On the point of presenting his new work at the Champs-Élysées, *L'Opinion* tells us, M. Claudel had an attack of nerves. He was shaking and kept saying to his friends that he was going to be "torn to pieces". That this was the last time he would be writing a ballet. But M. Darius Milhaud gave him encouragement: the whistles had such an important role in his orchestra, he said, that those of the spectators would sound like no more than an inoffensive echo. Contrary to what one might have expected, it was the frenetic Claudelians who in fact disrupted the performance: unable to believe that so many whistles could be coming from the orchestra alone, they sought to drown them out at all costs with their clapping. M. Darius Milhaud was distraught.... When the curtain was lowered, there was a volley of protests. And yet M. Claudel's friends were there to defend him! While the black hours filed past in slow procession, they could be heard muttering remarks like the following. – It's like in the mystery plays: there's the sky above, hell below, and the Earth in the middle. – No, no! Read the programme: it's a page of music.... – It looks like three lines of Egyptian hieroglyphics to me.... – Is that big white ball up there the Moon? – Of course not! The Moon is the lady carrying a yellowy-coloured disc.... – He's got great muscles.... – There's a grandeur about it, you must admit!... And when the curtain was lowered, the same people shouted: "Vive Claudel! Vive Claudel!"'

——— PRESS CUTTING ———

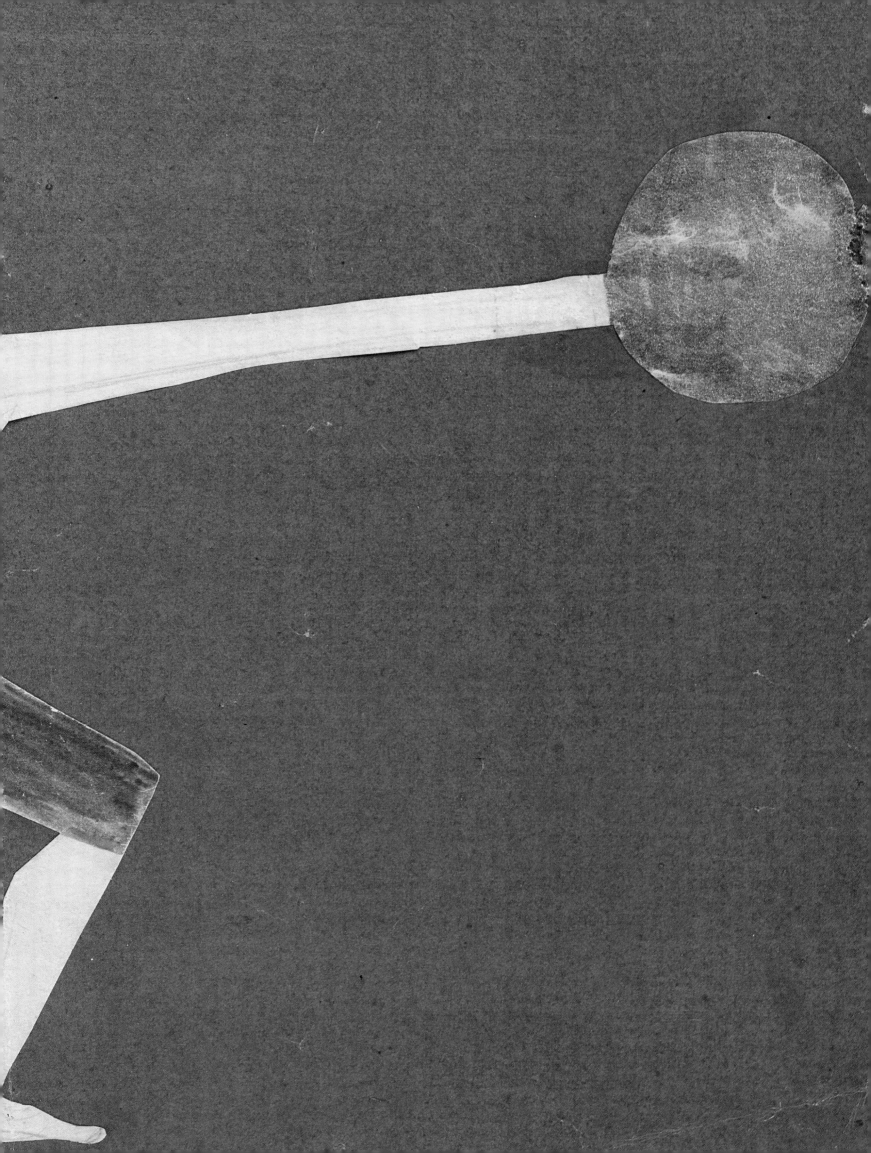

Paul Claudel

Andrée Parr

Darius Milhaud

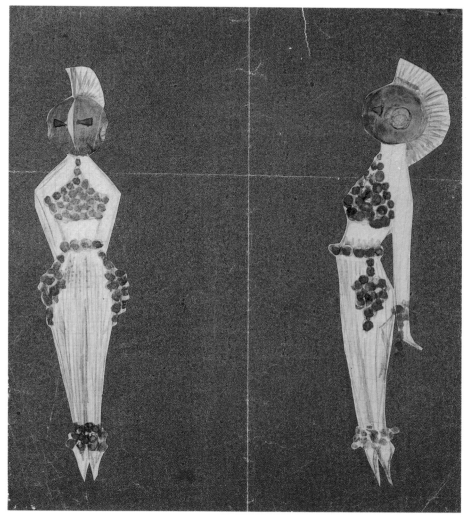

LES MARIÉS DE LA TOUR EIFFEL

DEVISED BY *JEAN COCTEAU*. MUSIC BY *GERMAINE TAILLEFERRE, GEORGES AURIC, ARTHUR HONEGGER, DARIUS MILHAUD* AND *FRANCIS POULENC*. CHOREOGRAPHY BY *JEAN BÖRLIN*. SCENERY BY *IRÈNE LAGUT*, EXECUTED BY *MOUVEAU*. COSTUMES BY *JEAN HUGO*, EXECUTED BY *BERTHELIN* AND *MAX WELDY*. PAINTED MASKS BY *JEAN HUGO*. THÉÂTRE DES CHAMPS-ÉLYSÉES ORCHESTRA CONDUCTED BY *D. E. INGHELBRECHT* AND *E. BIGOT*.

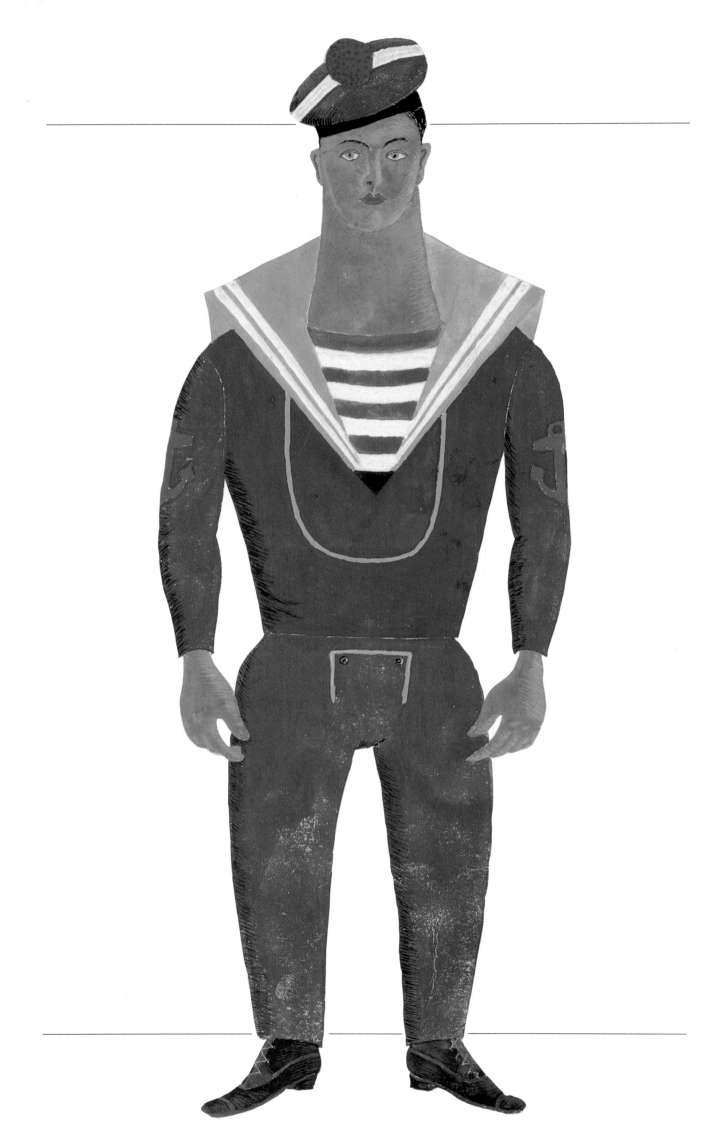

GRAMOPHONE ONE *JEAN COCTEAU* / GRAMOPHONE TWO *PIERRE BERTIN* / THE
OSTRICH *THERESE PETTERSON* / THE HUNTSMAN *KAJ SMITH* / THE DIRECTOR OF
THE EIFFEL TOWER *HOLGER MEHNEN* / THE PHOTOGRAPHER *AXEL WITZANSKY* /
THE BRIDE *MARGIT WÅHLANDER* / THE BRIDEGROOM *PAUL ELTORP* / THE MOTHER-
IN-LAW *IRMA CALSON* / THE FATHER-IN-LAW *KRISTIAN DAHL* / THE GENERAL *PAUL
WITZANSKY* / 1ST BRIDESMAID *HELGA DAHL* / 2ND BRIDESMAID *KLARA KJELLBLAD* /
1ST PAGEBOY *NILS OSTMAN* / 2ND PAGEBOY *DAGMAR FORSLIN* / THE CYCLIST
ASTRID LINDGREN / THE CHILD *JOLANDA FIGONI* / THE TROUVILLE BATHING GIRL
CARINA ARI / THE LION *ERIC VIBER* / THE COLLECTOR *ROBERT FORD* / THE
PICTURE DEALER *TOR STETTLER* / 1ST TELEGRAM *THORBORG STJERNER* / 2ND
TELEGRAM *MARGARETA JOHANSON* / 3RD TELEGRAM *GRETA LUNDBERG* / 4TH
TELEGRAM *BERTA KRANTZ* / 5TH TELEGRAM *ASTRID LINDGREN*. ORDER OF MUSIC: 1.
OVERTURE 'THE 14TH OF JULY' *GEORGES AURIC* / 2. WEDDING MARCH (ARRIVAL)
DARIUS MILHAUD / 3. GENERAL'S SPEECH *FRANCIS POULENC* / 4. THE TROUVILLE
BATHING GIRL *FRANCIS POULENC* / 5. THE FAIRGROUND GAME (FUGUE) *DARIUS
MILHAUD* / 6. TELEGRAMS' DANCE *GERMAINE TAILLEFERRE* / 7. FUNERAL MARCH
ARTHUR HONEGGER / 8. IDIOTIC SONG *FRANCIS POULENC* / 9. QUADRILLE *GERMAINE
TAILLEFERRE* / 10. WEDDING MARCH (LEAVING) *DARIUS MILHAUD*. DURING THE
ACTION, THREE RITORNELLOS BY *GEORGES AURIC*. PREMIÈRE 18 JUNE 1921.

'*Décor:* first platform of the Eiffel Tower. The backdrop represents a bird's-eye view
of Paris. On the right, in the background, a human-size camera. The body of the
camera forms a corridor linking with the wings. The front of the apparatus opens
like a door, through which the characters come and go. In the foreground, to right
and left of the stage, two actors dressed as gramophones are stationed, half
concealed behind their frames: the base encloses the actor's body, the horn
corresponds to his mouth. It is these gramophones which comment on the action
and recite the characters' parts. They speak very loudly and very fast, clearly
enunciating each syllable. The scenes are performed in unison with their narration.

'*The curtain rises with a roll of drums, which marks the end of the overture. Bare
stage. Gramophone one.* – You are on the first platform of the Eiffel Tower.
Gramophone two. – Just look! An ostrich. It's crossing the stage. It's leaving. Here's
the huntsman. He's looking for the ostrich. He raises his head. He sees something. He
takes aim. He shoots. *Gramophone one.* – Heavens above! A telegram.

'*A large blue telegram falls out of the sky. Gramophone two.* – The detonation
wakes the director of the Eiffel Tower. He appears. *Gramophone one.* – Well then,
sir, so you think you're out hunting? . . . *Gramophone two.* – Here's the Eiffel Tower
photographer. He speaks. What is he saying? *Gramophone one.* – You wouldn't
happen to have seen an ostrich going this way, by any chance? *Gramophone two.* –
Indeed I have! I'm looking for it. *Gramophone one.* – Would you believe it? My
camera has broken. Usually when I say: "Don't move, watch the dicky-bird", a little
bird flies out. This morning, I said to a lady: "Watch the dicky-bird", and out came
an ostrich. I'm looking for the ostrich so that I can put it back in the camera.
Gramophone two. – Ladies and gentlemen, the plot thickens, since the director of the
Eiffel Tower suddenly realizes that the telegram bears his address. *Gramophone
one.* – He opens it. *Gramophone two.* – "Director Eiffel Tower. Coming wedding
lunch, request reserve table." *Gramophone one.* – But this telegram is dead [i.e. out
of date]. *Gramophone two.* – It's precisely because it's dead that everyone
understands it. *Gramophone one.* – Quick! Quick! We've just got time to set the table.
I'm cancelling your fine. I'm appointing you Eiffel Tower waiter. Photographer, to
your post! *Gramophone two.* – They are laying the tablecloth. *Gramophone one.* –
Wedding march. *Gramophone two.* – The procession.

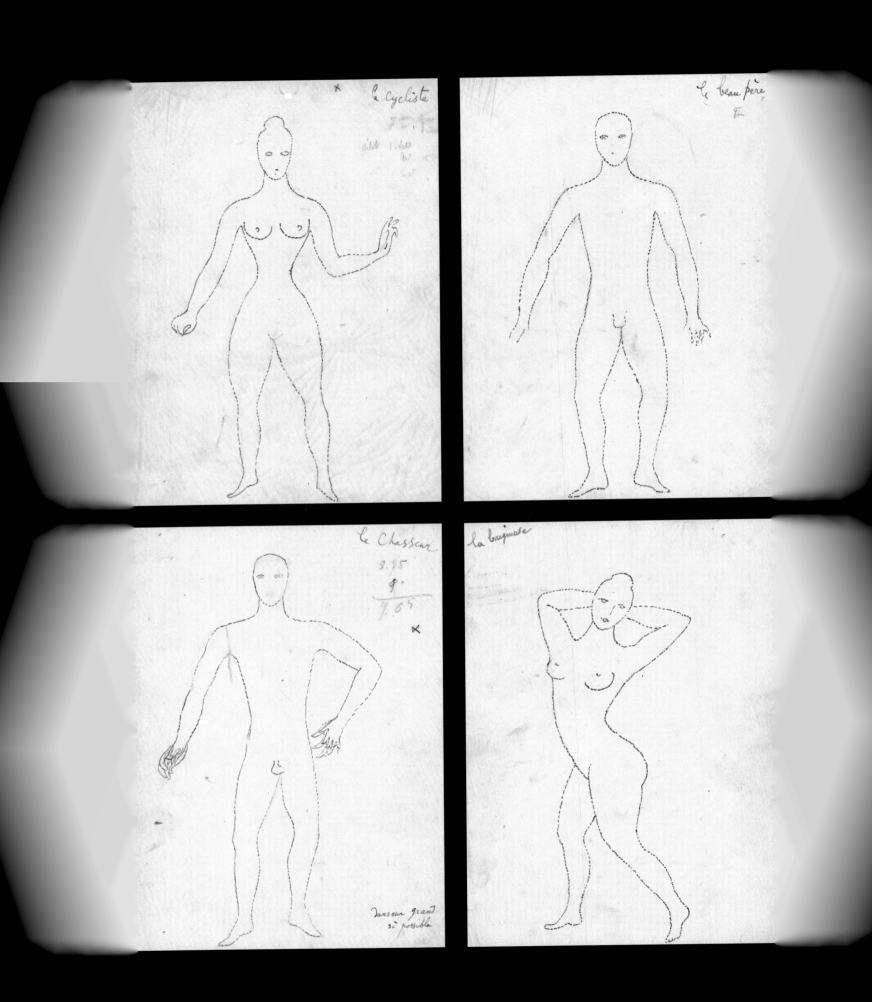

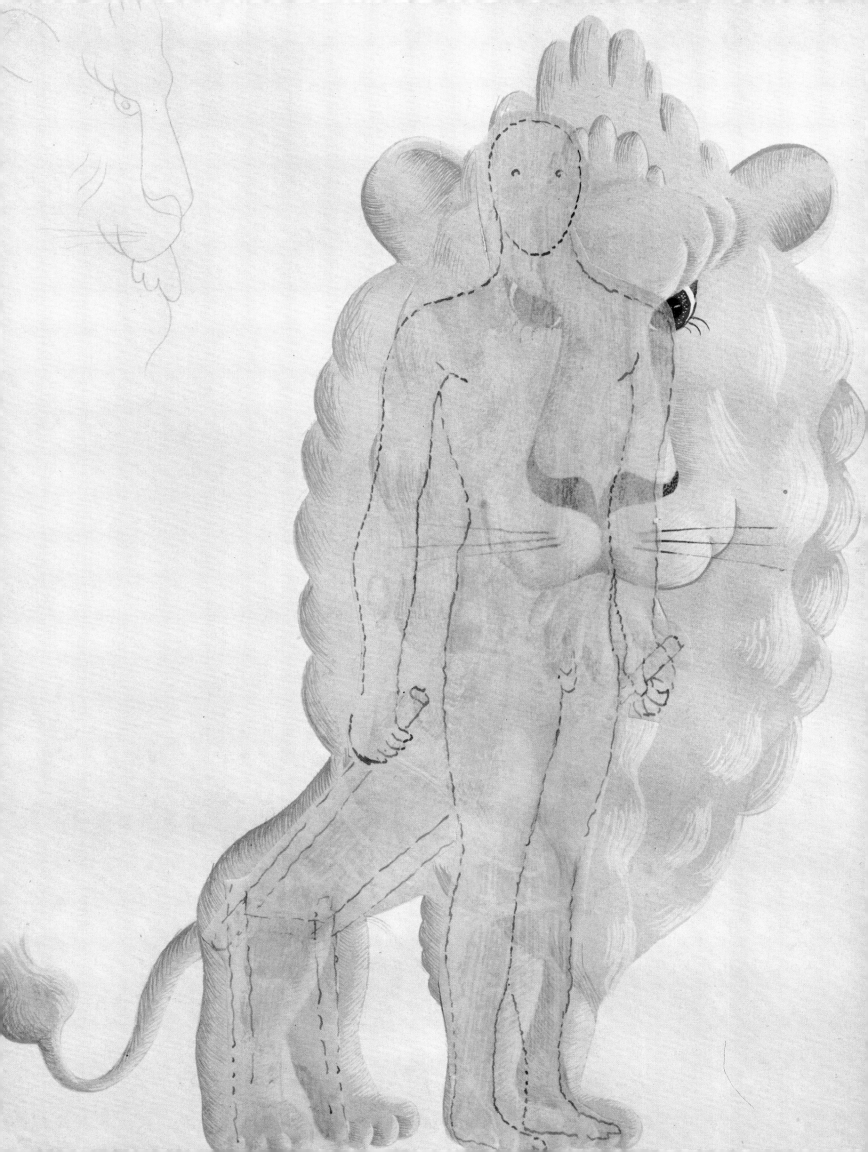

'Wedding march. The gramophones announce the dramatis personae of the wedding festivities, who enter in couples, walking like the dogs in doggy dramas. . . . Gramophone one. – The director of the Eiffel Tower shows them round the Eiffel Tower, pointing out the bird's-eye view of Paris. Gramophone two. – I feel dizzy!

'The huntsman and the director bring a table with plates painted on it. The tablecloth touches the floor. Gramophone one. – The general shouts: lunch is ready! Lunch is ready! And the wedding party sit down at the table. Gramophone two. – On one side of the table only, so that they can be seen by the audience. Gramophone one. – The general gets up. Gramophone two. – General's speech.

'The general's speech is played by the orchestra. He simply accompanies it with mime. . . . Gramophone one. – But who is this lovely cyclist in breeches?

'A cyclist enters. She gets off her bike. Gramophone two, in the cyclist's voice. – I beg your pardon, gentlemen. Gramophone one. – What can we do for you, madam? Gramophone two. – Am I on the right road for Chatou? Gramophone one. – Yes, madam. Just keep following the tram lines. . . . Gramophone two. – Don't move. Smile. Look at the camera. Watch the dicky-bird.

'Out comes a Trouville bathing girl. She is in a swimsuit, carrying a fishing net, and a basket slung across her back. Coloured lights. The wedding party raise their arms to heaven. Gramophone one. – Oh, what a pretty postcard! (The bathing girl dances.) The photographer is missing out on the wedding festivities. This is the second time since this morning that his camera has played tricks on him. He tries to get the Trouville bathing girl back inside. Gramophone one. – At last, the bathing girl goes back into the camera. The photographer tells her it's a bathing hut. End of the dance. The photographer flings a towelling wrap round the bather's shoulders. She goes back into the camera skipping and blowing kisses. . . . Gramophone two. – The wedding party compose themselves into a fresh tableau. Madam, your left foot on one of the spurs. Sir, attach the veil to your moustache. Perfect. Don't move. One. Two. Three. Look at the camera. Watch the dicky-bird. He presses the shutter button.

Out comes a fat child. He is wearing a green paper crown on his head and clutching prize books and a basket. Gramophone one. – Hello, mummy. *Gramophone two.* – Hello, daddy. . . . *Gramophone one.* – What's he looking for in his basket? *Gramophone two.* – Balls. *Gramophone one.* – What's he doing with the balls? It looks as if he's up to no good. *Gramophone two.* – He's playing at Aunt Sally. *Gramophone one.* – He's chucking balls at his family because he wants some macaroons.

'*The child bombards the wedding party, who collapse in a heap, yelling.* . . . *Gramophone two.* – The captured telegrams tumble down on to the stage and flounder about. The entire wedding party run after them and jump on top of them. *Gramophone one.* – Here, here, I've got one. Me too. Help! Over here! She's biting me! Keep a grip! Keep a grip! *Gramophone two.* – The telegrams calm down. They organize themselves into a line. The loveliest of them steps forward and does a military salute. *Gramophone one, in the voice of a revue compère.* – So, who are you, then? *Gramophone two.* – I am the wireless telegram and, like my sister the stork, I've come from New York. *Gramophone one, in the voice of a revue compère.* – New York! The city of lovers and blinds? *Gramophone two.* – On with the music! *Telegrams' dance. Exit the telegrams.* . . . *Gramophone two.* – Don't move. That's perfect. Watch the dicky-bird.

'*Out comes a lion. Gramophone two.* – Horrors! Oh, horrors! Ahhhhhh! *Gramophone one.* – What's he got in his mouth? *Gramophone two.* – A boot, with a spur on it. *Gramophone one.* – After eating the general, the lion goes back into the camera. *Gramophone one and gramophone two.* – Ahhhh! Ahhhh. . . . *Gramophone one.* – Poor general! *Gramophone two.* – He was such a jolly man, really young at heart. He'd have been tickled pink by a death like this. He'd have been the first to laugh about it. *Gramophone one.* – General's funeral. *Funeral procession.* . . . *Gramophone one.* – Listen! *Gramophone two.* – *The Newlyweds on the Eiffel Tower,* quadrille, by the Garde Républicaine band. *Gramophone one and gramophone two.* – Bravo! Bravo! Long live the Garde Républicaine.

'*Quadrille. End of the quadrille.* . . . *Gramophone two.* – Now then, ladies and gentlemen, I'm going to count up to five. Look at the camera. Watch the dicky-bird. *Gramophone one.* – A dove! *Gramophone two.* – The camera's working. *Gramophone one.* – All's well at last. *Gramophone two.* – One. (*The bride and groom leave the group, cross the stage and disappear into the camera.*) Two. (*The father- and mother-in-law do likewise.*) Three. (*The first pageboys and bridesmaids do likewise.*) Four. (*The second pageboys and bridesmaids do likewise.*) Five. (*The general and the child do likewise, the general walking with lowered head behind the child, who drags him by the hand.*) *Gramophone one.* – Enter the director of the Eiffel Tower. He is shaking a megaphone. . . . *Gramophone two.* – We're closing! We're closing! *Gramophone two.* – Enter the huntsman. He's hurrying. He runs up to the camera. What is the photographer saying? *Gramophone one.* – Where are you going? *Gramophone two.* – I want to catch the last train. *Gramophone one.* – No one else is allowed through. *Gramophone two.* – That's outrageous! I shall complain to the railways director. *Gramophone one.* – It's not my fault. Look, your train's leaving.

'*The camera begins to move to the left, followed, like a series of carriages, by its bellows. Through the openings, the wedding party can be seen waving handkerchiefs and, below, the feet of people walking. Curtain.*'

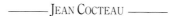

——— JEAN COCTEAU ———

'Ballet? No. Play? No. Revue? No. Tragedy? No. A sort of clandestine marriage, rather, between classical tragedy and the end-of-year revue, between the chorus

and the music-hall number. The whole thing already viewed at a distance, in perspective, modern antiquity, characters from our childhood, wedding party with a tendency to vanish into thin air, episode on the Eiffel Tower which, after being discovered by the painters, becomes once more what it should never have ceased to be: a lovely young woman in mittens, whose sole former employment was that of reigning over Paris and who, today, is simply the telegraph lady. What happens? Nothing that can readily be described. The sort of people one meets on a Sunday outing come and go while human gramophones, to right and left of the stage, comment on their actions. Thanks to Jean Hugo, these characters, instead of being – as tends to happen in the theatre – too small, too meagre in their reality, to hold their own against the luminous and decorative masses that make up the stage, are so ingeniously constructed, padded out, adjusted, touched up, that they do not go up like straw and fizzle out in the fire of the footlights and spotlights.

'Thanks to Irène Lagut, our Eiffel Tower conjures up the sort of Parisian postcards I have seen even little Arab girls in Africa sigh over. People ask me if the text is satirical. As soon as you have reality, you have satire, and I have no time for a work – even one embedded in the realms of subjective reality – which is not also deeply rooted in our common reality. Theatre must be direct. A masterpiece is a commonplace in disguise. The peril of the commonplace pure and simple is that eyes and ears no longer see or hear it, precisely because they are so used to seeing and hearing it. But commonplaces are tried and tested and should be universally approved. Anyone who systematically avoids them gets bogged down in the bizarre and the inhuman. In *Les Mariés* I am using commonplaces, but commonplaces connected and presented in such a way as to create surprise, striking us by their very youthfulness – as if they had never subsided into decrepit officialdom. I worked hard at avoiding studied effects, at not being original, at writing legibly.

'Georges Auric's overture, entitled "The 14th of July", conjures up the potent charm of the street, popular festivals, small platforms decked in Turkey-red cotton and evoking the guillotine, round which young women, sailors and shop assistants dance to the sound of drums and cornets. Its ritornellos provide a basic accompaniment to the pantomime in the same way that a circus orchestra repeats a motif *ad infinitum* during the acrobats' performance. The same atmosphere pervades the "Wedding March", the "Funeral March", the "Telegrams' Dance", the "Trouville Bathing Girl" and the "Quadrille" by Germaine Tailleferre, Arthur Honegger, Francis Poulenc and Darius Milhaud. Our friend Durey was prevented by illness from working with us. While the little boy, a product of the camera, born right into the awkward age, knocks over his relatives by hurling balls at them, his family's yells mingle with a fugue by Darius Milhaud – veritable imprecations of the Ancients interpreted for orchestra.'

——— Jean Cocteau, in *La Danse*, 1921 ———

'In *Les Mariés de la tour Eiffel*, there is a child who is bigger than the other characters. I have always seen him as bigger. The public, which understands things literally, is probably wondering why. I would no doubt have been wondering too, if it had not been for a stagehand who pointed him out to one of his mates saying: "Look at that kid! He really gets in the way! That's just like kids." . . . In our ballet, I have rehabilitated the commonplace. It was my job to place it, present it, in such a way that it rediscovered its lost youth. A generation of obscurity, of mystery, cannot just be shrugged off. I know that my text seems far too simple, far too *legibly written*, like the alphabet in school. The music accompanying it gives rise to a similar misapprehension. Out of nothing, a new limpidity, a new openness and

conviviality are created. An innocent is taken in by it, imagining that what he hears is a *café-concert* orchestra. His ear makes the same mistake as an eye wholly unable to distinguish between coarse material and the same fabric copied by Ingres.

'Whistles and ovations. Frightful press. A handful of articles. Surprise. Three years later, the detractors applaud, forgetting that they once whistled. . . . When Auric's overture – regiments crossing paths on 14 July, marching troops, whose music blares out on street corners, then fades into the distance – ends in a roll of drums and Irène Lagut's décor is revealed, pretty as a postcard decked with forget-me-nots and paper lace; when the costumes, sculpted, built and painted by Jean Hugo with an atavistically monstrous realism, appear; when the gramophones speak with voices coarser than nature's, do not balk, spectators! Do not look for double meanings. Do not imagine that you are being insulted. For weeks and weeks now, we have been working day and night for your pleasure.'

JEAN COCTEAU, LETTER TO JEAN BÖRLIN

'He had originally asked Irène Lagut to design the costumes. She was one of the guests at our Saturday dinners, a painter of delicate harlequins and circus horses. When he read the piece to her, she exclaimed, with that child-like laugh of hers: "We can use electric lights for the lion's eyes." A few days later, Cocteau came to my place with Radiguet and read me *La Noce*. He had balked at the puerile idea of a lion with luminous eyes, and thinking, perhaps, of the cyclist that I had done for *Les Joues en feu*, he asked me to design the costumes instead. Irène was rather put out about it – in as far as such an easy-going person could be – and Georges Auric, who was in love with her, flew into a rage and refused to collaborate further on the score for *La Noce*.

'Cocteau continued working on his décor. . . . But he was getting rather bogged down with all those red, green, yellow and blue triangles, rhombuses and trapeziums. In the end, he gave up and asked Irène to make the model for the stage setting. She agreed. Auric immediately promised to write the overture and everyone was happy. . . . In *La Noce* – which, from now on, we were to call *Les Mariés* – Cocteau's aim was, as he put it, to "rehabilitate commonplaces". So, I looked up the words *bather, boot, cyclist, lion, bride*, etc. in Larousse, where I found bathing girls in little skirts, wasp-waisted brides, a lion similar to the sort you see in the shops near the Louvre, a cyclist in breeches and button-up boots – an entire wardrobe, in fact!

'Most of the models were designed at the first attempt. The director of the Eiffel Tower was the only one I had trouble getting to grips with. . . . Initially, he was a sort of mustachioed hotel porter wearing a bowler hat. But Cocteau said: "No, the director is a Guépratte [French First World War admiral]!" So, the porter turned into an admiral with a fan-shaped beard, before ending up as the stout civil servant in an alpaca jacket, chewing the end of his cigar and hopping around on a pair of tiny feet. We took the masks and the pasteboards to the theatre, together with the costumes, padded or stretched on wire frames. (According to Cocteau, these costumes were intended to endow the characters with "an epic look".) With Valentine's help, I distempered them, matching them up perfectly with the décor, and treating them sufficiently carefully that they could be viewed from close quarters. Cocteau insisted that – contrary to accepted opinion – everything, in theatre, is seen. We took virtually no time at all organizing the lighting. "Here I'm abandoning mystery," Cocteau said, "illuminating everything, accentuating everything." This was how we came to use our much-decried "full lights".

'Cocteau knew how to "arrange an audience". He had taken great care in positioning his friends and his enemies. The press preview was stormy and the

applause mixed with whistles. But Cocteau would probably not have enjoyed the "bravos" without the boos.

'Before the Ballets Suédois left, Rolf de Maré gave a luncheon on the first platform of the Eiffel Tower for the dancers and all those who had collaborated on the ballet. . . . After the meal, the lion, the ostrich, the photographer and the lovely telegrams – the whole wedding party, in other words – climbed to the top of the tower, where the sea breeze was blowing. A boundary marker told us the distance from there to Chatou, and we thought of *the dreamy cyclist with her heart between her legs* who asked the general the way there.'

———— Jean Hugo, *Le Regard de la Mémoire*, Paris, 1984 ————

'. . . And what label should we give it, this work at once simple and complex, this veritable cocktail, in which all the genres of theatre are mixed so as to reappear in a new form, this simultaneous classical tragedy and music-hall revue – though not end-of-year revue; more one that sums up a whole era. Two human gramophones recite the text, each using different tones of voice, which are to diction what capital letters, italics, etc. are to typography. No embellishments, no "fancy lettering". Everything, here, is as simple, as "crude", as the sentences in a child's spelling book. An item like "The Trouville Bathing Girl", composed by Francis Poulenc, and marvellously danced by Mlle Carina Ari, is a colour postcard with the potency of an allegory. During the climax of the piece, when the little boy hurls balls at his relatives and knocks them over, a fugue by Darius Milhaud plunges us into the atmosphere of classical drama. Georges Auric's overture, entitled "The 14th of July", on the other hand, evokes torchlight tattoos, and fairgrounds, whose pomp and simplicity should not be mistaken for banality. Thanks to Jean Hugo, whose sense of the "monstrously real" amazes us, and to Irène Lagut, whose tower is what it ought to be in reality – the cage enclosing those bluebirds, the telegrams – *Les Mariés de la tour Eiffel* never for a moment loses that air of a picture postcard, a veritable "souvenir of Paris". . . .'

———— Raymond Radiguet ————

'*Les Mariés de la Tour Eiffel* completes the trilogy of experiment by Cocteau, of which the two previous works were *Parade*, the ballet written for Diaghilev, and *Le Boeuf sur le Toit*. The *Mariés*, a trenchant satire on bourgeois traditions, caused an uproar on its first performance, but, the first shock over, it gradually won its way to success.

'Just as the antique Greek Theatre made use of gigantic masks, so the characteristics of the types in the ballet were stressed and magnified by the dancers' wearing special masks and padded costumes. . . . The use of masks, however, involved many difficulties for the choreographer, since the dancers could neither hear the music nor the voice of the announcer. All the movements, therefore, had to be worked out with mathematical precision.

'Another innovation was the use of the human phonograph. At each side of the stage was placed a two-sided booth, fitted with a megaphone, in which the announcer, hidden from the audience, made the necessary introductions for the entrance of each character.'

C.W. Beaumont
———— *The Complete Book of Ballets*, London, 1937 ————

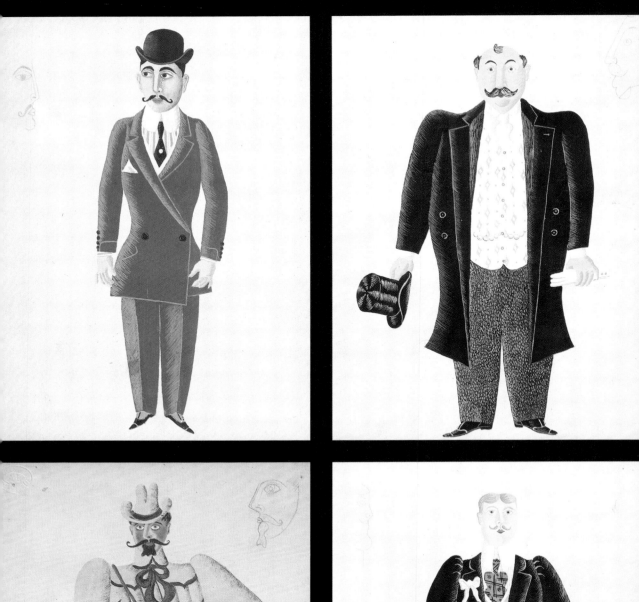

DANSGILLE

MUSIC BY *EUGÈNE BIGOT*, ADAPTED FROM SWEDISH FOLK TUNES. SETS BASED ON
A PAINTING IN STOCKHOLM'S NORDIC MUSEUM. SWEDISH NATIONAL COSTUMES.
CHOREOGRAPHY BY *JEAN BÖRLIN*. ORCHESTRA CONDUCTED BY *EUGÈNE BIGOT*.

GOTTLÄNDSK QUADRILLE / CORPS DE BALLET / FOLKVISA *CARINA ARI, THORBORG STJERNER, DAGMAR FORSLIN, JEAN BÖRLIN, KAJ SMITH, PAUL ELTORP* / GÅNGLÅT *HELGA DAHL, MARGARETA JOHANSON, AXEL WITZANSKY* / SLUTDANS *CARINA ARI, JEAN BÖRLIN* AND THE CORPS DE BALLET. PREMIÈRE 20 NOVEMBER 1921.

Each item was based on an authentic dance, characteristic of a particular region of Sweden, and involving only the original steps and figures.

'This colourful, fresh and wholesome sequence of rustic dances is both relaxing and absorbing.'

——— G. LE FÈVRE ———

'Their opening programme contained something new for the Paris public, the rustic entertainment *Dansgille*, already successfully staged in the provinces. *Dansgille* (actually pronounced "dansguillé") is a selection of popular peasant dances still performed along traditional lines in Swedish villages. The costumes are cheerful, gaudy; movements comically puppet-like; gestures stylized. And the whole is interspersed with little heavy-footed gallopades, and loud heel tapping on the floorboards to mark the downbeats. This pleasing piece frames a staggeringly virtuoso performance from M. Axel Witzansky, a young dancer whose lightness, rhythmical precision and musical intelligence, as displayed in the course of an entertaining acrobatic variation, drew enthusiastic and well-deserved applause. With a laudable sense of artistic fairness, M. Jean Börlin played second fiddle to Witzansky, thus personally giving a little lesson in tact to star dancers who un-fortunately and all too frequently demand a monopoly on success as their natural right.'

——— ÉMILE VUILLERMOZ ———

'*Dansgille* reproduces the motif of Swedish peasant dances in a richer and technically superior artistic guise.'

——— GOTTHARD JOHANSSON, IN *ARES*, NO. 18, 1922 ———

S K A T I N G
R I N K

POEM BY *RICIOTTO CANUDO*. MUSIC BY *ARTHUR HONEGGER*.

CURTAIN, SCENERY AND COSTUMES BY *FERNAND LÉGER*.

CHOREOGRAPHY AND STAGING BY *JEAN BÖRLIN*.

The Madman *Jean Börlin* / The Woman *Jolanda Figoni* / The Man *Kaj Smith* / Men and Women. Première 20 January 1922.

'This "danced poem" represents an unprecedented experiment in modern choreography, since movements, steps, gestures and attitudes are all inspired here by skating. In a dramatic setting that is deliberately kept very simple, reduced to essentials, Canudo has expressed one of life's major, elemental forms of anguish. That is, sensual longing, which thrusts living beings towards and counter to one another and creates collisions, unions, all the harmonies and all the disharmonies of love and hate. The scene evokes a modern skating environment, the *skating rink*, where crowds of men and women meet, mingle and separate, in a musical, luminous, fairy-tale atmosphere.'

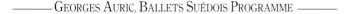

———— Georges Auric, Ballets Suédois Programme ————

1. They turn. They turn. They *turn*. / In vague eddies of madness, / they spin the desperate meaning of life. 2. Skating rink. A little *vortex of flesh*, / somewhere, in the city. / No gestures. Above all, no words. / The full, round whine of skates under the airless vault. / Suffocating carnal smells / in the whining shriek of steel. . . . 5. A handful of couples have entered the lists. / Five, ten, very few. And they fill the space with the wind of their moving flesh. / They have no faces. / A double-sided form of sliding flesh. / An image. / *Lightness*. / Exasperating image of *sexuality*. / Two bodies combine to make one. The joint undulation / of hips and loins is the undulation of the sexual embrace. 6. In their midst, all of a sudden, a man appears. / Tall, straight-backed, lean. Ineluctable like the will to rhythm / in the hands of the conductor. / A man alone, on his *skates*. / Like the actors of ancient Greece in their buskins. / The end of the red scarf at his neck / flutters, like the flame of a candle that is shaken. / We glimpse how pale, how emaciated, he is – like an anchorite. / He is the leader of the *skating dance*. / He captures in his swirling motion / the metallic glare of the fairground organ, and all the movement. / His bones vibrate like an instrument. / Visible, tangible, cords stretched beneath supple muscles. / In his open arms he holds the rhythm of those couples / who spin and spin the desperate meaning of life. / Frenzied Corybant. / Poet. / Madman. . . . 9. A woman, dizzy with turning, / leaves the dance. / In one bound, the madman catches hold of her, / mesmerized by his red scarf. / He carries her off in a glorious flourish of leaps and veils. / He hurls himself with her into a more flexuous frenzy / in the midst of the skaters. / *Spider* at the heart of its web. . . . 11. A man inflamed with jealous anger / springs towards the woman and the madman. / He extends his whole slender body towards a CHIMERA. / He stretches out his hands towards the elusive / couple, the woman and the madman. / He turns, and turns, in ever-diminishing circles, / round the woman and the madman. / And finds nothing. He cannot seize hold of what is elusive. / The couple escape, playing, / drawing close, drifting away again. / And the man pursues them, trembling with unbearable longing. . . . 13. No voice. No gesture to indicate desire. / The undulation of three bodies, / of one body and another dual body, / in the same circle of *lightness*, / bounding, each fading out in turn. / One, with its desire / for *death*. / The other with its desire / for *love*. . . . 15. *Fate has entered the fray*. / The man brandished his knife, / fierce as a cinema villain. But his gesture was useless. / As useless as his claim / to this lovely, distant female flesh. / Fate has made its pronouncement. / There is too much carefree *lightness* in the madman's beauty. / And, one by one, all the women's faces light up / like candle flames / twirled by invisible hands. / Spectre-like. / All of them, every one, / gravitate towards the centre of the world, / towards *the woman and the madman*. / One by one,

scything the air with their sweeping circular lines in which bodies no longer move, but spread outwards like waves. / All of them, every one, round the woman and the madman! / Humble carnal platform. . . . 18. The two masses of humanity come and go, / draw close and drift apart, / embrace in the *dance of hatred*, / and immediately withdraw. / The mass of *men*. The mass of *women*. / The men have won. The women are theirs. / Exasperated, the women begin their game again. / And alone, at the centre once more, the *couple* reappear, / the madman and the woman in love. / Alone, at the centre of all the hatred that encircles them. 19. And so, they all turn, / in an endless dance, / *they spin the crazy-meaning-of-life*. 20. When, with a great cry, sharp, and luminous as a flare, / the woman falls in a faint at the madman's feet. / Fainting from the languor of clasping too close / in the most mortal voluptuousness / the sublime oblivion of her being / through the supreme *lightness*, / the supreme *dance* / *of elegance*. / The circle of attacking couples opens up / in pitying and expectant terror. . . . And, in silence, as if in response to the eternal sign of new beginnings, all the couples begin once more, in a mild frenzy, spinning *the desperate meaning of life*.'

—— RICCIOTTO CANUDO, IN *MERCURE DE FRANCE*, 5.5.1920 ——

'I endeavoured to obtain maximum scenic intensity using one technique alone: the application of pure colour with no attempt at creating perspective. . . . When it came to staging *Skating Rink*, the characters were inspired by working-class venues like the popular dance halls, which we visited with Börlin and Rolf de Maré. The innovativeness of the production inevitably caused some ructions with the public, prompting one wit to remark that he saw no need whatsoever for an orchestra, given the racket that was unleashed in the auditorium. Rehearsals, he added, are money down the drain.'

—— FERNAND LÉGER, IN *LES BALLETS SUÉDOIS*, PARIS, 1932 ——

'The success of *Skating Rink* prompted me to ask Léger, who painted the curtain, scenery and costumes for it, to define what he had been seeking to achieve. Léger's aim is to provide an intense "visual emotion" thanks to the interplay of coloured shapes in movement. To which end, he rejects the merely anecdotal, the studied effect. In order to eliminate all fantasy, his characters retain their realistic type value. But there is a difficulty here: how to obtain a unity between the realistic nature of the character and the inventive quality with which the painter seeks to endow the grouped elements of his décor. Showing the dancer's art to advantage, at the cost of the décor's immobility, constitutes a blending of barely theatrical reality with creative elements which are indeed the characteristic of a scenic spectacle. There is an imbalance here between two opposing ideas, or rather a harmonizing endeavour that lacks adequate cohesion. Such duality may inevitably cause sympathetic attention to waver.

'Now, for Fernand Léger, a vital question has to be asked at this point, one that is never sufficiently considered: how to move the audience emotionally via a purely visual spectacle; in other words, how to add a visual emotion to that procured by the music and the dancers' movements. In a theatre, there are, according to Léger, three actual positions: a dead surface, the auditorium; a focal point of intensity, the stage; and a neutral sector, the footlights. Léger's aim has been to override this status quo. According to him, the stage must extend beyond the footlights, penetrate the auditorium and envelop the spectators (eighty per cent of whom are distracted), thereby creating a more perfect unity, with the result that the spectator becomes actor, the spectacle comes down into the auditorium, and the subject ceases to be a

museum piece, passing instead into general hands. In order to achieve this, Léger does away with the dancer as a representation of human elements. The dancer, in his view, should become an integral part of the décor; a plastic element that will be a moving part of the décor's plastic elements.

'A further difficulty arises at this point: the conflict between the mobility of the dancer and the immobility of the décor. One day, perhaps, ballets will be endowed with mobile décors which will evolve in the manner of films, presenting a spectacle that is repeatedly renewed. Léger, for his part, has recourse to essentially pictorial means. First of all, he reduces the stage to its minimum depth. From this restricted space, he banishes all perspective, or rather he creates, of necessity, a reverse perspective. As for the *mobile décor* – the dancers – he arranges it in parallel and contrasting masses, the only means of avoiding the monotony which the absence of precise types would otherwise produce. The desired effect is obtained by, for example, the opposition of ten characters *in red, moving at speed* set against ten characters *in yellow, moving slowly*. As for movements, they follow a set of mechanical and geometric rules, their duration rigorously determined in order to avoid delays and *mistimings*. Finally, from the point of view of colour, Léger deems that the absolute law in such a case is the application of local colour full strength. Any visual blend, any linking of complementary colours, is liable to evoke an emotion that has more to do with charm and less to do with plastic intensity, an emotion which seems to amount merely to that agreeable art of display, or window dressing – the very opposite of what the painter is seeking to achieve.'

——— Maurice Raynal, in *Der Querschnitt*, 1922 ———

'A poem with noble philosophical tendencies disappears beneath the systematically debauched garb of a freakish costume designer, and a curtain which so thoroughly creates the effect of movement that it becomes a substitute for the dancers themselves, who appear not to move at all, so little variation is there in their endless revolutions. A composer brings to this improvisation the weight of a logical score, one sure of its power to sweep us along with it, and which, without a backward glance, starts up its engine and drives off, boldly heading for the appointed goal without ever imagining that its companions will never reach the rendezvous. All this vaguely creates the impression of a dream in which a picnic trip suddenly turns into a race, with one of the competitors emerging as the victor, while the others are still several yards behind the starting line.'

——— Maurice Bex, in *Revue Hebdomadaire*, 25.2.1922 ———

'Here, at last, is a ballet in which the most enlightened have uncovered a new formula, that of the *foliage which aspires to be flower*, the mass of humanity which aspires to the perfection of the couple; and in which others have sought a face familiar to art, and have not found it, being utterly unqualified to respond to the supreme beauty of Honegger's music, or to the new choreographic experiment that *Skating Rink* inspired in Jean Börlin, and which the dazzling Fernand Léger enveloped in "Cubist" lights.'

——— Riciotto Canudo, in *Comœdia* ———

MARCHAND D'OISEAUX

BALLET BY *HÉLÈNE PERDRIAT*. MUSIC BY *GERMAINE TAILLEFERRE*.

SETS AND COSTUMES BY *HÉLÈNE PERDRIAT*. CHOREOGRAPHY BY *JEAN BÖRLIN*.

THE YOUNGER SISTER *GRETA LUNDBERG* / THE ELDER SISTER *CARINA ARI* / THE BIRD SELLER *JEAN BÖRLIN* / THE CHILDREN OF MARY *MLLES FORSLIN, SELID, MALMBERG, LARSON* / THE SCHOOLGIRLS *MLLES FRIIS, KÄHR, SCHWARCK, BLOM-KVIST* / THE GARDENERS *MLLES BONSDORFF, PETTERSON, ALLAN* / THE STRANGER *TURE ANDERSSON* / THE SERVANT *MLLE ALLAN*. PREMIÈRE 25 MAY 1923.

The theme of this delightful ballet is the punishment of false pride. It tells the simple story of two sisters who discover two bouquets on their doorstep, and each chooses one. The elder sister scorns the wild flowers, but her younger sister sees them as the lovelier of the two bunches. She loves and is loved in return by a simple bird seller, whereas her sister is courted by a wealthy masked stranger, whose attentions she welcomes. A naughty schoolgirl suddenly snatches away the stranger's mask, revealing … the old merchant from the port. There is general shock and confusion. Meanwhile, to loud applause, the younger sister – performing the most graceful of dances – exits on the arm of the bird seller.

'Mlle Germaine Tailleferre's subtle, idiosyncratic music complemented the Futurist boldness of the sets and costumes. Mlles Greta Lundberg and Carina Ari, in the roles of the younger and elder sister, displayed perfect technique and agility. They were a tremendous success with the audience.'

——— RENÉ D'IXELLES ———

'*Marchand d'oiseaux* takes place in a rustic setting that is a little overdone, designed – like the novel costumes – by Mme Hélène Perdriat, whose painted brows get lost in her hairline [meaning that she is "low-brow"].'

——— ALBERT DU MOULIN ———

'Though Mme Perdriat's libretto for *Marchand d'oiseaux* is rather a summary affair, and though it is easy to imagine (without wishing to sound malicious) that our poets could offer a thousand richer topics, yet the décor and costumes devised by the same artist, blending as they do influences from Persia and contemporary colourists, convey a charm that alternates between the delicate and the acid. An impression which may not move but which nevertheless pleases us, and is all the more satisfying since M. Börlin's choreography is grounded on this occasion in a free classicism, Mlle Tailleferre's music is fresh and agreeable, threaded with delightful reminiscences, and Mlles Carina Ari, with her Goya-esque lace, and Greta Lundberg, with her playful candour, are, quite simply, perfect.'

——— GABRIEL BOISSY ———

'Quick, let us smile at *Marchand d'oiseaux*, at its fresh, acid décor, its ironic costumes, its Children of Mary, with their straight backs and crimped hair, its mischievous schoolgirls, its red-headed coquette, rival of a dreamy brunette. A scenario? You want a scenario? Why? The handsome young man who sells birds embraces one of the most beautiful young women in the world, and that is in every way enough. This little divertissement is the triumph of Mlle Germaine Tailleferre,

Le jeune marchand d'oiseaux.

author of a sharp musical score, in which the popular motif and the child's round game sparkle, run for cover, and reappear, ribbons tying up an orchestral bouquet.'

——— COLETTE ———

'The choreography of *Marchand d'oiseaux* is as traditional as choreography ever was, with its ballerinas plying their points at every turn, like a class exercise, and it requires all Mlle Carina Ari's talent to make it bearable. M. Jean Börlin is graceful, but his dancing is always rather commonplace.'

——— ANDRÉ MESSAGER ———

lières

OFFERLUNDEN

BALLET PANTOMIME BY *JEAN BÖRLIN*. MUSIC BY *ALGOT HAQUINIUS*.

DÉCOR AND COSTUMES BY *GUNNAR HALLSTRÖM*.

CHOREOGRAPHY AND STAGING BY *JEAN BÖRLIN*. PREMIÈRE 25 MAY 1923.

In a prehistoric grove, the sacred fire has gone out. Following a succession of rites, dances and prayers, the tribal chieftain chooses to offer himself up as a sacrifice, and the flame bursts forth once more.

'The entire tribe invokes the gods, but in vain: the ashes remain cold. The guardians of the Fire summon the priests and the warriors with horn blasts; but the ashes remain ashes. Finally, the queen appears, ready to relight the Flame by killing herself, and thus avoiding other human sacrifices. This is where we see what a marvellous invention matches are! . . . But the queen is not required to give up her life, since the chieftain sacrifices himself in her stead, and the sacred fire burns once more.'

——— ÉDOUARD FONTEYNE ———

'More of a pantomime than a ballet, employing deliberate complexities and exaggerations, *Offerlunden* was staged in a magnificent setting. Mlle Thorborg Stjerner was the great sacrificer at whose feet Jean Börlin, self-appointed victim, fell. Mlle Margit Wåhlander was the queen, whose sacrifice is intended to placate the gods. She, too, was enthusiastically applauded. And for more than two dances, Börlin held us utterly spellbound.'

——— RENÉ D'IXELLES ———

'*Offerlunden* takes place in a wooded setting and uses strange costumes that have an element of the grotesque about them (fat white beans!): the creation of Dadaist Gunnar Hallström. A sombrely painted stage set by Darlot and Boue.'

——— ALBERT DU MOULIN ———

'The pantomime ballet which followed *Marchand d'oiseaux* was as sombre, symbolic and Wagnerian – with a cool, tempered Wagnerianism – as *Marchand d'oiseaux* had been light and easy. Messieurs de Maré and Börlin have made a huge effort to get to grips with a theme which must needs leave us indifferent, our feelings already dulled by so many similar legends. . . . Beautiful costumes, following a primitive schematism, a deliberately heavy-footed Börlin wearing a magnificent helmet, and a rather rousing war dance, fail to enliven the heavily oppressive prehistoric forest scene painted by M. Hallström.'

——— GABRIEL BOISSY ———

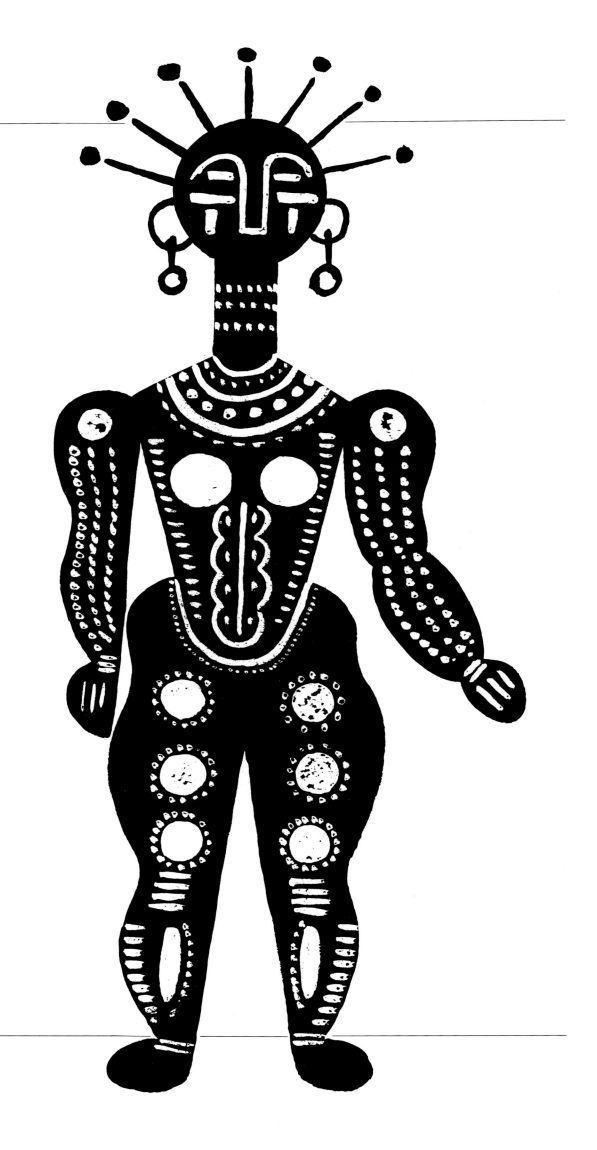

LA CRÉATION DU MONDE

BALLET BY *BLAISE CENDRARS*. MUSIC BY *DARIUS MILHAUD*.

CURTAIN, SETS AND COSTUMES BY *FERNAND LÉGER*. SETS PAINTED BY

MARCEL GUÉRIN. COSTUMES MADE BY *MUELLE*.

CHOREOGRAPHY BY *JEAN BÖRLIN*.

Man *Jean Börlin* / Woman *Ebon Strandin*. Insects, Monkeys, Birds, Herons, Men, Women. Première 25 October 1923.

'1. The curtain slowly rises on a dark stage. In the middle of the stage, we see a confused mass of intertwined bodies: chaos prior to creation. Three giant deities move slowly round the periphery. These are Nzame, Medere and N'kva, the masters of creation. They hold counsel together, circle round the formless mass, and utter magic incantations. 2. There is movement in the central mass, a series of convulsions. A tree gradually begins to grow, gets taller and taller, rising up straight, and when one of its seeds falls to the ground, a new tree sprouts. When one of the tree's leaves touches the ground, it lengthens, swells, rocks back and forth, begins to walk, becomes an animal. An elephant hanging in mid-air, a creeping tortoise, a crab, monkeys sliding down from the ceiling. The stage has gradually become lighter in the course of creation, and with each new animal it is brilliantly illuminated. 3. Each creature, with a dancer bursting from its centre, evolves in its own individual way, takes a few steps, then gently begins to move in a circle, gradually gathering speed as it revolves round the three initial deities. An opening appears in the circle, the three deities utter fresh incantations, and we see the formless mass seething. Everything vibrates. A monstrous leg appears, backs quiver, a hairy head emerges, arms are extended. All of a sudden, two torsos straighten, cling together: this is man and woman, suddenly upright. They recognize one another; they come face to face. 4. And while the couple perform the dance of desire, followed by the mating dance, all the formless beings that remained on the ground stealthily creep up and join in the round dance, leading it at a frenetic, dizzy pace. These are the N'guils, the invokers, the sorcerers and sorceresses, the fetishists. 5. The round's frenzy abates; it checks and slows and fades right out. The figures disperse in little groups. The couple stand apart in an embrace which lifts them up like a wave. Spring has arrived.'

———— Blaise Cendrars, Ballets Suédois Programme ————

'Notes on rules for staging. General rhythm grave and slow; accentuated at moments, but remaining rather solemn and ceremonial. Local colour: white, black, ochre. Mobile stage lighting intermittent (chiaroscuro effects), partial lighting (avoid total lighting). Continuous mobility of stage via displacement of mobile sets and real or fictitious characters. Animation of stage through birth of a tree and of various animals.'

———— B. Cendrars, F. Léger, Ballets Suédois Programme ————

'While strolling round Paris in this way, Léger, Cendrars and I worked out the details of our ballet. Léger wanted to provide an interpretation of primitive Negro art and paint the curtain and the sets with African divinities expressing a kind of dark power. But he never found the finished effects sufficiently frightening. He gave me a sketch for the curtain, black on dark brown, because he found it too light and a little bit too "cosy". What a charming euphemism! He would have liked to use goldbeater's skins, representing flowers, trees and a whole variety of animals, which we would have blown up with gas and let loose like balloons at the moment of creation. But such a project was impracticable, since it required a complicated arrangement of gas cylinders in each corner of the stage, and the sound of the balloons being inflated would have drowned out the music. Léger had to make do with drawing his inspiration from animal costumes like those worn by African dancers during their religious ceremonies.

'*La Création du monde* finally gave me the opportunity to put to use those jazz elements which I had studied so seriously. I arranged my orchestra like the Harlem ones, employing seventeen solo musicians, and exploited the jazz style unreservedly, blending it with a classical feel.'

———— Darius Milhaud, *Ma Vie Heureuse*, Paris, 1973 ————

'The ballet is based on the birth of the Negro world. When the curtain goes up, the three deities are on stage facing the audience. Behind them, as scenery, *mountains*, *clouds*, the *moon*, *stars*. Their job is to create plants, animals and humans. The three deities – statues in high-relief and relief fragment – will be between five and six metres tall. Colour: ochre and black, and blue. Some white. These huge figures will have *mobile sections*. Same with the décor. Thus, throughout the ballet, continual, slow movement of the scenic *Figure with four revolving faces*. Possible [tilting] of certain parts of the body. The *birth of the trees and the animals* achieved via an apparatus involving a goldbeater's skin which can be blown up. Dancers slipping down from one of the trees *as monkeys*. (As a surprise element.) Figures (dancers) heavily disguised, wearing carapaces, with the result that no dancers will have human proportions. By this means, we will achieve a *grandiose*, *dramatic* ballet, with, moreover, lighting effects which allow for alterations of light and dark.'

———— Fernand Léger ————

'For some years previous to the production of this ballet, Börlin had taken a great interest in native dances, and in 1919 had arranged for himself a solo dance which he called "*Sculpture Nègre*". From that day he always contemplated the production of a negro ballet.

'*La Création du Monde* is the story of Creation and the birth of Man as an aboriginal might conceive it. There were several new elements in the choreography, for instance the dancers who suggested herons moved on stilts, others who took the part of animals walked on all-fours. Again, the action took place in semi-darkness, with occasional dimming and lightening which produced an interesting play of light and shade.'

C.W. Beaumont
———— *The Complete Book of Ballets*, London, 1937 ————

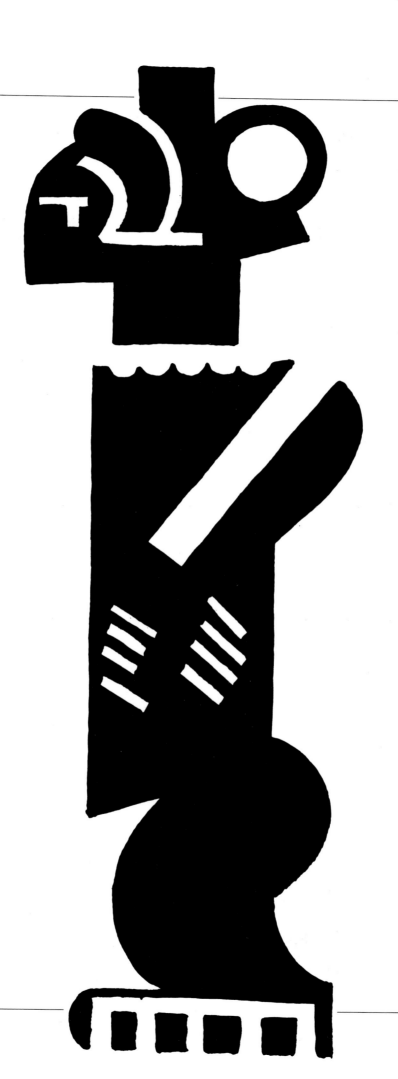

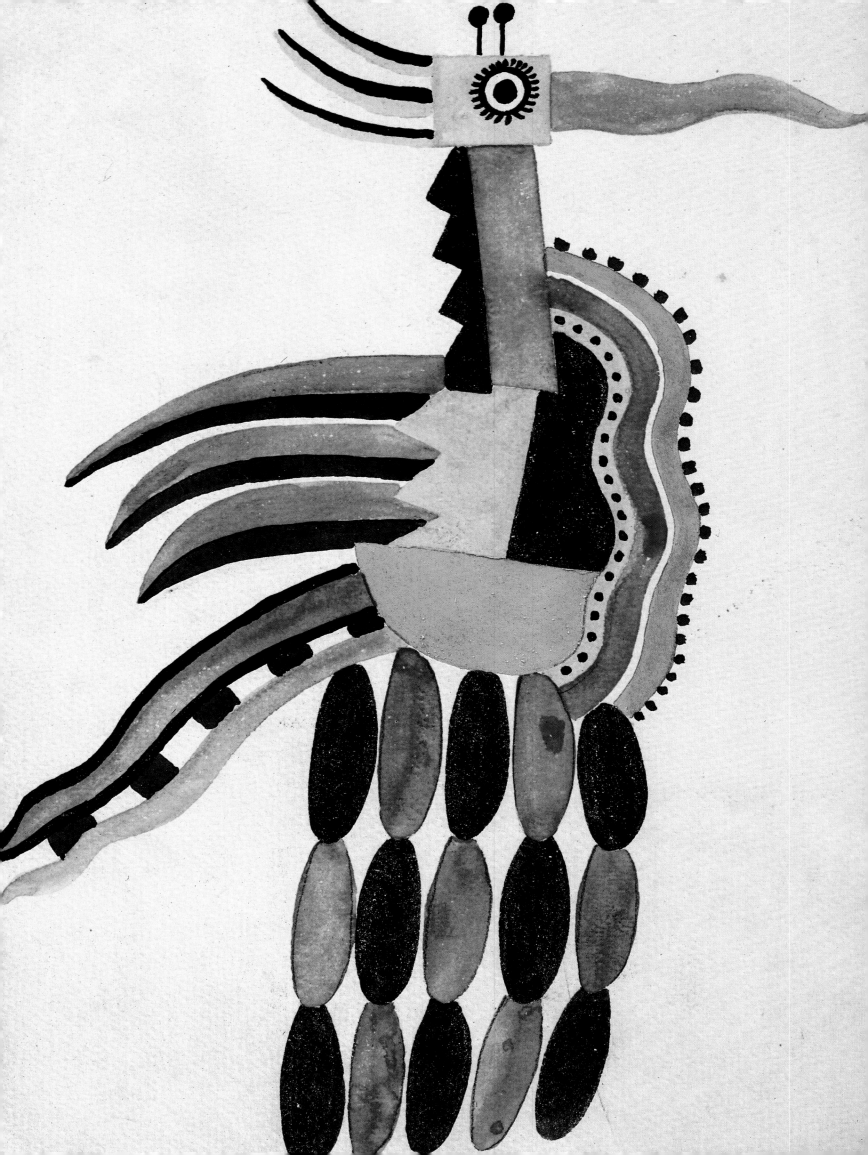

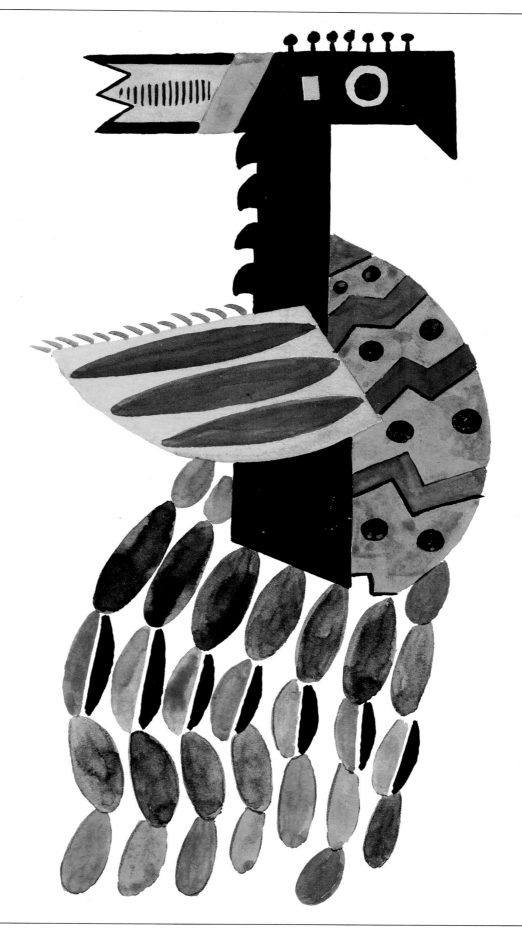

WITHIN
THE QUOTA

BALLET SKETCH BY *GERALD MURPHY*. MUSIC BY *COLE PORTER*.

ORCHESTRATED BY *CHARLES KOECHLIN*. SETS AND COSTUMES BY *GERALD*

MURPHY. CHOREOGRAPHY BY *JEAN BÖRLIN*.

THE IMMIGRANT *JEAN BÖRLIN* / THE MULTI-MILLIONAIRESS *KLARA KJELLBLAD* / THE PURITAN *TOIVO NISKANEN* / THE COLOURED GENTLEMAN *KAJ SMITH* / THE JAZZBABY *EBON STRANDIN* / THE COWBOY *PAUL ELTORP* / THE QUEEN OF HEARTS *EDITH BONSDORFF.* PREMIÈRE 25 OCTOBER 1923.

'*Within the Quota* is properly speaking an American ballet, the first to be staged by a foreign company and the first in which popular American music is used to illustrate an American theme. It is in the course of the action itself that the most interesting theme evolves: the possibility of reducing this little comedy "how the Scandinavians are integrated" to eighteen minutes. The figures passing before the immigrant's eyes are the mythical heroes of modern American life, in part as the average European imagines them from the cinema, in part as they really are. The intention is satirical, the method exaggeration. There is nothing more delightful than Cole Porter's talent as a jazz composer. Parody and comic exaggeration are second nature to him. In the cowboy, the "coloured gentleman" and the finale, he has used syncopation to sum up almost every detail.

'Technical interest is the last thing one would miss here (it is in fact very great). But when the five-strain chorus is added to the combination of shimmy, *Jazzbaby*, and nostalgic Swedish waltz, there is reason to believe this music worthy of a great composer. The concision, the arrangement, the general confidence of the score are admirable. The choreography for such a ballet must borrow its steps from American dancing and its movements from American daily life. In dealing with an American theme, it is absolutely crucial that traditional European ballet steps give way to the foxtrot and the shimmy, to steps from those body-jerking dances performed in soft shoes. The ballet's sets and costumes achieve their aim, which is to avoid distracting attention from the action and the music. It is on these two elements that this ballet, with its innate lightness and gaiety, is founded.'

———— GILBERT SELDES, IN *PARIS-JOURNAL*, 1923 ————

'De Maré, about to tour the United States, was anxious to put on an authentic American work, but did not know whose help to enlist. He was afraid of landing himself with a composer still in the Debussy or Ravel mould or a musician who would compose "à la Brahms" or "à la Reyer". Now, I had met Cole Porter many times at the Princesse de Polignac's. This elegant young American, who always wore a white carnation in the buttonhole of his immaculate dinner-jacket, used to sing – in his grave, husky voice – songs he had written himself and which possessed the exact qualities de Maré was looking for. I introduced him to de Maré, who immediately proposed that he handle a theme marvellously attuned to his own music: the arrival of a young Swede in New York. Since Cole Porter had no experience as yet of orchestra, it was Charles Koechlin who instrumented his score, a pure emanation of Manhattan, in which nostalgic blues alternated with throbbing ragtime rhythms. This strange collaboration between the technician of counterpoint and fugue and the brilliant future "king of Broadway" was a wonderful success. Fernand Léger got Gerald Murphy, an American, to make the sets and we saw the skyscrapers of Times Square rearing up on the Champs-Élysées stage.'

———— DARIUS MILHAUD, *MA VIE HEUREUSE*, PARIS, 1973 ————

EXTRA!
CHICAGOA
FINAL EDITION
eart-Balm Love-Tangle
WN BANKER
S ATLANTIC
Auto King Pledges Boom
MAMMOTH PLANE UP
THRONGS AT DEAL
SHOE-MAGNATE
SPLIT

LE ROSEAU

BALLET BASED ON A PERSIAN STORY. MUSIC BY *DANIEL LAZARUS*.
SETS AND COSTUMES BY *ALEKSANDR ALEKSEEV* FROM PERSIAN
MINIATURES. CHOREOGRAPHY BY *JEAN BÖRLIN*.

Khedad *Jean Börlin* / Suleika *Inger Friis* / The Slaves *Mlles Schwarck, Malmberg, Kähr, Allan* / The Old Musician *Kaarlo Eronen.* Première 19 November 1924.

Le Roseau is based on an old Persian legend, in which a young man falls in love with a woman playing a flute. Hearing another melody, however, he has a mystical experience and recognizes that his longing is spiritual in origin; he renounces earthly love and devotes himself to a life of prayer.

'The flute weeps and sighs, but heavier, more bitter still, is man's lament. Like the fingers which hold the flute and draw forth mysterious sounds, so woman holds man. She says to him: "Your flame is for me alone; I am your sole desire; all your longings can be satisfied in me. The tiny vibration of the earth before the rising of the sun, the imminence of the first rays, are no more than a foreshadowing of myself." Her hand rests lightly on him as he kneels at her feet, his brow against the earth. But the man who truly hears in time the telltale pangs of the flute will burst his chains and raise himself up to God, his source, crying: "My one desire is to be myself."'

——— Daniel Lazarus, in *La Danse*, 1924 ———

'I have trouble envisaging M. Lazarus's muse. No doubt, she has armour-plated breasts, an aluminium crown and tinted spectacles. God, what a tedious evocation! And what can be the name of that which we love and serve so passionately, if the unfortunate pages which constitute the score of *Le Roseau* call themselves music?'

——— Henri Sauguet, in *La Vie des Lettres et des Arts*, 1925 ———

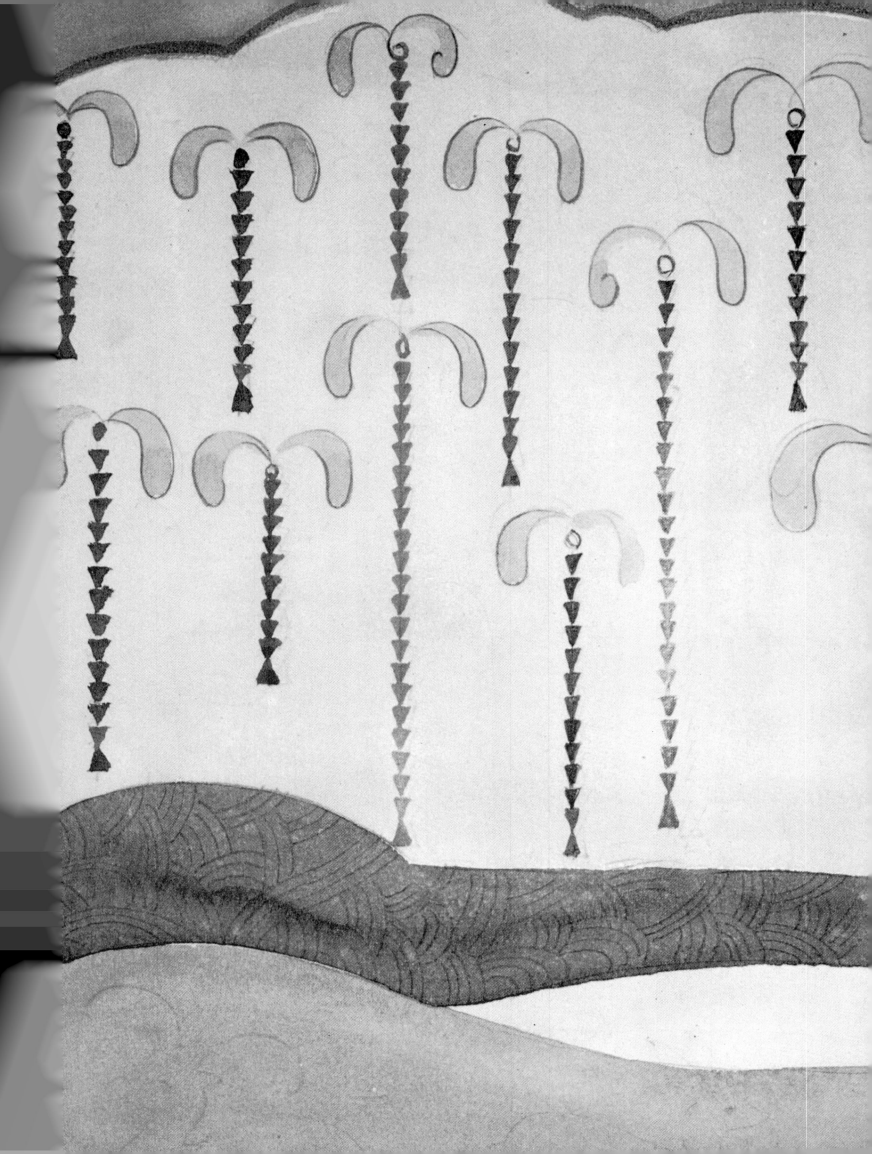

LE PORCHER

BALLET INSPIRED BY A *HANS CHRISTIAN ANDERSEN* FAIRY TALE. MUSIC BASED
ON OLD SWEDISH MELODIES, ORCHESTRATED BY *PIERRE-OCTAVE FERROUD*. SETS
AND COSTUMES BY *ALEKSEEV*. CHOREOGRAPHY AND STAGING BY *JEAN BÖRLIN*.

THE EMPEROR *TURE ANDERSSON* / THE PRINCESS *GRETA LUNDBERG* / THE PRINCE *JEAN BÖRLIN* / LADIES IN WAITING *MLLES CALSON, FORSLIN, SELID, PETTERSON* / THE CHAMBERLAIN *M. GILLER*. PREMIÈRE 19 NOVEMBER 1924.

'On the prince's father's grave there grew a rose tree, oh, such a lovely rose tree! It only flowered once every five years. And the prince also had a nightingale, which sang as if all the fairest tunes in the world were stored in its breast. This rose and this nightingale were for the princess.

'When the princess saw the big boxes with the presents in them, she clapped her hands with joy. "For shame, father, it's not artificial, it's a real rose!" "For shame", said all the ladies in waiting, "it's a real rose!" And then they saw the nightingale. It sang so sweetly that no one said anything at first. "All the same, I can't believe it's real", said the princess. "Yes, it's a real bird", said those who had brought it. "Well, let it fly away then", said the princess, and she refused point-blank to receive the prince.

'But he was not to be put off. He smeared his face black and brown, pulled his hood down low, and came and knocked at the door. And so the prince was appointed imperial swineherd. He spent all day working, and by evening he had made a pretty little cooking pot surrounded with little bells. As soon as the pot boiled, the bells rang, sweetly playing an old tune. The princess came walking by with all her ladies in waiting, and when she heard the tune, she stopped. "What do you want in exchange for that cooking pot?" asked the lady in waiting. "I want ten kisses from the princess", replied the swineherd. "How tiresome", said the princess. "You had better stand in front of me, so that no one sees". The ladies in waiting placed themselves in front of her, holding out their skirts, and the swineherd got his ten kisses, and the princess got the cooking pot.

'He made a rattle which, when it was shaken, rattled out all the polkas and waltzes that had ever been invented since the beginning of time. "It's wonderful", said the princess when she passed by. "I've never heard a nicer piece of music! Listen! Go and ask him what the instrument costs. But no kisses!" "He wants a hundred kisses from the princess", said the lady in waiting who had gone to ask. "Make a circle round me", she said. All the ladies in waiting made a circle around her, and she began to kiss him.

'"What's that cluster of people over there, on the pig track?" asked the emperor, who had stepped out on to his terrace. "What's this?" he asked, when he saw the two kissing , and he hit them over the head with his slipper, just as the swineherd was receiving his eighty-sixth kiss. "Out of here!" commanded the emperor.

'"Oh, how unhappy I am", said the princess. "Why didn't I accept the charming prince? I am so unhappy!" "I have come here to shame you", he said. "You scorned a loyal prince. You didn't appreciate the rose and the nightingale, but you gave your kisses to a swineherd for a musical toy. You can find your own amusement now."'

——— HANS CHRISTIAN ANDERSEN, *THE SWINEHERD* ———

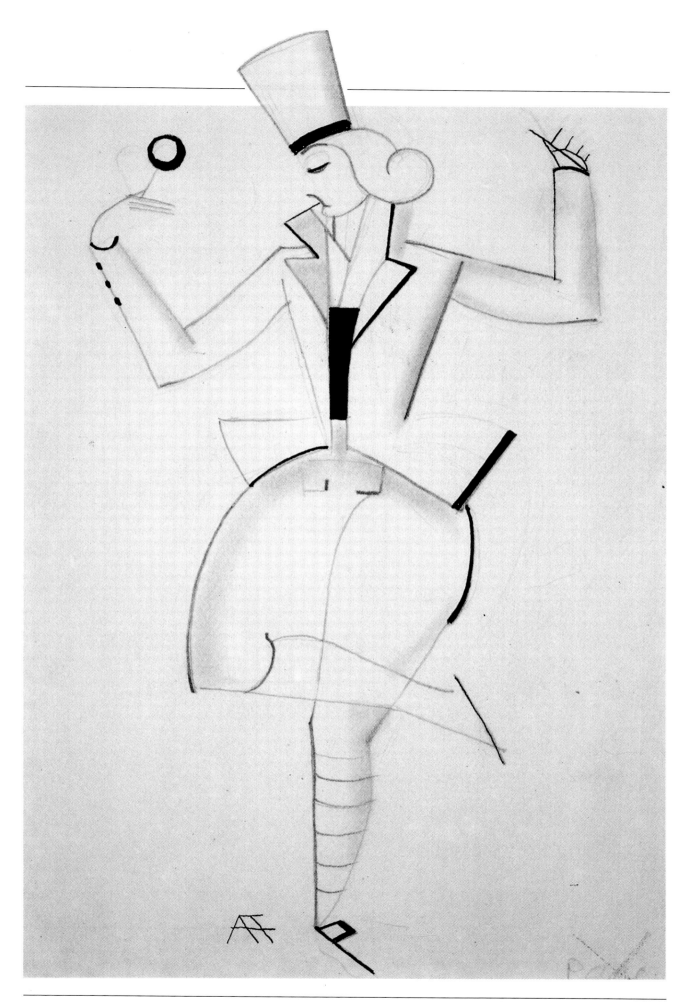

La folie

LE TOURNOI
SINGULIER

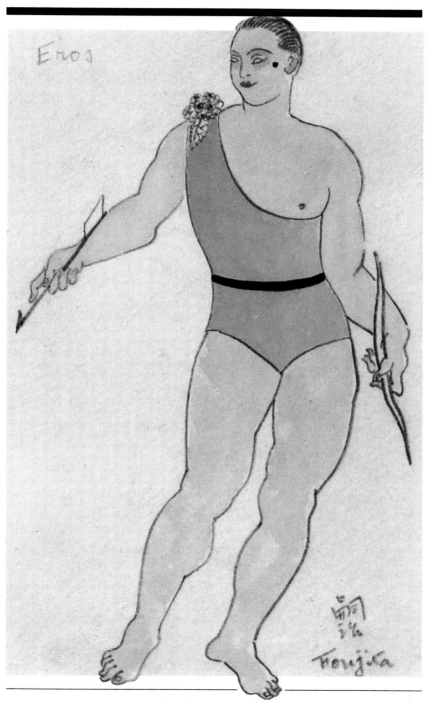

BALLET BASED ON A WORK BY *LOUISE LABÉ*. MUSIC BY *ROLAND-MANUEL*.

SETS AND COSTUMES BY *FOUJITA*. CHOREOGRAPHY BY *JEAN BÖRLIN*.

Eros *Jean Börlin* / Folly *Irma Calson* / Two Caddies *Signe Selid, Siva Blomkvist* / Venus *Edith Bonsdorff* / Iris *Valborg Larson* / Zephyrus *John Carlberg* / Soprano *Marthe Brega.* Première 19 November 1924.

'Roland-Manuel has staged the famous allegory of *Love and Folly*. Folly, playing, or arguing, with Love, blinds the young god, whereupon she is condemned by Olympus to serve him henceforth as a guide. Roland-Manuel gives us his own version of the legend. . . . The little drama is set on a golf course by the sea. Eros himself is a bather in a swimsuit. Caddies, walking in front of Folly, carry Anglo-Saxon golf clubs, and it is while playing a game of golf that Folly wounds Love. The appearance of Venus, flanked by Zephyrus and Iris, and the judgment scene (the judgment being pronounced here by the goddess) take us back, however, to a more "ancient" mythology. Once the sentence has been passed, Love is given back his bow and arrows and the charming blind boy begins shooting at random – a pastime he will indulge in for eternity. . . .

'The brief introduction is a slow Fauré-esque lullaby, which creates an atmosphere of charm, nobility and refinement. Five pages later, Folly dances to a *tempo di blues*, with a very precise rhythm, interwoven moreover with clever harmonies. . . . The author has supplemented the orchestra with a human voice (a soprano), "singing without words", like another instrument, and performing wonders in certain passages: thus, Venus's lament or that beautiful last page echoing the theme of the introduction, with its melancholy, softly twilit poetry.'

———— Maurice Brillant, in *Le Correspondant*, 25.12.1924 ————

'It seems that dance has arrived at an important turning point in its history. It is undergoing the effects of that irresistible movement prompting all the arts – which had merged for a moment in the romantic mêlée – to seize their respective independence once more, and to return each to its rightful place. One need only observe the fluctuations in the choreographic aesthetic to be convinced of this fact. The ballets we have now been applauding for fifteen years almost all belong to the heretical tradition of artistic fusion. Dazzled by so many juxtaposed riches, we have ignored the danger. But by dint of welcoming so many strangers into its house, dance is now under threat of being evicted by those same painters, men of letters and musicians, guests whose insolence matches their ingratitude.

'Jean Börlin said to me one day that the dancer must cease to be the sandwich-man condemned to carry the great painters' advertisement boards. Even less should he continue a trembling slave to the musicians. So let us rid ourselves of the erroneous view that dance is symphony interpreted in terms of movement. Let us imitate the modesty and the forbearance of the choreographers. The moment has come to repay so much courtesy. Servants of the caprice that soars in rhythmic flight, to use the words of Stéphane Mallarmé, why should we blush at such a noble servitude? Let us offer to Terpsichore the carpet she requests and which she so clearly requires. May it receive the imprint of the lightest feet in the world and may it congratulate itself, in emulation of a rather over-quoted line, at being trodden underfoot by an empress.'

———— Roland-Manuel ————

'*Le Tournoi singulier* is the old legend of Love and Folly, as seen through the eyes of Roland-Manuel. Here, it is during a game of golf, by the sea, that Folly, dressed for the event by the Japanese painter Foujita, blinds Eros in a soft-pink swimsuit. . . . It is not difficult to imagine just what possibilities such a mélange offered the musician!

Thanks to this compromise between mythology and sport, he was able to blend the most tender strains of his sensitive, thoroughly refined, thoroughly subtle muse with the droll and unexpected rhythms coming straight across the Ocean. This short ballet thus presents us with, side by side, a "Folly ragtime" and the complaints and lamentations of Venus.

'I confess, however, to regretting the brevity of Roland-Manuel's divertissement. I expected a less sketchy work from him, and a little more breadth of detail. The quality of these pages, displaying an orchestration that is unusual, but also simple, throughout, will amaze none of those who were so enchanted by *Isabelle et Pantalon* at the Trianon or the *Tempo di Ballo* at the Concerts Koussevitzky. For my part, I could happily have heard double its length. The importance of this *Tournoi singulier* would have been substantially increased thereby. Let us have greater generosity from Roland-Manuel next time: this is what I have no hesitation in asking of him! . . .'

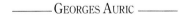

——— Georges Auric ———

Zephir

Foujita

paysanne

LA JARRE

Ballet Based on a Libretto by *Luigi Pirandello*. Music by *Alfredo Casella*. Sets and Costumes by *Giorgio de Chirico*. Choreography and Staging by *Jean Börlin*.

THE MASTER ... / HIS DAUGHTER *INGER FRIIS* / THE HUNCHBACK *ERIC VIBER* / A YOUNG LAD *JEAN BÖRLIN* / THE 'CHIOVU' DANCED BY *SIGNE SELID, JEAN BÖRLIN* AND THE CORPS DE BALLET. STORY OF THE YOUNG GIRL ABDUCTED BY PIRATES SUNG BY *MAX MOUTIA*. PREMIÈRE 19 NOVEMBER 1924.

'A flat area in front of a large house (farm). In the background, the house surrounded by trees, etc. The end of the day. The peasants employed by Don Lollo', a wealthy and not very likable farmer, come bursting in on their return from work and dance to a popular Sicilian tune. General merriment.

'Enter three young girls, looking frightened, apparently with the announcement of some bad news. Solemnly, several men arrive bearing an enormous oil jar, cracked down the front. The peasants are afraid. A few of them decide to call Don Lollo', who appears, furious. His daughter arrives in her turn and succeeds in calming him down. The old repairs man is sent for.

'After examining it closely, he agrees to mend the jar. He makes a hole in the pieces with the help of a brace, a woe-begone expression on his face. Afterwards, he gets inside the jar and the young peasant girls fit the broken piece in place. Then Zi' Dima tries to get out through the neck of the jar, but is prevented from doing so by his hump. The peasants gather round. General hilarity. Reappearance of Don Lollo'. Heated discussion between him and the peasants, who advise him to break the jar again in order to free Zi' Dima. Don Lollo', furious, grabs hold of the jar and shakes it violently. Jeering from the peasants. Don Lollo' goes away, angrier than ever.

'Zi' Dima hands his pipe out of the jar, and a peasant fills it for him, lights it and hands it back. The peasants leave. Night falls. Total darkness. Moonlight. Puffs of smoke waft from the jar. Nela comes out of the house and dances round the jar. The old man reaches out his arm and makes a sign to her. In among the olive trees, over the tops of the walls, appear the heads of the peasants, come to take a look at what is happening to the extraordinary jar. Nela gathers the men and women together. Someone fetches something to drink. They begin a headlong dance around the jar, in which the old man is singing at the top of his voice.

'Don Lollo', woken by the racket, appears on the balcony and comes down on stage, furious. He gives the jar an almighty kick and sends it rolling off-stage. The peasants, horrified, rush to Zi' Dima's aid and triumphantly bring him back on stage, to the sound of glorious music. Finale dance. Don Lollo', exasperated, takes refuge in his house.'

———— LUIGI PIRANDELLO, IN *LA DANSE*, NOVEMBER–DECEMBER 1924 ————

'These dazzling décors by de Chirico, these scarlet walls, this shimmering crowd, plunge us suddenly in the fairy-tale atmosphere of Girgenti. Round an innocent but witty piece of clowning by Pirandello, who had previously given us theatre of a different complexity, Alfredo Casella has woven a brisk and joyful piece of music, treated with a virtuosity which does not scorn (beneath a highly contemporary exterior, moreover) the paternal camaraderie of a barber.'

———— FLORENT SCHMITT ————

'In his search for a style, M. Casella had successively and a little too obviously borrowed from the masters of the hour certain of their more superficial working methods, and that, we believe, at the expense of the character, expression and intimate feeling of his art. Mahler, Debussy, Schönberg and Stravinsky.... We were baffled by so many successive influences, as well as amazed by the virtuosity of the man who thus brought them into play. And that is why it was such a pleasure for me to listen to *La Jarre*. Here, the Italian Casella speaks his own language at last, expressing himself in phrases, an accent and inflexions which are his homeland's and which will be every bit his own, if he can only succeed now in cultivating and developing them in the manner they require.'

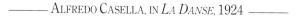 GEORGES AURIC

'The music of *La Giara* was composed in obedience to the fundamental idea of uniting in a single modern synthesis the style of Italian musical comedy (the Neapolitan school, Rossini, *Falstaff*, etc.) with elements derived from Italian, and more particularly Sicilian, folklore. The composer has thus sought to "fashion" his melody and his rhythm on the basis of this Southern music, which displays powerful traces of Hellenism and is, in more than one respect, reminiscent of Arabic and Iberian music. "Rustic comedy" would have been the most apt description for this theatrical work, which was suggested by one of Luigi Pirandello's most colourful and picaresque narratives. Let us note, too, that this ballet is the first to bring together the names of a poet, a musician and a painter all three of whom are Italian.'

ALFREDO CASELLA, IN *LA DANSE*, 1924

la fille du
patron

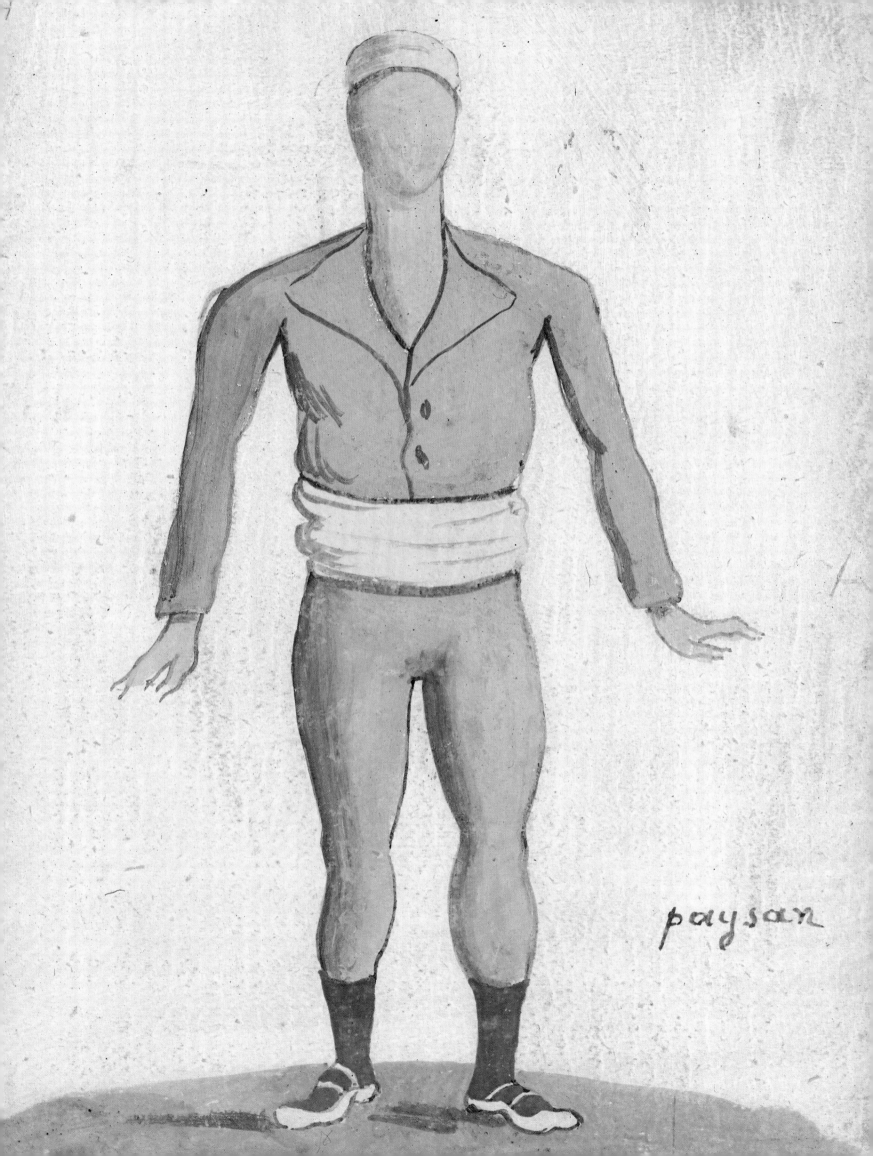

paysan

paysanne

paysan

paysanne

paysanne

g. de Chirico
se ipsum delineavit

Mes idées sur les bal-lets? Je trouve que lorsqu'ils se-ront délivrés com-plètement d'un certain esthétisme qui les cor-rompt encore et qu'ils se seront enrichis d'éléments nouveaux, ils pourront, avec le cinéma, rempla-cer le théâtre de prose et d'opéra qui dispa-raît lentement. Mais ce ne sont pas là choses à écrire sur un pro-gramme.

Chirico

... J'ai demandé
à Pirandello d'é=
crire un sujet de bal=
let pour nous, non point
seulement parce que
Pirandello est le grand
auteur du jour, mais
aussi parce que nul
mieux que lui ne
pouvait dépein=
dre l'atmosphè=
re pittoresque
de cette Sicile
pleine de Soleil
dont les dan=
ses paysannes
m'avaient tou=
jours séduit...   ROLF DE MARÉ

RELÂCHE

Instantaneous Ballet in Two Acts with a Cinematographic
Entr'acte, and the 'Dog's Tail', by *Francis Picabia*. Music by
Erik Satie. Scenery by *Francis Picabia*. Cinematographic
Entr'acte by *René Clair*. Choreography by *Jean Börlin*.

A Woman *Edith Bonsdorff* / A Man *Jean Börlin* / The Other Man *Kaj Smith* / Orchestra of the Association des Concerts Pasdeloup, Conducted by *Roger Désormière*. Première Scheduled for 27 November 1924, Postponed to 4 December 1924 Due to Indisposition on the Part of Jean Börlin.

The original title, typewritten like the rest of the text, was *Après dîner*. It was deleted by Picabia and the following note appended: 'by Erik Satie, Jean Börlin and Picabia'.

'Flat, white screen. Film projection to be decided, lasting around thirty seconds and accompanied by music. The curtain rises on a domed stage shaped like an egg and entirely lined with big white balloons. White carpet. At the back, a revolving door. The music continues for a further thirty seconds after the curtain rises. A woman in full evening dress gets up from the stalls and steps on to the stage. Music: thirty-five seconds. The moment she appears on stage, the music ends. The woman comes to a halt in the middle of the stage and looks around at the décor, then remains standing perfectly still. At which point, the music starts up again for approximately another minute. When it finishes, the woman begins to dance. (Choreography to be arranged.) The music starts up again for a further minute and a half. The woman walks to the back of the stage and passes through the revolving door three times, ending up facing the auditorium.

'Meanwhile, thirty men in evening dress, with white cravats, white gloves and opera hats, leave their seats in the auditorium one after the other and step up on to the stage in single file. Duration of music: one and a half minutes. The music stops the moment they start to perform a dance (to be arranged) around the woman, now in her former position centre stage. They circle round her while she undresses to reveal clinging, pink silk tights. Music for forty seconds. The men draw back and line up against the décor; the woman remains motionless for a few seconds, while the music starts up again (thirty-five seconds). A few balloons burst at the back of the stage. General dance. The woman is lifted up to the flies. *Curtain*.

'No entr'acte properly speaking. Five minutes of music. A film of the authors sitting talking face to face will be projected and the text of their conversation will appear on the screen for ten minutes. No music during the written projection.

'*Second act*. The curtain rises. One minute's music. Against a black backdrop is an arrangement of signs which light up intermittently, with the names of Erik Satie, Francis Picabia and Blaise Cendrars alternating in large coloured letters. Three or four very powerful projectors are directed from the stage into the auditorium. They illuminate the audience and produce black and white effects through the medium of pierced discs. The men return one by one and arrange themselves in a circle round the woman's clothes. Twenty seconds of music. The woman comes down from the flies, still in her all-over tights and wearing a crown of orange blossom on her head. She gets dressed again while the men undress in their turn, to reveal white silk tights. Twenty seconds of music. Dance to be arranged.

'One by one the men return to their places, where they pick up their overcoats. Thirty seconds of music. The woman, left on her own, takes hold of a wheelbarrow, piles the men's clothes in it and goes and tips them in a heap in the corner. Then, coming as close as she can to the forestage, she removes her bridal crown and throws it to one of the dancers, who will go and place it on the head of a specified woman in the audience. Music: fifteen seconds. The woman herself returns to her seat. The white screen comes down, and in front of it another little woman appears, dancing and singing a song. Music: forty-five seconds.'

———— Preliminary Plan by Francis Picabia ————

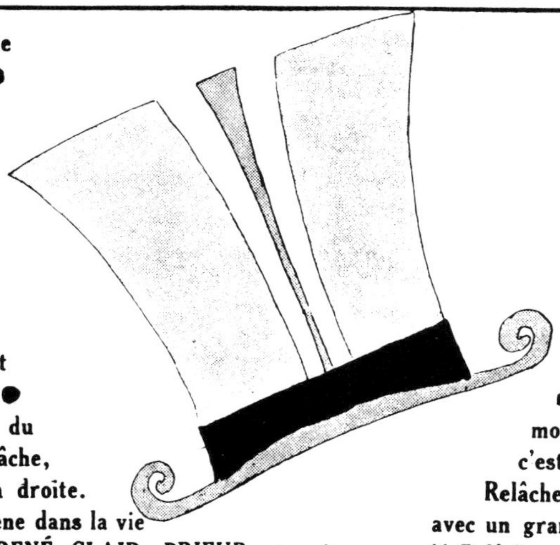

Relâche, rose de feuille — feuille de
guêpe, cul de lampe, etc..... ● ●
Relâche est un passage à niveau, un
table — ou l'amant-chaise ! Et puis
l'aime ; la vie sans lendemain, la vie
rien pour hier, rien pour demain.
Les phares d'automobiles, les colliers
des femmes, la publicité, la musique,
habit noir, le mouvement, le bruit,
plaisir de rire, voilà Relâche.
Relâche a été fait comme l'on abat
maquillé les cartes. ● ●
Relâche a les plus belles jambes du
jarretières noires et blanches. Relâche,
ni en arrière, ni à gauche ni à droite.
pas tout droit ; Relâche se promène dans la vie

rose ; guêpe de taille — taille de
● ● ● ● ●
passage à nivache ; Relâche est lamen-
Relâche est la vie, la vie comme je
d'aujourd'hui, tout pour aujourd'hui,
● ● ● ● ●
de perles, les formes rondes et fines
l'automobile, quelques hommes en
le jeu, l'eau transparente et claire, le
● ● ● ● ●
neuf dix-sept fois de suite sans avoir
● ● ● ●
monde, ses bas sont champagne, ses
c'est le mouvement sans but, ni en avant
Relâche ne tourne pas et pourtant ne va
avec un grand éclat de rire ; ERIK SATIE,

BORLIN, ROLF DE MARÉ, RENÉ CLAIR, PRIEUR et moi avons créé Relâche un peu comme Dieu créa la vie.
Il n'y a pas de décors, il n'y a pas de costumes, il n'y a pas de nu, il n'y a qu'espace, l'espace que notre
imagination aime à parcourir ; Relâche est le bonheur des instants sans réflexion ; pourquoi réfléchir,
pourquoi avoir une convention de beauté ou de joie ? ● ● ● ● ●
Il faut risquer les indigestions si l'on a envie de manger ! ● ● ● ●
Pourquoi ne pas se ruiner ? Pourquoi ne pas travailler quarante-huit heures de suite
si c'est notre plaisir ? Pourquoi ne pas avoir quinze femmes et pourquoi une
femme n'aurait-elle pas cinquante-deux hommes si cela peut lui plaire ?
Relâche vous conseille d'être des viveurs, car la vie sera toujours
plus longue à l'école du plaisir qu'à l'école de la morale, à
l'école de l'art, à l'école religieuse, à l'école
des conventions mondaines.

**FRANCIS
PICA-
BIA.**

La musique de "Relâche" ? J'y dépeins des personnages
"en vadrouille". Pour cela, je me suis servi de thèmes populaires.
Ces thèmes sont fortement "évocateurs"... Oui ! très "évocateurs". "Spéciaux", même.
....
Les "timorés" — & autres "moralistes" — me reprocheront l'emploi de
ces thèmes. Je n'ai pas à m'occuper de l'opinion de telles gens....
.... Les "têtes de veau" réactionnaires lanceront leurs fulminations.
Veuh !... Je ne tolère qu'un juge : le public. Il reconnaîtra ces thèmes,
& ne sera nullement choqué de les entendre .... N'est-il pas "humain" ?...
.... Je ne voudrais pas faire rougir un homard, ni un œuf.
Que ceux, qui auraient la crainte de ces "évocations", se retirent :....
J'aurais honte de troubler les eaux tranquilles & suaves de leur sereine
candeur ...Je suis trop aimable, pour désirer leur déplaire.

EriK SATiE

'On the theatre's advertisement boards, a huge *Relâche* [Cancelled] notice was clearly displayed. It referred to the ballet of which it was also the title. So, the public, thoroughly confused, obstinately tried to force the doors, which remained no less obstinately shut. Finally, a man dressed in black (was this [the fictional villain] Fantômas?) came and announced in a lifeless voice that the performance really had been "cancelled" and that the première of *Relâche* had been postponed to a later date. Everybody was convinced that this was another practical joke on the part of that prankster Picabia. . . .

'However, on 4 December, the curtain rose, to reveal a truly astonishing sight. The décor consisted of an immense panel, almost triangular in shape, on which were fixed a hundred or so powerful reflectors, which shone their blinding light into the spectators' eyes. After a few minutes, as our eyes adjusted to the light, we could make out dancers in white tights and tall hats. Then came the ballerinas [*sic*] (Swedish women really are beautiful!). . . . A ballet defies description. I will just say, though, that at the end Erik Satie and Francis Picabia did a tour of the stage in a tiny motorcar (a Citroën, if I remember correctly), yelled at by a large section of the audience and rowdily applauded by the rest.'

———— Maurice Sachs, *La Décade de l'Illusion*, Paris, 1950 ————

'My first is a pretty woman wearing a dress and coat from Jacques Doucet's. My second is a handsome lad, as dazzling as a diamond. My third is a fireman wearing the order of the Legion of Honour, present in case of fire. My fourth is a camel. My fifth, these are the men in evening dress. My sixth is the dog's tail. My all is a success. What is that?'

———— Francis Picabia, Programme for *Relâche* ————

'Now, what can I tell you about *Relâche* itself? It is perpetual movement, life, the quest for happiness; it is light, riches, luxury, love, removed from prudery and convention; without a moral for the fools, without studied artistic effects for the snobs. *Relâche* is also alcohol and opium, as much as it is sport, strength and health; it is baccarat and maths. *Relâche* is the optimism of happy people. You will see in it a very lovely woman, a handsome man, many handsome men, in fact; dazzling lights; the whole thing evolving in as rapid and agreeable a movement as that procured by a 300 HP engine on the best road, lined with trees slanting in the illusion created by speed. . . .

'*Relâche* is black and white, night and day, day and night. *Relâche*, I hope, will set off in life like a beautiful woman who dares to display the prettiest pair of legs in the loveliest silk stockings, while walking on the arm of the most perfect athlete! And yet, I already hear "intelligent" folk, the folk who know, the Protestant ministers, saying: "But it's not a ballet, is it?" or "It's only a Swedish ballet!" And again: "It's not music." And again: "Francis Picabia is poking fun at the world, poking fun at us!" And again: "It's not a patch on our good Opéra ballets!" And yet again: "It's easy to make music like that; and the painter hasn't gone to much trouble over the sets." Total success, at last! But there is one thing that some people will feel, perhaps: that is, a sensation of *newness*, of pleasure, the sensation of forgetting that one has to "think" and "know" in order to like something. . . .'

———— Francis Picabia, in *Les Ballets Suédois*, Paris, 1932 ————

'A rupture, a break, with traditional ballet. Light as mistress of the world and of the stage. Surprise effects. Rhythms of men in black, men in white – the handsome fireman – the lovely dancer. An amusing, whimsical, burlesque screen. To the Devil, scenarios and all literature! *Relâche* is a lot of kicks up a lot of backsides, hallowed or otherwise. It is a homogeneous and precise piece of theatre. The watertight division between ballet and music hall has burst. Actor, dancer, acrobat, screen, stage, all these different means for creating a spectacle come together and rearrange themselves. The sole aim: to bring a scene to life. All the prejudices come tumbling down.

'In all of that, through all of that, a music which is no longer music, which is all new music; something imponderable, clear-cut, not situated, precisely situated, we no longer know. It does not come from the orchestra; it is above the orchestra, on the stage – in the auditorium – beneath the auditorium – in the dancers' legs, in the electric lights, behind the projectors. It is the music of the youngest French musician. A luminous, electric, cinematographic music. Very new, entirely new, possessing an incredible lightness and confident design. And perfectly arranged, without appearing to be. A homogeneous spectacle, an infinitely elastic block.

'J. Börlin moving nicely in this highly contemporary mirage, moving with ease, dazzling, brilliant, participating in the action, without acting the star, without "stealing the show". He is the first dancer to have understood the value of personal sacrifice for the sake of collective qualities. He appears, disappears, in white, in black, metallic, dazzling, discreet, and fades into the background, to make way for other, equal, talent. Mme Bonsdorff: as supple as a cascade under the spotlights, cruel, real, life in all its graceful movement; the light bath that blinds, that intoxicates, the eyes; the glitter, hard and fluid, of a princess's dress behind a white wooden wheelbarrow.

'The electrician in blue overalls: modern god, emperor, king, master of us all; tucked away in his compartment, lean, cold, lucid, framed by perspectives of gleaming levers and little red, blue and green indicators. A skilful orchestration. A prodigious conductor, who creates day and night, cold and heat, on his metallic keyboard. Everyone is afraid of him, dependent on him. In front of the chronometer, a second, a quarter of a second, a tenth of a second. He is going to play out the whole of this charming fantasy, which appears not to have been arranged at all, which appears that way . . . for everything is arranged, deliberate – the mechanisms of gesture, movement and lighting.

'For several months Picabia was arranging the tempo, the fractions, the tenths of a fraction – a whole world in miniature where everything functions with discipline, precision, rigidity, mechanically – and still it does not appear that way. . . . The luminous design which scoots over a black velvet backdrop, the mobile image framed in the square of cloth with all the enormous fantasies it permits – the prodigious new means to limitless consequences – and which we are only just beginning to glimpse. The cinema is going to develop, just pay attention – open your eyes – from slow to ultra-fast motion, from the close-up to the infinite. All human fantasy harnessed in books and theatre will be let loose. The scenario flies off, useless now. The star dancer wishes us good luck and disappears. And then the real fun begins, then we begin to use our eyes for the things that really count. Believe me, go to the oculist, have your eyes, your spectacles, remade. Cinema is about to begin . . . it is beginning . . . watch out, here it is now!

'The scene shifters, [Henri] Prieur, all those lovely people involved in carting things about, jokers, who could not care less about anything – in their proper place – who, at the precise moment, stick at the job, and how! – the artisans of the theatre. Everyone in his proper place for *Relâche*, without appearing to be. . . . Rolf de Maré: everywhere and nowhere. Bound to his stage, always ahead, always upright, tireless in his quest for newness. Follow him. Go from *Les Mariés de la tour Eiffel* to *Relâche*.

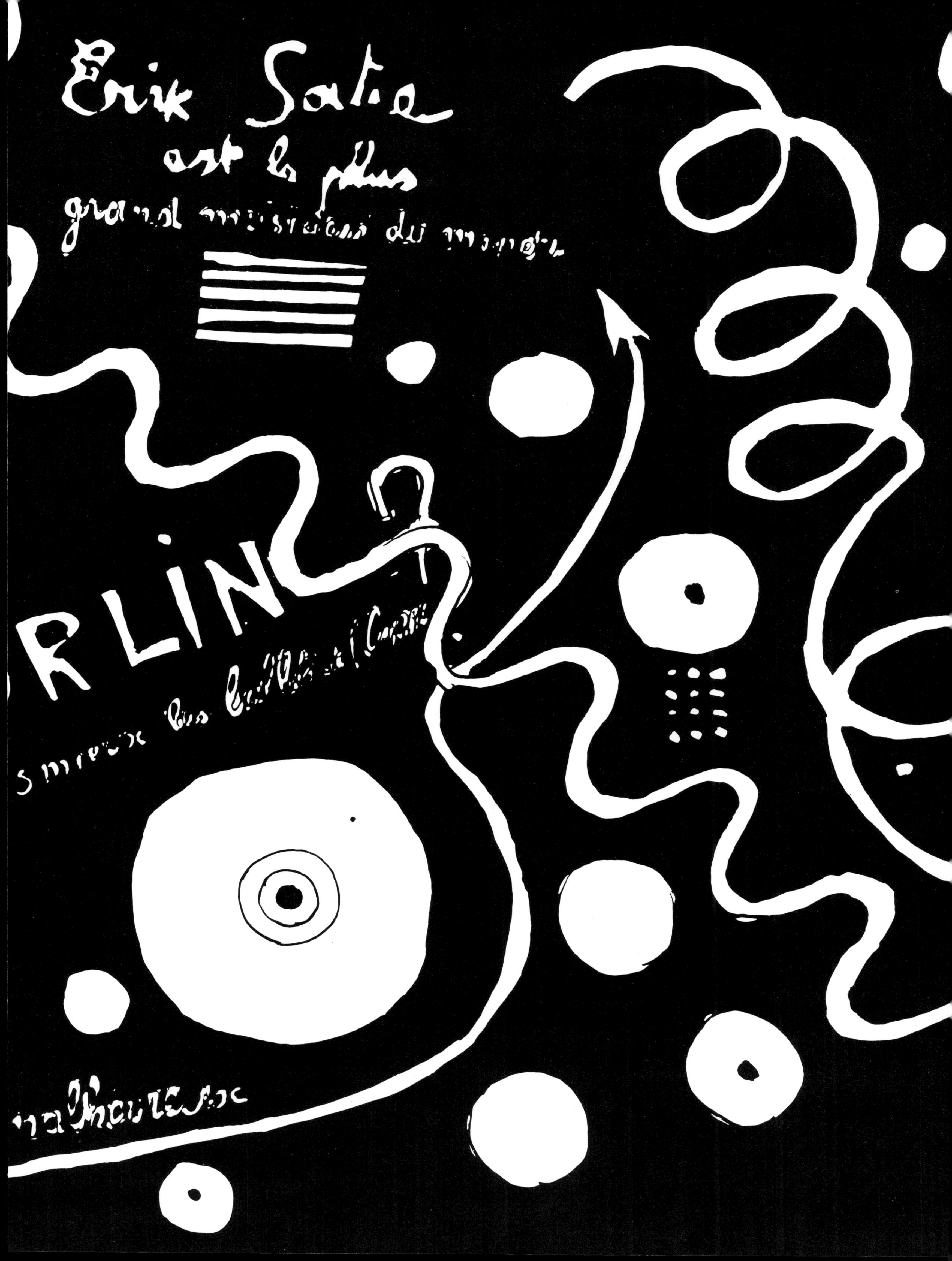
Erik Satie
est le plus
RLIN

The path is uphill all the way. He does not know how to go downhill. And if he needs to sit down, it is never in a Louis XV chair! He is global in his efforts, persevering, tireless. He is a winner. Bravo *Relâche* – Satie – Picabia – Clair – the electrician – the scene shifter – the lovely audience, young already, or else rejuvenated – the beautiful auditorium – de Maré – Börlin – de Maré. I take my hat off to you.'

——— Fernand Léger ———

'Postscript: by wandering off in search of food, you lose your place at table. The ballet that I had sent Satie from La Pallice was staged by Rolf de Maré's "Ballets Suédois" at Paris's Théâtre des Champs-Élysées, under the title *Relâche*. My name did not appear on the bill. Taking advantage of my trip to Brazil, Francis Picabia (whom I had been considering for the sets, and who had received the libretto from Satie) had pinched the idea for my ballet and arranged it in his own way, and his name alone figured on the bill. Satie was a friend of mine, so was Rolf de Maré: I did not intend to start legal proceedings against them. But on my return from Brazil, I tried, unsuccessfully, to have it out with Picabia. He was my neighbour in the country, but he had the good sense to clear off.

'It was from the lips of that great coward that we first heard the pronouncement, which several others have since repeated, "Cendrars is exaggerating! He knows perfectly well that, since he's only got one arm, no one's going to challenge him to a duel." . . . Of course, of course, but I could have booted his backside with my two feet. . . . I have not done so because the dear gentleman has always scarpered . . . and then I was so pleased to see cinema participating in an artistic theatrical production, if only in the entr'acte . . . something I was also the first to think of.

'And so, René Clair has made his début as a producer, unaware to this day that he owes this lucky break to me. I make no claims. It has been a wonderful success and I am really happy for him, for myself, for Satie, for everyone.'

——— Blaise Cendrars ———

'Such a work, which plumbs the depths of aesthetic paltriness, carries within it an incomparable lesson. A heresy which boasts many converts illustrates its downfall here. Let us thank it for proclaiming its own bankruptcy, for committing suicide so cleanly, and for dying gracelessly, no doubt in order to discourage the last of its proselytes from martyrdom. The vague musical religion whose birth and death we will have witnessed bore no name before offering its allegiance to M. Picabia's "instantaneity". Its fundamental dogma was the dogma of non-resistance to evil, transferred on to the aesthetic plane. Its clearest aim: the pursuit of originality, with the collaboration of chance. Cult of liberty, disdaining all the refinements of the craft, though not a certain scholastic rigidity; affectation, finally, of a preposterous simplicity. Thanks to a misunderstanding, this bizarre romanticism enjoyed some success at first in the circles least fitted to appreciate it.' (A few years later, in the margin of this article, Roland-Manuel wrote: 'Unjust! A momentary whim. With regard to Picabia, I concede it all. But not where Satie is concerned.')

——— Roland-Manuel, *Adieu à Satie*, Paris, 1924 ———

'The music for *Relâche*? I was portraying people "out on a spree". Using popular themes for the purpose. These themes are powerfully "evocative". . . . Yes, very "evocative". "Special", even. "Faint-hearts" – and other "moralists" – will reproach me for making use of these themes. Why should I bother with such people's opinions? . . . The reactionary "sourpusses" will rant and rail. Pooh! . . . There is only one judge I defer to: the public. It will recognize these themes and will not be in the least shocked to hear them.... Aren't they "human", after all? ... I have no wish to make a lobster blush, or an egg, for that matter. Let anyone who dreads such "evocations" retire. ... I would be ashamed to disturb the smooth and tranquil waters of their serene innocence.... I am too nice to want to displease them.'

——— Erik Satie, Ballets Suédois Programme ———

'Gentlemen, critics, I am inclined to think that what you baptize as new is the new of three years ago, to which you are just beginning to grow accustomed! Moreover, it has to be signed by names which have the same dimensions as your own: Messager, Levinson, Roland-Manuel, Félix Potin, Auric, Vuillermoz, Georges Pioch, Dufayel! And many more, too many! Although *Relâche* is "empty", "idiotic" and "futile", everyone has written columns and columns about it: what a waste of everyone's time, above all the readers'!

'*Relâche* was not created for you, but for a handful of very dear friends, and for the public at large, the majority of whose members have become our friends. You see, whatever you may do – or rather as a result of what you do – criticism is daily losing ground, and you will not be the ones to prevent Rolf de Maré from soon being the only person in Paris who – free of all idiotic constraints – succeeds in putting on the sole productions with any real value or originality, any more than you will prevent the public from enjoying the performance of a work, simply because you have proclaimed it tiresome!

'It is an easy thing, gentlemen, when talking about Erik Satie, to predict his past! I, on the other hand, am going to predict the future for you, just like Freya. I do not see this future being as brilliant as the author of *Parade*'s! Give me your hand, Monsieur Messager. You are an artist whose train has left ... but you have broken down! There is nothing for it but to get moving again: the Morgue is not far. Monsieur Roland-Manuel, you are in real danger of making the same trip, but on foot, and in *such* boots! ... Auric, you are too like Beethoven at his deaf and blind stage. I have trouble, as a result, following the lines in your hand. Monsieur Aymard, Monsieur Aymard, do not speak so airily of artificial paradises. ... Levinson, you will go down with a serious illness that will kill you off next year. Before you get too thin, sell yourself off by weight! Since you refuse to pay more than a few pence for your consultation, Vuillermoz, I refuse to tell you a thing!

'And the others? They declined to open their hands; out of fear, I think. I shall not make the effort to see what they have got written there. In Satie's hand, I read something that gave me a certain pleasure: he will bury the lot of them and go and visit their anonymous graves, which will simply bear the following inscription: "Here lies a critic!" I was about to write "a cretin"! My apologies.'

——— Francis Picabia, in *Les Ballets Suédois*, Paris, 1932 ———

'We know how hard Rolf de Maré had to work to get the Ballets Suédois accepted.... There was a lot of noisy whistling at the première of *Relâche*, but M. de Maré kept his cool. The next day, through his good offices, each spectator was given a little whistle "offering him the opportunity to express his opinion if he felt so inclined".'

——— Georges Schmitt ———

'*Relâche*: music takes a holiday here.... The void, a laborious void in two acts.... A foolish rhapsody in which not one harmony, not one stress, falls in its rightful place. ... It is a miserable pastiche, lacking any lustre or warmth, and in which everything is false, awkward and outdated. An orchestration of exceptional poverty adds to our embarrassment. . . . A half hour during which our depression increases to the point of nausea. The few amusing highlights which we might, with a great deal of good will, note in passing are all ones we have seen executed a thousand times better at the Paris Casino. Look round a bar door at midnight. Witness the noise, the movement, a whole mixture of violent and corrupt ingredients, fermenting in there, but with what different potency! I would quickly have dismissed this wretched *Relâche*, but for those perfect moments in which I got to know and love a charming side to Picabia (and he will never succeed in making me forget it), and for the knowledge that accompanying it is a "score" by a musician for whose extraordinary talent I have felt immense admiration: Erik Satie.'

——— Georges Auric, in *Les Nouvelles Littéraires*, 13.12.1924 ———

LES BALLETS SUÉDOIS DONNERONT
LE 27 NOVEMBRE
AU THÉATRE DES CHAMPS ÉLYSÉES
" RELÂCHE "
BALLET
INSTANTANÉISTE
EN DEUX ACTES, UN ENTR'ACTE CINÉMATOGRAPHIQUE
ET LA QUEUE DU CHIEN
PAR
FRANCIS PICABIA
MUSIQUE
D'
ERIK SATIE
CHORÉGRAPHIE DE JEAN BORLIN
Apportez des lunettes noires et de quoi vous boucher les oreilles.
RETENEZ VOS PLACES

Messieurs les ex-Dadas sont priés de venir manifester et surtout de crier : « A BAS SATIE ! A BAS PICABIA ! VIVE LA NOUVELLE REVUE FRANCAISE ! »

BORLIN

Francis Picabia

Francis Picabia

ENTR'ACTE

AUTHOR *FRANCIS PICABIA*. ADAPTED BY *RENÉ CLAIR*.

PRODUCER *RENÉ CLAIR*. DIRECTOR OF PHOTOGRAPHY *JIMMY BERLIET*.

ASSISTANT PRODUCER *GEORGES LACOMBE*. COMPLETE ORIGINAL MUSIC

ERIK SATIE. PRODUCTION *ROLF DE MARÉ*. YEAR OF PRODUCTION

1924. BLACK AND WHITE. LENGTH 22 MINUTES.

VERSION WITH SOUND-TRACK, 1968, PRODUCED BY RENÉ CLAIR IN COLLABORATION

WITH THE DANCE MUSEUM, STOCKHOLM (SHARING COPYRIGHT AND DISTRIBUTION).

Film script. A child's laugh. Chimneys leaning in all directions. The sky where the earth should be. Dolls whose heads expand and explode. A dancer so light that her feet do not touch the ground. A paper boat that floats over the rooftops and sinks. A ludicrous sportsman with a gun, trying unsuccessfully to hit an egg that is bouncing around on a jet of water. The egg escapes, divides, then remains more or less where it is. The sportsman cracks it. A pigeon flies out and alights on the delighted sportsman's head. Another sportsman arrives, tries to kill the pigeon, but kills the man instead. The sportsman's funeral takes place immediately. A crowd of grotesque dancing figures follows the hearse, which gathers speed and bolts off across the countryside. A mad chase begins, with cyclists, aeroplanes and boats joining in. Finally, the coffin falls to the ground. The sportsman steps out, transformed into a magician. With the aid of his wand, he magics away his pursuers: a bank clerk, an old lady, and a runner. Then he magics himself into thin air, too. A landscape is all that remains: the dream has faded.

'For the sake of future theatre historians, I ought to add that none of us ever knew precisely why this ballet was "instantaneous". Nor did we see the merest shadow of a dog's tail. But for Picabia, one of the great "inventors" of our time, one invention more or less was of little consequence. When I met him, he explained that he wanted to project a film between the two acts of his ballet, as was customary during *café-concert* entr'actes prior to 1914. And since I was the only one in the house who knew anything about cinema, it was my services that were enlisted. What a lucky break for someone just starting out!

'I got my team together quickly. I hired a cameraman, two young people styled assistants, who were responsible for a variety of odd jobs, and an assistant director, not the least of whose tasks was that of finding parking facilities each evening for a hearse hired from the undertakers. Few people cared to give a home for the night to a vehicle to which a camel was daily harnessed! But that was what the script demanded.

'With regard to this script, Picabia only knew what he had scribbled on a piece of *Maxim's* headed writing paper, and I was delighted when I showed him the finished film and he laughed at the additions I had made. As for Satie, the old master of the young music, he lavished meticulous care on each minute of each sequence, thus preparing the first musical composition written for the cinema "image by image" at a time when film was still silent. Conscientious in the extreme, he was afraid he might not complete the work by the appointed date. . . .

'A short filmed prologue, which I had shot at the authors' request, showed them – an unforgettable vision of Satie, with white goatee, pince-nez, bowler and umbrella – descending from the heavens in slow motion and firing a cannonball to announce the start of the show.

'The first section of the ballet was favourably received and the applause continued after the screen had been let down from the flies. Then began the projection of *Entr'acte*. With the appearance of the first images, a murmur of muffled growls interspersed with little bursts of laughter rose from the crowd and a faint tremor ran along the rows. Picabia, who had hoped to hear the audience shouting, was to have reason to feel satisfied. Yells and whistles mingled with Satie's melodious buffoonery, and the composer no doubt felt a connoisseur's appreciation of such sonorous reinforcement of his music. The bearded ballerina and the funeral camel were greeted in a fitting manner, and the Luna-Park scenic railway swept the entire auditorium, howling, along with it, maximizing the general disorder and our own personal delight. . . . Roger Désormière appeared to be simultaneously conducting the orchestra and unleashing a burlesque hurricane from his imperious baton.

'Thus was born, in the midst of noise and fury, this little film, whose conclusion was to be accompanied by as much applause as boos and whistles. Today, now that *Entr'acte* is shown in film clubs and film libraries, with the deference bestowed on antiques, it is tempting to pay homage to the people who once booed it.'

———— René Clair, in *L'Avant-Scène*, No. 86, November 1968 ————

'*Wednesday evening*. My dear friend, I am enclosing the film outline for the ballet. With all good wishes.

'*Rise of the curtain*. Satie and Picabia loading a cannon in slow motion; the explosion should be as loud as possible. Total duration: 1 minute.

'*During the entr'acte*. 1. Boxing match by white gloves on a black screen: 15 seconds' duration. Explanatory written projection: 10 seconds. 2. Game of chess between Duchamp and Man Ray. Jet of water directed over the game by Picabia: 30 seconds' duration. 3. Juggler and Father Lacolique: 30 seconds' duration. 4. Sportsman shooting at an ostrich egg balancing on Jet of water directed by Picabia. A pigeon flies out and settles on the sportsman's head; a second sportsman, aiming at the bird, kills the first sportsman: he falls to the ground; the bird flies off: 1 minute's duration. Written projection 20 seconds. 5. 21 people lying on their backs, showing us the soles of their feet. 10 seconds, manuscript projection 15 seconds. 6. Dancer on a transparent plate of glass, filmed from below: 1 minute's duration. Written projection 5 seconds. 7. Inflation of rubber balloons; props, on which various figures will be drawn, accompanied by inscriptions: 35 seconds' duration. 8. A funeral: hearse drawn by a camel, etc. 6 minutes' duration, written projection 1 minute.'

———— Francis Picabia ————

'Comic film, we might say in response to *Entr'acte*, but the inadequacy of such a definition will immediately be apparent: this is also, and not least, a lyrical film. The comic plot puts it in the same category as those wonderful films shown by Pathé in the early days of cinema – *L'Arroseur arrosé*, for example – but if the spirit remains the same, the application has been singularly improved. It is now an appeal to life by life, the negation of death by man confident in his authority and spiritually all-powerful.'

———— Robert Desnos, in *Le Journal Littéraire*, 13.12.1924 ————

'It is not possible to speak of cinema in connection with this reel of film. One can refer only to poetry. The spectator is surprised at every turn by the novelty of the images, and if the link between them sometimes eludes him, he has no time to reflect on this "anomaly", for yet another image comes to take hold of him, snatching him in passing, as it were, and swirling him along in its path in order to deposit him before a camel-drawn hearse, or at the feet of a dancer so light she almost seems a speck of dust in a ray of sunshine.'

———— Benjamin Péret, in *L'Humanité*, 3.4.1926 ————

'The audience hooted with delight, the evening I was there, and uttered the sort of cries peculiar to women when they are tickled or to those Sunday crowds one encounters on the scenic railways. We were in the grip of an absolutely new sensation: firmly ensconced in our seats and at the same time hurtling through space like an artillery shell.'

——— PIERRE SCIZE, IN *PARIS-JOURNAL*, 1924 ———

'Film and script both incomprehensible. The production grotesque. Nothing which might raise the level of our awareness, mentally or emotionally, or even succeed in achieving some degree of expressiveness.'

——— LA LIBERTÉ, 1924 ———

'Such novelties were acclaimed with rapture by the advance-guard just as they were ferociously attacked by the conservative critics. In after years it is sometimes difficult to understand the clamour excited by certain productions, so often is the sensation of to-day the commonplace of to-morrow. But the pioneers are sacrificed on the altar of progress, and Börlin suffered from being in advance of his time. His activity was so feverish there was no time to prepare the public for these iconoclastic productions.'

C.W. BEAUMONT
——— *THE COMPLETE BOOK OF BALLETS*, LONDON, 1937 ———

Francis Picabia

J'ai donné à René Clair un tout petit scénario de rien du tout; il en a fait un chef-d'œuvre : *Entr'acte*. L'entr'acte de *Relâche* est un film qui traduit nos rêves et les événements non matérialisés qui se passent dans notre cerveau; pourquoi raconter ce que tout le monde voit, ou peut voir chaque jour? :-: *Entr'acte* est un véritable entr'acte, un entr'acte à l'ennui de la vie monotone et des conventions pleines de respect hypocrite et ridicule. *Entr'acte* est une réclame en faveur du plaisir d'aujourd'hui, une réclame aussi pour l'art de la réclame, si vous voulez. Pourquoi ne mettrait-on pas ces mots sur un corbillard : "Il est mort parce qu'il ne buvait pas de quinquina Dubonnet"; ou encore : "Il ne portait pas de chaussures Raoul". Les gens superstitieux permettraient ainsi de faire fortune à bien des industries nationales.

Entr'acte ne croit pas à grand chose, au plaisir de la vie, peut être; il croit au plaisir d'inventer, il ne respecte rien si ce n'est le désir d'*éclater de rire*, car rire, penser, travailler ont une même valeur et sont indispensables l'un à l'autre.

Je suis heureux d'écrire ces lignes, de dire ici publiquement combien j'ai été ravi de la collaboration de René Clair que je considère comme un des meilleurs metteurs en scène de notre époque; grâce à lui, notre film *Entr'acte* est une merveille.

F R A N C I S   P I C A B I A.

Le cinéma n'est en ce moment qu'un "devenir". Les gens cultivés aiment peu les ciné=romans; mais est=il possible d'affir=mer que les ciné=romans soient d'une valeur artistique inférieure à tel film " pour l'élite " ? Au nom de quoi jugerez=vous, esprits délicats, le réjouissant chaos d'images qui menace le monde d'une mesure nouvelle ? Patientez. Le cinéma a compté quelques œuvres dignes de lui : *l'Arroseur arrosé* (vers 1900), *le Voyage dans la Lune* (vers 1904) et certains comiques américains. Les autres films (quelques millions de kilomètres) ont été plus ou moins gâtés par l'art obligatoire. Voici *Entr'acte* qui prétend donner une nouvelle valeur à l'image. Il appartenait à Francis Picabia, qui a tant fait pour la libération du mot, de libé=rer l'image. Dans *Entr'acte*, l'image " détournée de son devoir de signifier " naît " à une exis=tence concrète ". Rien ne me semble plus respectueux de l'avenir du film que ces bal=butiements visuels dont il a réglé l'harmonie. Ma tâche s'est bornée à réaliser techniquement les desseins de Francis Picabia. Je le remercie et je remercie Rolf de Maré de lui a la joie que ce travail fait éprouver. L'in=dignation de cer=taines per sonnes ne sera pas pour moi une récom=pense plus douce que la satisfaction qu'ils ont bien vou=lu m'exprimer. RENÉ CLAIR.

CERCLE
ÉTERNEL

BALLET BY *JEAN BÖRLIN*. MUSIC BY *ALEXANDRE TANSMAN*.

SETS AND COSTUMES BY *SERGE GLADKY*. CHOREOGRAPHY BY

JEAN BÖRLIN. PREMIÈRE 30 NOVEMBER 1929.

JEAN BÖRLIN

'Every tableau which creates an impression on me is channelled, through me, directly into dance. This is why I owe so much to both the old and the modern masters. They have helped me enormously. Not that I have ever tried to copy them by creating "tableaux vivants". But they make me think, inspire me with new ideas, new dances. I envy painters. Their works are immortal. They carry their own life within them, independently of their creators'. A dance is fairly short-lived. As short-lived as the dancer himself.'

————— Jean Börlin —————

'The choreographer, the ballet master and the dancer must be not just artists, but also artisans bound by the strictest rules. In the Ballets Suédois, that trinity is embodied in one person: Jean Börlin. The audience who applaud him have no idea that this dancer doubles up as the mathematician responsible for putting in place each of the physical elements that compose the finished ballet in all its splendour. They have even less idea that Rolf de Maré's company, by helping to defend and illustrate the new artistic tendencies (which it aims to synthesize), refuses to subordinate everything to dance and never seeks to shine on its own account alone while elbowing out the décor or neglecting the music.

'One has only to attend one of the Swedes' daily rehearsals to grasp the secret of this art which incorporates so much fantasy within such a very solid framework (Börlin being the great enemy of improvisation). Each morning, in the rehearsal room at the Champs-Élysées, Börlin, in his role as ballet master, patiently takes his company through those laborious exercises indispensable to a dancer's healthy functioning. To an unflagging piano accompaniment of Schubert, the ballet master demonstrates the movements which each member of his company, from the prima ballerina to the most minor extra, must imitate with precision. Each of them works conscientiously, joyfully. Torso and arm movements are rehearsed with particular care, since Börlin attaches especial importance to their execution.

'Then, the dancer leaves the *barre* in order to practise group figures. The academic lesson is followed by an in-depth study of the ballet, with Börlin now wearing his choreographer's hat. There is an immediate change of quality in the movements, for rehearsed movements are to ballet what words in the dictionary are to the language of poetry. This is the moment of truth regarding the theory behind the joint authority of choreographer and ballet master: the choreographer knows exactly what he can expect of the ballet master; the ballet master knows what he can expect of the dancers.

'It is excellent discipline such as this which has enabled the Ballets Suédois to express – using an astonishing range of movements – the multiple face of contemporary art and to interpret successfully the works so different in technique and tendency with which, over the last five years, poets, musicians and painters have fuelled Jean Börlin's tireless endeavours. None of the ballets resembles its predecessors; and yet each of them was scenically realized *by* Börlin, if not *for* Börlin.'

————— Roland-Manuel —————

'Alas, Jean, I will not be seeing you dance in the ballet *Outre-Atlantique*, the great ballet of the *Democratic Masses*, nor in that open-air spectacle, *Les Sports*, we so often spoke about. It was to be performed in a stadium and, to accompany it, along with motorcar horns and aeroplane engines, we had already found a magnificent orchestra we were utterly thrilled with!'

————— Blaise Cendrars —————

'My earliest memory of Jean Börlin relates to a spring morning in 1919. In the school gymnasium attached to the charming Swedish church in rue Guyot, the man who was to be the driving force behind the Ballets Suédois gave me a preview of his first recital at the Comédie des Champs-Élysées. The first dances did no more than "reassure" me: here was a professional dancer – raised since childhood in the strict school of opera – and not one of those innumerable amateurs cluttering up Paris. But when Börlin danced his *Arlequin*, whose gracefully spiralling "fall" from a slow, easy pirouette clearly marked him out as a pupil and disciple of Fokine, I could not refrain from saying as much to him . . . and my remark brought a smile of satisfaction to the young man's thoughtful face, sealing between us a collaboration which was to last almost four years. . . .

'It was not always possible to tell how much his triple role as interpreter, author and choreographer cost this young Scandinavian who had been responsible for bringing together and teaching, in a matter of months, a company capable of performing such an excellent and extraordinarily eclectic repertoire. . . . It has rarely been possible to dissociate Börlin the interpreter from Börlin the creator. It is in this dual role that he has been discussed, accepted and celebrated. . . . Indeed, from his very first productions, where other artists take only tentative steps, he created unforgettable masterpieces such as *Les Vierges folles* and *El Greco*, handling with equal skill the Toledo painter's sombre crowds and Nerman's ingenuous round dances. His hallucinatory *Maison de fous* was a masterpiece of rare imaginativeness, *Marchand d'oiseaux* a masterpiece of humour and grace. Despite the thankless task and illustrious precedent he inherited, the new choreographer of *Jeux* succeeded in moulding himself more precisely to the spirit and adhering more closely to the wishes of Debussy than even Nijinsky had done. *Jeux* revealed him as a genuine innovator in the adaptation of classical dance to the modern spirit. As Carina Ari commented, no one has the least idea what courage Börlin displayed or how few of his fellow ballet masters knew how to serve, with equal discernment, the evolution of the classical school towards *natural* grace.

'The role of the Ballets Suédois and their contribution will undoubtedly become increasingly apparent. With hindsight, it will be clearer to us how absolute their influence was. We might go so far as to say that it extended to the Ballets Russes themselves, for Serge Diaghilev's final creations showed the marked influence of *Les Mariés de la tour Eiffel, L'Homme et son désir, Skating Rink,* and *La Création du monde,* itself already foreshadowed by Börlin's *Danse nègre.*

——— D.E. INGHELBRECHT ———

'My first memories of Jean Börlin date from 1911. I was just beginning to stage ballets with Stockholm's Royal Opera company. The company was small, but very talented, and of its twenty-five or thirty members at that time, several later went on to become famous dancers, ballerinas or ballet teachers. For me, it was a real godsend, and of all the company's dancers, it was Jean Börlin who thrilled me the most. He was still a boy and had not made a name for himself yet: he was an unknown. I remember seeing him in the role of a young faun, in a rehearsal for *Cléopâtre.* He crossed the stage with great bounds, landed with all his force and glided over the boards among the group of bacchantes. What character! What ecstasy! It was the fanatical sacrifice of a body, bruised and battered in the quest for maximum choreographic expressiveness. It was a revelation....

'His short life was an ardent, single, soaring burst of creativity. He moved from one style to another, one form to another, constantly seeking the best expression for his chosen subject. This is why, for him, there was not, and could not be, a definitive form of dance, gesture, and mime: "You have to begin again each time and stage each thing in a new way." This principle demands that the ballet master create, rather than repeat. A new form is not conceived in order to submit to new requirements, but to express as perfectly as possible a new idea, a new conception.'

——— MICHEL FOKINE ———

'I said to Jean Börlin one day: "Listen, old man, you don't know how to dance." And I explained to him what I meant: "You have to understand. You're on a footing with sailors, half-castes, Negroes and savages, and that is what I admire most about you. You've planted yourself, on those Swedish peasant feet of yours, diametrically opposite the Ballets Russes, and you're jostling aside the French ballet tradition that has come down to us from St Petersburg via the *ancien régime* and Italianism. Listen to Whitman's great heartbeat now and let yourself go in the arms of motorcar and aeroplane mechanics." And I dragged him along with me to see how dancing is done in Paris. The Paris dance venues, once you have left rue de Lappe and rue de la Roquette behind you, are the great boulevards, the stations, Le Bourget airport, the Vel' d'Hiv', the Salle Wagram, and Linas-Montlhéry motor-racing track. Thanks to the notices and loudspeakers there, you forget the teachings of the Académie de Danse, sciatica and time, tempo and fashion, virtuosity and affectation. Once you have forgotten everything, you have made it, you have found rhythm, the lovely rhythm of today, on which float the five new continents: discipline, balance, health, strength and speed.'

——— BLAISE CENDRARS ———

Per Krohg - 1920

Jean Börlin

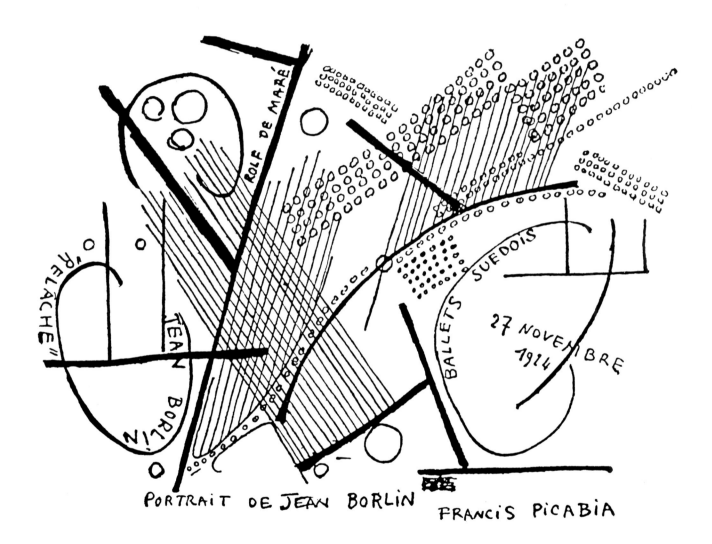

"RELÂCHE"

ROLF DE MARÉ

JEAN BORLIN

BALLETS SUÉDOIS

27 NOVEMBRE 1924

PORTRAIT DE JEAN BORLIN

FRANCIS PICABIA

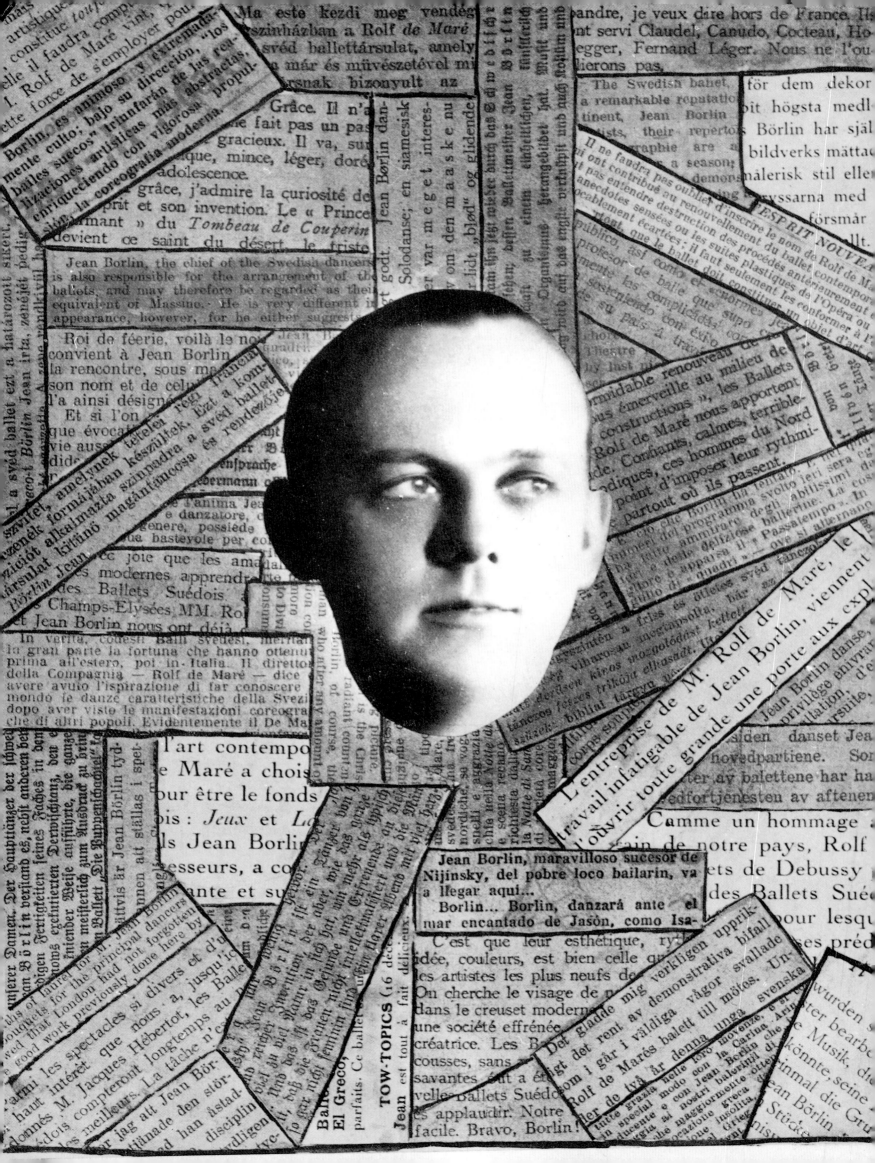

Jean Borlin

Jean Borlin est au niveau des matelots, des soldats, des mulâtres, des nègres, des hawaïens, des sauvages ; aux antipodes des russes, de la tradition française émigrée à Saint-Pétersbourg, de l'ancien régime, de la régence, de l'italianisme ; il se penche sur le grand cœur de Whitman qui éclate comme un gramophone géant, et part dans les bras des ouvriers de la voiture-aviation. Les endroits où l'on danse à Paris sont les Grands Boulevards, les Gares, le port du Bourget, le Vel'-d'Hiv', la salle Wagram, l'Autodrome Linas-Monthéry. Affiches et hauts-parleurs vous y font oublier les enseignements de l'Académie de la Danse, la sciatique et le temps, la mesure et le goût, la mièvrerie et la virtuosité. Quand on a tout oublié, ça y est on a trouvé le rythme, le beau rythme d'aujourd'hui qui porte les cinq continents nouveaux, la discipline, l'équilibre, la santé, la force, la vitesse. Les trois grandes créations de Jean Borlin sont *Skating-Ring. Les Mariés de la Tour Eiffel* et le ballet nègre *La Création du Monde.* A quand le ballet *Outre-Atlantique*, le grand ballet des *Foules Démocratiques*, le grand ballet *Sportif* en plein air ?

BLAISE CENDRARS.

MEMBERS OF THE COMPANY

Conductors: D.E. Inghelbrecht, E. Bigot, V. Golschmann, R. Désormière. *Stage Director:* Henri Prieur. *Company Manager:* E. Kjellblad. *Chief Electricians:* Étienne Bouvier, M. Henriot. *Cashier:* V. Johanneson. *Rehearsal Pianist:* Oscar Gustafson. *Wardrobe Mistress:* Lily Asberg. *Secretary:* Eric Viber. *The Dancers:* Jean Börlin, Jenny Hasselquist, Ebon Strandin, Carina Ari, Jolanda Figoni, Margareta Johanson, Klara Kjellblad, Irma Calson, Greta Lundberg, Edith Bonsdorff, Helga Dahl, Anna Wikstrom, Margit Wåhlander, Thorborg Stjerner, Dagmar Forslin, Astrid Lindgren, Berta Krantz, Ingeborg Kahr, Greta Kähr, Valborg Larson, Elsie Schwarck, Signe Selid, Signe Malmberg, Inger Friis, Siva Blomkvist, Therese Patterson, Axel Witzansky, Holger Mehnen, Kaj Smith, Paul Eltorp, Kristian Dahl, Paul Witzansky, Eric Viber, Nils Östman, Robert Ford, Tor Stettler, Toivo Niskanen, Ture Andersson, Kaarlo Eronen, John Carlberg, Rupert Doone, Walther Junk, Sam Blomkvist.

TOURS BY THE BALLETS SUÉDOIS

1920: Paris, London.

1921: Paris, Barcelona, Valencia, Madrid, Valladolid, Bilbao, Santander, Corunna, El Ferrol, Orense, Vigo, Pontevedra, Santiago, Brussels, Paris, Roubaix, Douai, Valenciennes, Lille, Orléans, Nantes, Le Mans, Rochefort, Limoges, Périgueux, Bordeaux, Pau, Tarbes, Carcassonne, Sète, Nîmes, Montpellier, Narbonne, Toulouse, Perpignan, Béziers, Avignon, Nice, Nîmes, Saint-Étienne, Dijon, Troyes, Nancy.

1922: Paris, Berlin, Vienna, Budapest, Berlin, Cologne, Düsseldorf, Hamburg, Stockholm, Besançon, Montreux, Geneva, Lausanne, Évian, Aix-les-Bains, Dijon, Le Havre, Trouville, Cabourg, Caen, Cherbourg, Paramé, Rennes, Saint-Nazaire, La Rochelle, Fouras, Royan, Arcachon, Biarritz, Angoulême, Malmö, Copenhagen, Hälsingborg, Gothenburg, Oslo, London, Brighton, Hull, Newcastle, Glasgow.

1923: Étampes, Milan, Brescia, Genoa, Florence, Forlì, Ravenna, Pesaro, Bologna, Verona, Udine, Trieste, Gorizia, Venice, Treviso, Vicenza, Mantua, Modena, Piacenza, Turin, Paris, New York, Philadelphia, Washington, New York.

1924: (USA) Easton, Reading, Allentown, Scranton, Harrisburg, Wilmington, York, Lebanon, Williamsport, Wilkes-Barre, Albany, Geneva, Oswego, Syracuse, Rochester, Utica, Batavia, Elyria, Toledo, Lima, Dayton, Columbus, Cohocton, New Philadelphia, Newcastle, Cumberland, Altoona, Allentown; Paris.

1925: Paris, Brussels, Namur, Brest, Lorient, Rennes, Le Mans, Nantes, Angers, Nantes, Saint-Nazaire, La Rochelle, Angoulême, Limoges, Brive, Arcachon, Bordeaux, Bayonne, Pau, Toulouse, Nice, Menton, Grasse, Cannes, Saint-Raphaël, Toulon, Hyères, Salon, Marseilles, Avignon, Lyons, Dijon, Troyes, Épinal, Verdun, Épernay.

TABLE OF PERFORMANCES

No.	Ballets	Seasons					
		1st	2nd	3rd	4th	5th	Total
1	Les Vierges folles	140	73	69	71	22	375
2	Divertissements		75	155	87	39	356
3	Chopiniana	96	82	107			285
4	La Boîte à joujoux	51	52	139	34	4	280
5	Nuit de Saint-Jean	134	21	43	55		253
6	Dansgille		76	104	27	35	242
7	El Greco	102	27	43		4	176
8	Le Tombeau de Couperin	102	30	35			167
9	Iberia	63	28	13			104
10	Marchand d'oiseaux			28	22	43	93
11	Within the Quota				69		69
12	L'Homme et son désir	17	19	10	10		56
13	Derviches	53					53

No.	Ballets	Seasons					
		1st	2nd	3rd	4th	5th	Total
14	Skating Rink		17	15	14	4	50
15	Le Porcher					38	38
16	Maison de fous	30	7				37
17	Jeux	29	2				31
18	Les Mariés de la tour Eiffel	10	8	9	3		30
19	La Jarre					13	13
20	Relâche				3	9	12
21	La Création du monde					12	12
22	Le Roseau					11	11
23	Le Tournoi singulier					10	10
24	Offerlunden			5			5
		827	517	775	395	244	2758

GLOSSARY OF NAMES

A

ALBÉNIZ, Isaac: Spanish pianist and composer (1860–1909). He studied in Leipzig, and in 1893 moved to Paris. In 1906, he published the first *Iberia* suite (Debussy was to compose his *Iberia* suite between 1910 and 1912). Orchestrated by Inghelbrecht, these *Images de l'Espagne* inspired Jean Börlin to create a ballet for the company's début performance on 25 October 1920.

ALEKSEEV, Aleksandr: Russian painter (1901–1982). Famous for his striking book illustrations. He also designed posters and made avant-garde animated films, exhibiting at the Venice Biennale in 1951. The sets and costumes for the Ballets Suédois' *Le Roseau* (1924) were designed by Alekseev from Persian miniatures.

ALFVÉN, Hugo: Swedish violinist, composer and conductor (1872–1960). Several ballets have been arranged to his music, which is very popular in Sweden. His *Nuit de Saint-Jean* (1920) drew its inspiration from Swedish musical folklore. His other works include a number of vocal pieces, as well as four symphonies and an oratorio.

ANDERSEN, Hans Christian: Danish writer (1805–1875). Famous for his *Fairy-Tales*, from which the Ballets Suédois borrowed *Le Porcher* in 1924. Stravinsky's opera *Feu d'artifice* and ballet *Le Baiser de la fée* are also based on Hans Christian Andersen fairy-tales. The writer, son of a shoemaker, had originally tried his hand at a whole variety of jobs – principally in the theatre, as a dancer, then as a chorus singer! – and literary genres. Author, in turn, of tragedies, poems and novels, he was finally acclaimed, during his own lifetime, for his *Fairy-Tales*, one of the greatest literary successes of all time.

ARCUEIL SCHOOL: the name adopted by a group of musicians who congregated around the composer Erik Satie (who went to live in Arcueil at the end of his life). In a letter to Rolf de Maré dated 12 October 1923, Satie announced the creation of the group in the following terms: 'What is the Arcueil school? ... On 14 June last, it was my privilege to present – to the Collège de France – four young musicians: Henri Cliquet-Pleyel, Roger Désormière, Maxime Jacob and Henri Sauguet. They have called themselves the Arcueil school out of friendship for an old inhabitant of that suburban commune. Yes, indeed. I shan't talk about their talent – being neither a pawn nor a critic (fortunately).' In 1924, Rolf de Maré presented the group by organizing a concert for them at the Théâtre des Champs-Élysées.

ARI, Carina: Swedish dancer and choreographer (1897–1970). She studied at Stockholm Opera Ballet School, then with Fokine in Copenhagen, and became prima ballerina with the Ballets Suédois, partnering Jean Börlin. Her own choreographic compositions draw on the two styles of classical and free dance, blending them with humorous and lyrical elements. Very popular with Paris audiences, she became the star dancer and director of dance at the Opéra-Comique, where she choreographed and danced in the first production of *Sousmarine* (Honegger) in 1925. Then, having become the star of the Paris Opéra, she staged several of her own ballets there, including *Rayon de lune* (Fauré) in 1928, *Ode à la rose* and *Ève*. Her final performance was in *Le Cantique des cantiques*, with Lifar, in 1938.

ATTERBERG, Kurt: Swedish composer and conductor (1887–1974). He drew much of his inspiration from Swedish folklore, to which he gave a romantic interpretation. In 1920, the Ballets Suédois produced his *Les Vierges folles*. He also wrote operas and symphonic music.

AURIC, Georges: French composer (1899–1983). Satie's most direct heir, in a sense he personified the spirit of the Six. Auric was, without doubt, the clearest embodiment of Cocteau's 'French musician' at the time of *Les Mariés de la tour Eiffel* (1921), for which he composed the overture. His lively, caustic wit, his detachment and ready sense of irony were naturally attuned to that bizarre, light-hearted and sceptical ballet. He was to go on and write the music for Cocteau's films *Le Sang d'un poète*, *L'Éternel retour* and *Orphée*, and Diaghilev enlisted his services for *Les Fâcheux* (1924), *Les Matelots* (1925) and *La Pastorale* (1926). He wrote the *Enchantements d'Alcine* (1929) for Ida Rubinstein, *Concurrence* (1932) for the Ballets de Monte-Carlo, *Quadrille* (1946) and *Le Peintre et son modèle* (1949) for the Ballets des Champs-Élysées, and *Phèdre* (1950) for Lifar at the Paris Opéra, where he was to take up the post of administrator.

B

BIGOT, Eugène: French conductor and composer (1888-1965). He was hired by the Théâtre des Champs-Élysées in 1913 to conduct the Ballets Suédois (along with Inghelbrecht). He was also to accompany the Ballets on tour and, in 1921, composed *Dansgille* for them, based on Swedish folk-dances. In 1925, he was made musical director of the Théâtre des Champs-Élysées, henceforth managed by Rolf de Maré. Later, he became director of the Concerts Lamoureux and conducted the Opéra-Comique and Radio-France orchestras.

BONNARD, Pierre: French painter (1867–1947). While studying law, he attended the Académie Jullian. He formed ties with Vuillard, Félix Vallotton and Maurice Denis, with whom, in 1889, under the aegis of Paul Sérusier, his first teacher, he founded the group known as the Nabis, which in Hebrew means 'the Prophets'. Like all the 'pupils of Gauguin', he 'simplified line and gave first place to colour' – to such a degree that, on the occasion of his first exhibition at the Salon des Indépendants in 1891, one critic spoke of his *tachisme violent* (tendency to create violent blobs of colour). He built up a personal style by endowing his decorative motifs with an abstract quality (which he owed to his predilection for Japanese painting), and it was this abstract decorative quality to which he gave triumphant expression in the great splash of blue he painted for *Jeux* in 1920.

BÖRLIN, Jean: Swedish dancer and choreographer (1893–1930). As well as having a brilliant career as a choreographer and dancer, Börlin appeared in two films by René Clair: *Entr'acte* (1924) and *Le Voyage imaginaire* (1925). Following the disbanding of the Ballets Suédois he continued his dancing career in Paris and New York. He died in New York while in the midst of preparations (aided by his last pupil Zita Fiord) for a ballet with a Lapland setting commissioned by the Metropolitan Opera. His notion of dance was radically different from that of the Ballets Russes, and even from his teacher Fokine's. From classical ballet, which he mastered to perfection, he retained the demand for muscular training pushed to its absolute limit, but as a creator he invented a new aesthetic of movement, freed from the old academic rules. With this new art of dance, he endeavoured to express the new age, modern man and his radically changed life-style.

C

CANUDO, Riciotto: Italian poet (1877–1923). He settled in Paris, where he formed friendships with Apollinaire and Cendrars. Canudo encouraged the inception of Dante studies in France by publishing essays on *The Divine Comedy*, large portions of which he also translated. He also translated into French works by Gabriele D'Annunzio, with whom he was on intimate terms. He was one of the very first serious writers to recognize the immense scope of cinema and, in 1922, founded *La Gazette des sept arts*. In 1920, he published, in *Le Mercure de France*, a 'Skating Ballet': *Skating Rink*. This poem, intended to be set to music, was turned into a ballet by Jean Börlin in 1922, with music by Honegger and scenery by Léger.

CAPLET, André: French composer and conductor (1878–1925). He completed Debussy's instrumentation for *La Boîte à joujoux*, performed by the Ballets Suédois in 1921.

CASELLA, Alfredo: Italian composer and conductor (1883–1947). A pupil of Diemer and Fauré, he lived in Paris at the start of his career and was actively involved in the avant-garde musical movement. Initially responsive to the influence of Debussy, Milhaud and Stravinsky, following his return to Italy in 1915 he renewed his ties with the old Italian tradition. As music critic, conductor and teacher, he exerted a powerful influence on the next generation of Italian musicians.

CENDRARS, Blaise: French poet and novelist, born in Switzerland (1887–1961). A dedicated traveller, whose entire work celebrates the passion for *bourlinguer*: treating every journey as an allegory of literature, he lived his writing like a voyage of initiation. Before the war, he befriended Chagall, Soutine, the Delaunays (Sonia illustrated the famous first edition of his *Transsibérien*, which opened out to a length of several metres), Modigliani (who painted his portrait), Léger (who illustrated several of his books), Cocteau, Max Jacob and Apollinaire. In July 1914, he and Canudo signed an appeal to foreigners resident in France; published in all the papers, it was met with tremendous enthusiasm. In 1915, while fighting in France's Foreign Legion, he was badly wounded in his right arm, which had to be amputated. After working with Abel Gance on *J'accuse* and *La Roue* (1920–21), he produced a film single-handed: *La Venere nera* (1923, with music by Honegger). During the thirties, he became friendly with Dos Passos, Hemingway and Arthur Miller.

In writing *La Création du monde* (1923) for Rolf de Maré, he drew his inspiration from a legend in his famous *Anthologie nègre*, published two years earlier. Léger designed the sets and costumes and Milhaud wrote the music for the ballet.

CHASTEL, Roger: French painter (1879–1981). After a lengthy period of military service (1916–19), a recommendation by the caricaturist Sem established him in a career publishing fashion designs and cartoons in the newspapers. His drawings of the Ballets Suédois date from this period. From 1925, he decided to devote his efforts exclusively to painting. Since he had just won the Grand Prix National de Peinture, in 1932 he was commissioned, along with Vuillard, Roussel and Maurice Denis, to paint one of the four panels in the Palais de la Société des Nations in Geneva. He taught at the École des Beaux-Arts in Paris until 1968.

CLAIR, René: French film maker (1898–1981). For Picabia's ballet *Relâche* (1924), he created his famous *Entr'acte*, accompanied by a cheerful score by Erik Satie: *musique d'ameublement* ('music as furniture') thus found its very first employment in the film industry. This film – which presented itself as a veritable modernist manifesto – also marked the first occasion that film had been incorporated into choreography. The sequence of bold and rapidly changing images, obtained by the close interaction between dance and film, was governed entirely by rhythm. The programme stated: 'Anyone who doesn't like it has our permission to clear off home', and 'Some people prefer the ballets at the Opéra, poor fools ...'. The challenge was immediately taken up in a series of heated debates and the attempt at bringing life and image face to face was to be heralded as an artistic landmark. (Massine echoed the attempt in 1928, when he created *Ode*, involving the projection of a film by Charbonnier.) *Entr'acte* marked the end of the era of the Ballets Suédois, and the start of his career for René Clair, who went on to produce *Le Million* (1931), *À nous la liberté* (1931), *Le Silence est d'or* (1947), *Les Grandes Manœuvres* (1955), *Tout l'or du monde* (1961) and *Les Fêtes galantes* (1965).

CLAUDEL, Paul: French diplomat, poet and dramatist (1868–1955). Claudel, who was converted to Roman Catholicism after a sudden mystical experience in 1886, depended for his literary success on the powerful lyricism of his dramatic works. His poetic vocation never suf-

fered as a result of the brilliant diplomatic career which took him, successively, as consul general to China, Prague, Rome and Hamburg, as minister plenipotentiary to Brazil and Denmark, and as ambassador to Japan and the United States. Darius Milhaud was appointed his secretary during Claudel's posting to Rio de Janeiro in 1917, and it was there that, in collaboration with Milhaud and Andrée Parr, Claudel composed a ballet evoking the sombre beauty of the Amazonian forest: *L'Homme et son désir*. During his long ambassadorship in Japan, Claudel wrote his major work, *Le Soulier de satin* (1924), the expression of his aim to create total theatre embracing 'this world and the next'. The play, with music by Honegger, was performed at the Comédie-Française in 1943.

COCTEAU, Jean: French writer, designer and film maker (1889–1963). The noisy scandal created by *Parade* (1917) gave Cocteau instant rite of passage into Parisian avant-garde circles. Staged under Diaghilev's auspices, the ballet established Satie (composing his first ever ballet score) as the standard-bearer of the new music, and represented Picabia's first involvement with ballet. Cocteau's book *Le Coq et l'Arlequin*, published the following year, was viewed as the aesthetic manifesto of this 'new spirit', which was soon to sweep beyond the borders of France.

He wrote *Le Dieu bleu* (1912), *Le Train bleu* (1924) and *Oedipus Rex* (1927) for Diaghilev's Ballets Russes; his *Le Boeuf sur le toit* (1920) was staged at the Comédie des Champs-Élysées; *Roméo et Juliette* (1924) by the Comte de Beaumont; *Le Jeune Homme et la Mort* (1946) by the Ballets des Champs-Élysées; *Phèdre* (1950) by the Paris Opéra, and *La Dame à la licorne* (1953) by the Munich Opera. His *Les Mariés de la tour Eiffel* (1921), which was a clear expression of his modernist tendencies, marked one of the highpoints in the career of the Ballets Suédois. This work, which fell somewhere between classical tragedy and the music-hall revue, presented a picture of the mediocrity, paltriness and vulgarity of a middle class that was at once sinister and ridiculous: 'We made no concessions', he was to recall, forty-five years later. 'The oldest among us was not yet twenty-five.' Cocteau also created numerous stage sets: for, among others, *Phèdre* and *La Dame à la licorne*, as well as for *Antigone* (Paris Opéra, 1943) and *L'Amour et son amour* (Théâtre des Champs-Élysées, 1947).

Satie, Milhaud, Auric, Honegger and Stravinsky wrote the scores for his ballets, operas and, later, for his screenplays, including *Le Sang d'un poète*, *L'Éternel Retour*, *La Belle et la Bête* and *Orphée*. Acting as spokesman for the Six, Cocteau attacked the elder musical generation – as represented by Debussy and Ravel – with passionate ferocity, drawing on a whole range of images and paradoxes, and expressing the desire to have done with 'musical impressionism'.

COLIN, Paul: French poster designer, scenographer and painter (1892–1985). Together with Cassandre, he was the creator of the modern poster, in which colour predominates over form. The poster he executed for the Ballets Suédois was one of his very first works. He was acclaimed in 1925 for his posters for the *Revue nègre* (he produced, in fact, almost all the Théâtre des Champs-Élysées' posters), for which, at Rolf de

Maré's request, he also created the stage sets. From that day on, he received a regular stream of commissions and is said to have designed nearly five hundred posters of lasting artistic value. He created the costume for Börlin's *Sculpture nègre* (1920), the scenography for the Opéra's *Prélude dominical* (1931), *L'Orchestre en liberté* (1931) and *Le Cantique des cantiques* (1938), and for the Opéra-Comique's *Comme ils s'aiment* (1941), *Casse-Noisette* (1947) and *Guignol* (1949).

D

DAHL, Viking: Swedish composer (1895–1945). Dahl, who wrote the score for *Maison de fous* (1920), was one of the most original young Swedish composers of the early twenties. A minister's son from Skåne, he studied at the Stockholm Conservatoire and, in 1917, made a name for himself with his *Oriental suite for orchestra*. But it was in Paris, studying under Ravel, that he spent his most important apprenticeship years. He also tried his hand at painting and writing. *Maison de fous* represented the peak, but also the finish, of his career: little understood or appreciated, he ended his days as a music teacher in a school in a small Swedish town.

DARDEL, Nils (von): Swedish painter (1888–1942). He lived in Paris in the twenties and rubbed shoulders with members of the Paris school and Parisian intellectuals of his generation. Born, like Rolf de Maré, into an aristocratic family, Dardel was to be one of the really great names in Swedish painting. He created the sets for *Nuit de Saint-Jean* and *Maison de fous*, and he and his wife Thora, a writer, were friends and important advisers to the Ballets Suédois.

DEBUSSY, Claude: French composer (1862–1918). Impressed by Nijinsky's choreography for *L'Après-midi d'un faune*, Debussy wrote *Jeux* for him: a 'danced poem', which was first performed on 15 May 1913. This marvellous piece of music 'in every respect, an astonishing work' (A. Schaeffner), the last orchestral piece Debussy was to write, was revived by the Ballets Suédois in 1920, during their first season in Paris.

Enchanted by the originality of *La Boîte à joujoux*, proposed to him by André Hellé in 1913, Debussy proceeded to compose the music for this ballet, which was later orchestrated by André Caplet and staged by the Ballets Suédois on 15 February 1921.

DE CHIRICO, Giorgio: Italian painter (1888–1978). In Paris, he made the acquaintance of Apollinaire (whom he depicted, prophetically, with a bullet hole in his head), Max Jacob and Picasso, who brought him into contact with the artistic and literary avant-garde. He studied at the Academy in Athens, and, most importantly, at the Munich Academy (1906–9). In Paris, he painted his first 'Places d'Italie', whose deserted spaces are borrowed from the arcades of Ferrara and Turin. During the summer of 1915, following his success at the 1914 Salon des Indépendants in Paris, he was obliged to return to Ferrara, on account of the war, and was almost immediately hospitalized for nervous depression.

It was during this stay in Ferrara that he formulated the principles of his 'metaphysical painting'. This movement, which was polemically opposed to Futurism and the 'modern spirit', sought to achieve a spirituality of form linking Uccello or Piero della Francesca's mathematical composition with Cubist recomposition. In 1919, de Chirico was one of the leaders of the Valori Plastici group, which sought a deliberate return to classical tradition; and – an unexpected shift in an artist of his calibre – he began copying works by Raphael, Botticelli and Michelangelo.

Rolf de Maré was the first to enlist the help of this artist, whom the avant-garde claimed as one of its own, for the purposes of designing a ballet: *La Jarre* (1924). In 1929, Diaghilev commissioned him to design the sets and costumes for *Le Bal*, in a more 'Surrealist' vein. De Chirico's other contributions to ballet were to follow his own changing preferences: *Pulcinella* (1930), *Bacchus et Ariane*, a mythological fantasy (1931), *Les Bacchantes* (1937), and *Protée*, for the Ballets du Colonel de Basil (1938). For Milan's La Scala, he executed *The Legend of Joseph* (1951), and *Don Quichotte* (1953) for the Florence Festival.

DÉSORMIÈRE, Roger: French conductor and composer (1898–1963). In 1921, he was appointed head of the Concerts Pleyel, and he conducted the premières of *Salade* (Milhaud) and *Mercure* (Satie) given by Massine at the Comte de Beaumont's Soirées de Paris in 1924. That same year, he was made conductor of the Ballets Suédois, and, from 1925, he conducted the Ballets Russes orchestra. Following the death of Diaghilev, he won acclaim as guest conductor all over Europe and in the USSR, defending French music, past and present, with great sensitivity. From 1937, he was conductor with the Opéra-Comique, of which he was later to become director (1944–45), before being appointed associate director of the Paris Opéra (1945–46). He proved himself an ardent supporter of contemporary music, which led him, *inter alia*, to conduct the first version of Boulez's *Soleil des eaux* (1950). He also composed the music for numerous screenplays.

DIAGHILEV, Serge: Russian ballet impresario (1872–1929). Forming friendships with the painters Bakst and Benois, he organized musical soirées with the aim of introducing contemporary musicians, such as Debussy, Ravel and Dukas, to St Petersburg society. He also organized art exhibitions: 'Two centuries of Russian painting and sculpture' in St Petersburg in 1905 and, the following year, an exhibition introducing Russian art to Paris at the Salon d'Automne. He presented a series of concerts at the Paris Opéra in 1907 and, the following year, staged a version of the opera *Boris Godunov*, in which he introduced the Russian bass Fyodor Chaliapin.

Having been assistant to the director of the Imperial Theatres for a short period at the turn of the century, he had come into contact with the dancers of the Maryinsky Theatre and with the choreographer Fokine, whose creativity was stifled under the restraints imposed by a board of conformist directors. Diaghilev seized his opportunity to present a new type of ballet in Paris: during the summer vacation he formed a company drawn from the best dancers at the Imperial Theatres and, on 19 May 1909, presented his first programme, at Paris's Théâtre du Châtelet. Fokine created the choreography, Bakst and Benois painted the sets, Nijinsky and Pavlova danced. It was a sensation, and the springboard for an international renewal in classical ballet. The 'Ballets Russes de Serge de Diaghilev', having eventually severed their ties with the still traditional ballet in the USSR, continued until the impresario's death in 1929. Under Diaghilev's aegis, ballet was recognized anew as a major art.

F

FERROUD, Pierre-Octave: French composer (1900–1936). He orchestrated some old Swedish folk melodies to accompany the ballet *Le Porcher*, based on a Hans Christian Andersen fairy-tale and staged by Börlin in 1924.

FOKINE, Michel: Russian choreographer (1880–1942), the great reformer of academic dance. His technique is a further development of Marius Petipa's style. Fokine's choreographic principles form the groundwork for the new classical repertoire, which has been constantly reinterpreted ever since.

The Maryinsky Theatre engaged him as a member of its corps de ballet in 1898, and in 1904 he was promoted first soloist. That same year, he wrote a ballet scenario from Longus's *Daphnis and Chloe*, already embodying a new outlook and the philosophy of a reformed ballet, partly based on the ideas of his older colleague Gorsky. In an open letter to *The Times*, published on 6 July 1914, Fokine defined his 'rules' for ballet. He insisted on 'the absolute and harmonious unity of three elements: music, painting and choreography', which must replace 'the traditional duality music/dance': 'Dance must be expressive, and cannot confine itself to a limited language of conventional gestures. It must never degenerate into a display of technical virtuosity. It must interpret the dancers' inmost feelings. Above all, it must be the expression of the time and place evoked by the scenario.' In 1904, Isadora Duncan's visit revealed to him 'something which is as important for dance as professional skill: spirit, the emanation of pure emotion'.

He married his partner Vera Antonova, and, in 1907, choreographed *The Dying Swan* (Saint-Saëns) for Anna Pavlova, a ballet that assumed symbolic status and was repeatedly performed by Pavlova up until the end of her career. It was to affect the interpretation of all the old classical ballets, which became henceforth softer and more soulful. Like Diaghilev, Fokine fell out with the director of the Imperial Theatres, and it was at about this time that the painter Alexandre Benois introduced him to Diaghilev. Diaghilev engaged him for the memorable 1909 Paris season, for which he choreographed *Le Pavillon d'Armide*, *Polovtsian Dances*, *Les Sylphides* and *Cléopâtre*. He followed these with *Le Carnaval*, *Sheherazade* and *Firebird* in 1910; *Le Spectre de la rose*, *Narcisse* and *Petrushka* in 1911; *Le Dieu bleu*, *Thamar* and *Daphnis and Chloe* in 1912; then *Papillons*, *The Legend of Joseph*, *Midas* and *The Golden Cockerel* in 1914.

In 1912, Nijinsky, who was increasingly monopolizing Diaghilev's attention, was appointed choreographer in Fokine's stead, and Fokine broke his ties with the company, returning to Russia, where he staged a few ballets. In 1913–14, he was director of the Royal Swedish Ballet, to which he returned in 1918 after leaving Russia for good. It was here that he trained Börlin and all the other artistes whom Rolf de Maré was to hire. For a time, he opened a private school in Denmark. He spent the last years of his life in the United States without producing anything as distinguished as the works of his youth.

FOUJITA, Léonard: Japanese-born painter and engraver (1886–1968). Though destined for a brilliant official career in Japan, he apparently felt the pull of the West and, in 1913, moved to Paris. As a book illustrator, he illustrated works by, among others, Claudel, Loti and Tagore. In 1924, the year he designed the sets and costumes for *Le Tournoi singulier*, he exhibited at Paris's Salon d'Automne and at the Tuileries and was elected a member of Tokyo's Academy of Fine Arts.

The fascination of Foujita's art lay in its modernism combined with an underlay of Japanese traditionalism. Best known for his many nudes, his cats and still lifes, he used loosely flowing lines, leaving large areas of his canvas bare, and blending traditional Japanese techniques with European ones to create his own original style of painting.

G

GLAZUNOV, Aleksandr: Russian composer (1865–1936). He was admired in Russian musical circles for his precocious talent, his *First Symphony* being performed in 1882. Glazunov helped to make Russian music better known in Western Europe. In 1909, he collaborated on the Ballets Russes' first Paris season, and, in 1920, composed the score for *Derviches*. In 1928, he directed the St Petersburg Conservatoire, where the quality of his teaching exerted a profound influence on Stravinsky, Prokofiev, Scriabin and Shostakovich.

GOLSCHMANN, Vladimir: American conductor of Russian origin, born in France (1893–1972). He studied in Paris at the Schola Cantorum and made his début as a violinist. But it was as a conductor that he was to make a name for himself. He conducted the Ballets Russes orchestra (1919–23) and began his American career as conductor with the Ballets Suédois during their United States tour of 1923. In 1934, he settled for good in the United States, obtaining American citizenship in 1947.

GRECO, EL (real name Domenikos Theotocopoulos): Spanish painter, born in Crete (1541–1614). His highly personal work, which follows its own passionate inner logic, was met with profound incomprehension and long-term neglect, before the painter was rediscovered, as a forerunner of Expressionism, at the beginning of this century.

Rolf de Maré's private collection included a number of works by El Greco, on which the scenario of the 1920 ballet would be based. For Börlin, whose choreographies were so often guided by pictorial references, these canvases revealed an expressivity of tremendous plastic force, giving him scope to effect an extreme radicalization of his own aesthetic. The public had reason indeed to be surprised by this ballet composed of mimed scenes which made El Greco's emotional world come alive.

If modern critics have been able to identify in the boldness of El Greco's technique an inspired vision of Expressionism, in his constructions involving small-scale cubic volumes (*Toledo*, 1610–14) the prefiguration of Cézannesque geometry, and in his dynamism, intensified by his use of colour and liberation of form, the potency of tormented Expressionism, if Cézanne and Van Gogh could perceive his attraction, it is because El Greco hazarded the sort of stakes in painting that none but modern art would match.

H

HALLSTRÖM, Gunnar: Swedish painter and illustrator (1875–1943). He painted mainly landscapes and subjects from Nordic antiquity. In 1923, he executed the sets and costumes for *Offerlunden*.

HAQUINIUS, Johan Algot: Swedish pianist and composer (1886–1966). He composed the music for *Offerlunden* (1923), whose particular interest lies in its Expressionist tonality. He studied the piano in Paris under Moszkowsky and came to be regarded as one of Sweden's most distinguished pianists.

HASSELQUIST, Jenny: Swedish dancer (1894–1978). She and Carina Ari were prima ballerinas with the Ballets Suédois. She was a soloist with the Royal Swedish Ballet before joining Börlin's troupe, with whom, as star dancer, she won huge public acclaim throughout Europe. After leaving the Ballets Suédois, she continued touring in Sweden and Europe, as a soloist or with a small ensemble of her pupils, rather like Pavlova. She also appeared in numerous Swedish and German silent films, including Lubitsch's famous *Sumurun* (1920). In 1932, she founded her own ballet school in Stockholm.

HÉBERTOT, Jacques: French theatre director (1886–1970). He founded the Théâtre d'Art Normand in Rouen in 1908, and later settled in Paris, where he worked successively as a music editor, journalist and drama critic, finally fixing on a permanent career as theatre director. From 1920 to 1925, he worked for Rolf de Maré as administrative director of the Théâtre des Champs-Élysées and Comédie des Champs-Élysées, and of the Studio from 1924. The Ballets Suédois staged all their creations at the main Théâtre des Champs-Élysées (though other artistes also performed there, including Pitoëff and the Ballets Russes) and de Maré finally handed over the direction of the Comédie des Champs-Élysées and Studio to Louis Jouvet and Gaston Baty, respectively. Hébertot went on to direct, in turn, the Théâtre des Mathurins (1926), the Théâtre de l'Oeuvre (1941) and, finally, the Théâtre des Arts, which became, under his management, the Théâtre-Hébertot. He staged the first productions of a large number of important works by the majority of contemporary authors, including Pirandello, Cocteau, Giraudoux, Camus, Montherlant, Bernanos and Mauriac.

HELLÉ, André: French designer, cartoonist and illustrator. He collaborated on the main Paris publications of the first half of the century and illustrated numerous childrens' books. He is best known, however, for his theatre scenography – in particular the sets and costumes for *La Boîte à joujoux*, for which he also wrote the libretto. Debussy composed the music for the ballet, and Börlin created the choreography: his detailed study of puppet movements produced 'Cubist', staccato dancing, like that of rigidly articulated dolls, each moving in a way that exactly fitted the individual character of the role.

HOFER, Carl: German painter and lithographer (1878–1955). He spent the years 1903–8 in Italy, and from then until 1913 in Paris. In around 1909, he became a member of the eclectic New Association of Munich Artists. His work, characterized by classical construction in the manner of Derain, was identified by the Nazis as 'degenerate'. Following the German defeat in 1945, he was appointed director of the School of Fine Arts in Berlin.

HONEGGER, Arthur: Swiss composer (1892–1955). A member of the Six, Honegger was the most sensitive of the group to romanticism and the Wagnerian aesthetic (and, thereby, the furthest removed from Satie). His work is marked by grandeur and solemnity, but not by irony, and though he may have identified himself with the Six out of friendship for its other members, he did not, however, subscribe to the new aesthetic preached by Cocteau: 'I don't go in for farce and music hall', he explained, 'but, rather, for chamber music and symphony music at its most solemn and austere.'

One of the very first works he wrote for a dance suite, *Les Dicts des jeux du monde* (1919), was commissioned by Jeanne Ronsay. Then, in 1921, he collaborated on *Les Mariés de la tour Eiffel*, for which he wrote a funeral march, before going on to compose his first real ballet: *Skating Rink* (1921). Here, his lyrical vein hovered between humour and drama. (One newspaper summed up the situation with typical Gallic wit: 'English title, Italian theme, Swedish ballet, Swiss music, very Parisian climax – everything went like clockwork [The witticism is partially lost in translation, since the French idiom *marcher comme sur des roulettes* literally means 'go as if on castors'].) That same year, his artistic originality was confirmed when he composed his ballet *Roi David*, which was choreographed by Serge Lifar under Rolf de Maré's sponsorship.

His other choreographic works included *L'Impératrice aux rochers* (1927), *Les Noces de l'amour et de Psyché* (1928) for Ida Rubinstein, *Amphion* (1931), based on a text by Paul Valéry, *Sémiramis* (1934), *L'Oiseau blanc* (1937, at the Salle Pleyel), *Le Cantique des cantiques* (1938) for Lifar at the Paris Opéra, with Carina Ari in the female lead, *Chota Roustaveli* (1946, at Monte Carlo), and, for the Paris Opéra, *L'Appel de la montagne* (1945) and *La Naissance des couleurs* (1949). T. Shawn choreographed his *Pacific 231* (1933) and A. Howard used some of his piano pieces for her *Lady into Fox* (1939).

HUGO, Jean: French painter, illustrator and scene painter (1894–1983). He was famous for his gouaches, which included landscapes, still lifes and book illustrations (for, among others, André Maurois's *Climats* and Radiguet's *Les Joues en feu*). He was initially known for his wonderful stage settings of plays by his great-grandfather, Victor Hugo, whose romantic leanings he had inherited. His collection of comical characters for Cocteau's *Les Mariés de la tour Eiffel* (1921) display his humorous, baroque inventiveness.

One of Hugo's original contributions to ballet related to his continued use of the kind of clinging tights that covered the whole body, whether it was for Cocteau's *Roméo et Juliette*, staged in 1924 at the Soirées de Paris arranged by the Comte de Beaumont, for *Les Cent Baisers* (Ballets de Monte-Carlo, 1935), or for his famous *Les Amours de Jupiter* (Roland Petit's Ballets des Champs-Élysées, 1946).

HUGO, Valentine: née Gross, French painter, illustrator and scene painter (1890–1968). She helped her fiancé Jean Hugo create the costumes and masks he designed for *Les Mariés de la tour Eiffel* (1921). She painted a number of famous portraits of her friends – including Satie, Stravinsky, Picasso, Max Ernst, Valéry and Éluard – and produced a magnificent wood engraving of Nijinsky, which Cocteau used as an inspiration for his poster. She also painted the sets for *Vogue* (1924) for the Comte de Beaumont, for *Quadrille* (Roland Petit, 1945) and for Debussy's *Pelléas et Mélisande* (1947) and *Les Malheurs de Sophie* (1948), at the Paris Opéra.

I

INGHELBRECHT, Désiré Émile: French conductor and composer (1880–1965). A pupil and friend of Debussy's, he was director of music with the Ballets Suédois, then conductor at the Opéra-Comique, before founding the Orchestre National de la Radiodiffusion Française (1934). As a composer, he worked in a wide range of genres: symphony, religious and chamber music, ballet, piano pieces and operettas.

J

JALĀL UD-DĪN RŪMĪ: Persian poet (1210–1273). Great Muslim mystic, born into a royal family; fleeing the vindictiveness of a jealous sultan, he was forced to leave Balkh and take up exile in Konya. There, he became the disciple of Shams of Tabriz and founded the order of the whirling dervishes. In the rules he laid down, an important role was given to dance as a means to inducing mystical fervour. He wrote a collection of lyric poems and is perhaps best known for his *Mathnawī* (Distichs), a vast poem comprising 25,000 distichs.

Jalāl ud-Dīn Rūmī's philosophy stresses the importance of creating a spiritual balance between heaven and earth by means of dance movements. Modern European dancers, in search of a similar outlook, adopted him as a forerunner and kindred soul. Börlin was an early European disciple of the dervish dance.

K

KROHG, Per: Norwegian painter (1889–1965). He went to Paris with his famous father, who ran a painting academy in Montparnasse. He studied under him (1903), then under Matisse (1907–9), and began exhibiting at the Salon des Indépendants in 1922. In 1924, he settled in Oslo, where he taught painting and occupied an influential position in artistic life. In 1952, he produced a vast decoration for the United Nations Security Council chamber in New York.

L

LABÉ, Louise: French poet (1524–1566). One of the greatest writers of the French Renaissance, she wrote some of the most beautiful and most candid love poems ever to have appeared in the French language. Famous as much for her beauty as for her literary talent, she gathered around her a circle of admiring fellow poets. In a collection which appeared in 1555, she explored the joys and sufferings of love in three *Elegies* and twenty-five

Sonnets, while her long prose poem in the form of a dialogue, *Le Débat de Folie et d'Amour*, was to provide the inspiration for La Fontaine's fable *L'Amour et la Folie*. It was this same poem on which Börlin based the scenario for his ballet *Le Tournoi singulier*, in 1924.

LAGERKVIST, Pär: Swedish poet, novelist and dramatist (1891–1952). An admirer of Baudelaire, Rimbaud and Strindberg, he sought through writing an outlet for that 'anguish' proclaimed by his first collected poems (1916), that genuine cry of terror and despair in the face of a senseless world. Lagerkvist provided the scenario for *Maison de fous* in 1920. For all his efforts to extol a sort of God-less faith, his great novels – *The Hangman* (1933, English translation 1936), *The Dwarf* (1944, 1945), *Barabbas* (1950, 1951) and *The Sibyl* (1956, 1958) – are all pessimistic works. Lagerkvist's dramatic oeuvre, which includes *The Man who Lived his Life Over* (1928, 1971) and *Victory in Darkness* (1939), is among the most important in twentieth-century Swedish theatre. In 1951, he received the Nobel prize for literature.

LAGUT, Irène: French painter and illustrator (b.1893). A student of Picasso, she exhibited at the Salon des Indépendants from 1920, and, in 1921, designed the sets for *Les Mariés de la tour Eiffel*.

LANVIN, Jeanne: French couturier (1867–1946). She founded the Lanvin house in 1889. She was the couturière of fashionable Paris, the stage and the cinema screen. She often designed dresses for the theatre or cinema, in fact, and created the costumes for Börlin's *Jeux* (1920), the Ballets Suédois' first production. She was friendly with a number of painters (Vuillard did a famous portrait of her) and with Cocteau and Christian Bérard, and in 1926, she opened the first *haute couture* firm for men.

LAPRADE, Pierre: French painter (1875–1931). His work combined an equal measure of eighteenth-century grace and Impressionist sensibility. He first exhibited at the Salon des Indépendants in 1901; shortly afterwards, the art dealer Vollard bought his entire collection of paintings, making him famous overnight. Laprade was responsible for the sets and costumes for *Le Tombeau de Couperin* (1920).

LAZARUS, Daniel: French composer and conductor (1898–1964). He was director of music at the Théâtre du Vieux-Colombier (1921–25) when he wrote *Le Roseau* (1924), whose theme was inspired by one of the Distichs of the great Sufi poet Jalāl ud-Dīn Rūmī. This precociously talented musician succeeded in occupying a double position as composer and conductor at the Opéra-Comique and the Paris Opéra, before going on to teach at the Schola Cantorum.

LÉGER, Fernand: French painter (1881–1955). He produced two important décors for the Ballets Suédois, which enabled him to perfect his notion of the spatial conflict occurring between the dynamic movement of lines and the static presence of objects, between the existence of man and the environment he inhabits. Starting out from the geometric precision of mechanics and the dynamism of industrial objects, he created movement by turning space into an abstraction, painting objects in close-up and eschewing the use of perspective.

During the preparations for *Skating Rink* (1922), Léger and Börlin would go along to the dance halls in rue de Lappe, where the Apaches were 'doing the Java', in order to gain some inspiration from their clothes and their dancing. It was undoubtedly for the 'African ballet' *La Création du monde* (1923), however, that Léger painted his finest sets: both décors and costumes created a sensation. That same year, he gave a lecture at the Collège de France; others followed at the Sorbonne. Thanks to its originality, Léger's contribution to the theatre was considerable. He fully grasped the necessity, and also the difficulty, of establishing a link between the décor (which was stable and occupied the entire volume of the scenic space) and the actors (who were mobile and only occupied the level of the stage floor). He solved this problem in *Skating Rink* by turning the dancer into part of the décor, and in *La Création du monde* by transforming the décor into an actor integrated into the very process whereby the theatrical production unfolded.

For the Paris Opéra, he designed and executed the sets and costumes for Lifar's *David triomphant* (1937) and *Bolivar* (1950).

M

MAN RAY: American painter and photographer (1890–1976). He co-founded the Dada movement in New York (1915) with Picabia and Marcel Duchamp. Though Man Ray's work showed the influence of Cézanne prior to that date, in 1915 the scandal-provoking Armory Show had an undoubted impact on the artist. That same year, the organizer of the show, Stieglitz, founded his own revue, *291*, in which he reproduced works by Duchamp and Picabia among others, and before long several by Man Ray himself. The following year Man Ray began showing abstract Dada paintings and 'ready-mades'.

In Paris, in 1921, he joined the Dada group formed by Tzara, Picabia and Breton, just as it was on the point of merging with the successful Surrealist movement. He was to live in Paris from now on – except during the years 1940–51, which he spent in Hollywood. And it was in Paris that he extended his activities to photography, inventing his famous 'Rayographs' or 'photograms', photographs taken without recourse to the mechanical medium of the lens: by placing objects directly on to sensitized paper. Surrealism continued to intrigue Man Ray, and its influence is apparent in the four films he made: *Le Retour à la raison* (1923), *Emak Bakia* (1926), *L'Étoile de mer* (1928), and *Les Mystères du Château de Dé* (1929).

In 1925, Léger wrote his *Ballet mécanique*, basing it on photographs by the artist, whom Breton described as: 'The indoor trapper, presser of the grapes of sight, captor of the sun and devotee of shadows, compass reader in the unknown and wrecker of predictability.'

MARÉ, Rolf de: Swedish founder and director of the Ballets Suédois (1888–1964). A collector of contemporary and non-European art, he also had an interest in Swedish folk-dance. He travelled widely, finally deciding to settle in Paris, where, from 1910 onwards, he formed friendships with Picasso and numerous other Paris-based artists. A glance at the list of musicians and painters whom he invited, in the years 1920 to 1924, to collaborate on his productions gives an idea of the invaluable inheritance he left ballet. At thirty-seven, following the creation of *Relâche*, he decided to disband his company, feeling that there were at that time no new channels to be explored, that he had taken this anti-ballet as far as it was possible to go: 'Since I had no wish to repeat myself, I decided to disband the Ballets Suédois.'

His efforts to express future trends had led to the creation of a work deemed blasphemous by an age it disorientated, and de Maré felt that it would be absurd to go any further. That did not mean abandoning the theatre, however, for he went on to create the Opéra-Music Hall des Champs-Élysées (1925–27), bringing over from New York the *Revue nègre*, which would introduce Josephine Baker to Europe. In 1931, he founded the Archives Internationales de la Danse, and, the following year, organized the first international choreographers' competition, which brought the young unknown Kurt Jooss instant world fame for his prize-winning *Green Table*. De Maré donated his collection of books, drawings and documents to France in 1950, where it is currently held in the Paris Opéra's museum library. The documents and around four hundred and fifty scenographic sketches relating to the Ballets Suédois are conserved at Stockholm's International Dance Museum, founded by Bengt Häger in 1950, which was also the beneficiary of de Maré's fortune. His important collection of contemporary paintings, meanwhile, forms a considerable part of the Museum of Modern Art in Stockholm.

MILHAUD, Darius: French composer (1892–1974). This immensely diverse and prolific composer was the author of more than five hundred works. Driven by a tremendous creative dynamism, he was the member of the Six most genuinely eager to discover new modes of expression. Deeply attracted by bold experimentalism and abstract theorizing alike, Milhaud had little regard for uncomprehending audiences.

His innovative impulses were to find their full expression in polytonality, and the modernity of his musical language unfolded most freely in the theatre – whether it be in Claudel's *L'Homme et son désir* (composed in 1919, when the two men had been posted to Brazil), where his highly original composition intensified the poignant mystery of Claudelian metaphysics; or in the fugue and wedding march he composed for Cocteau's *Les Mariés de la tour Eiffel* (1921). 'The first performance was greeted with what are generally called "mixed feelings"', he said of the latter. 'It was at the time when people thought of us as "jokers"; only Arthur Honegger was regarded as a serious musician. He had composed the *General's funeral march*. During its execution, someone shouted: "At last, some music . . . ", failing to realize that, as a joke, Arthur had used the theme of my *Wedding march*, in "minor" and "adagio", and that, later, in the paroxysm of the "fortissimo" he had introduced the *Faust waltz*, in counterpoint to the bass instruments and trombones. No one noticed, of course.'

In Cendrars's *La Création du monde* (1923), Milhaud was the first to introduce jazz music (thereby ratifying its existence) into a symphonic score, currently considered as one of his finest. The score followed a new orchestral arrangement, one that was typical of jazz, and represented the first use of the saxophone in symphony. The central theme resembles to a surprising degree Gershwin's *Rhapsody in Blue*, composed only a few months later.

MURPHY, Gerald: American painter (1888–1964). Aesthete and dilettante, Murphy lived the kind of brilliant life-style that fascinated friends such as Dos Passos and Scott Fitzgerald (who made him the hero of his novel *Tender is the Night*). In 1921, he settled in Paris, where he began to paint after six months of tuition with Natalia Goncharova, who introduced him to abstraction. But the paintings he exhibited at the Salon des Indépendants, from 1923, revealed more of his friend Picasso's influence with regard to colour, and that of his friend Léger regarding subject matter.

He painted utilitarian objects, which he enlarged out of all proportion, depicting them with a stylization that bordered on poster art. Thus, instead of fading out the object – razor, box of matches, or fountain pen – he emphasized its heroic aspect, down to the last detail. In 1925, for example, he painted the labyrinthine mechanism of a watch, on a two-by-two-metre canvas.

For Rolf de Maré, whom he met through Léger, he wrote an American ballet, *Within the Quota* (1923), for which he also created the sets and the costumes. With a humorousness and architectural precision characteristic of his style, he executed as a backdrop a huge enlargement of a page from an American newspaper. In 1929, deeply affected by his son's illness and convinced that he was no more than a second-rate painter, he gave up painting. Rediscovered by the United States in 1960, his work has found a place in the prestigious collection of the Dallas Museum of Contemporary Art.

N

NIJINSKY, Vaslav: Russian dancer and choreographer of Polish origin (1889–1950). Star performer with the Ballets Russes during their first period. His remarkable feats caused a sensation and his reputation was quickly established worldwide, rehabilitating the art of the male dancer. Henceforth, male ballet dancers were to enjoy a prestige and a role equal to that of their female counterparts (towards the end of the nineteenth century, the male dancer had been, by contrast, no more than a dismal foil for the prima ballerina). Nijinsky created the leading parts in several of Fokine's works, before producing his own choreography for *L'Après-midi d'un faune* (1912) – a ballet which provoked a violent scandal – based on the poem by Mallarmé, which inspired the music by Debussy. The following year, Nijinsky became the Ballets Russes' principal choreographer, creating *Jeux*, a 'sporting pas de trois', again written by Debussy (with sets by Bakst). But this work went more or less unnoticed, eclipsed shortly after by the tumultuous première of his *Le Sacre du printemps* (Stravinsky).

In 1913, Diaghilev dismissed Nijinsky from the company, partly on account of his marriage. (His sister, Nijinska, was to become one of the principal choreographers during the Ballets Russes' second period.) Unemployed now, in 1914 Nijinsky founded his own short-lived company in London. During the war, he was interned for two years in Hungary. In 1916, he linked up again for a time with Diaghilev, for whom he choreographed his final work, *Till Eulenspiegel*, in New York (to Richard Strauss's music from 1895). The ballet, too modernist for the public, was a flop, and in 1917, at the age of only twenty-eight, Nijinsky was forced to quit the stage for good due to a

deterioration in his already unstable psychological condition. His career had spanned only ten years, but he was to live for another thirty-three in complete mental isolation, before disappearing into the mists of legend.

O

ORSI: French painter and designer (1889–1947). After studying with Sérusier and Maurice Denis, he found his vocation, at a very early age, as a poster designer. His art occupies an important place in the history of the poster, thanks to its innovative approach – he was one of the first to simplify the material, expressing the basic idea through form and colour – and to the extent of his work (he produced more than a thousand posters). He also executed many posters for the theatre and the ballet, including ones for Carina Ari, Josephine Baker and Mistinguette.

P

PARR, Andrée: Wife of Raymond Parr, a counsellor with the British Legation in Brazil; of Polish origin. She was in Rio de Janeiro with her husband when Claudel (whom she knew from Rome) and Darius Milhaud (appointed Claudel's secretary) were both posted there. It was to the Parrs' beautiful residence in Petrópolis that Claudel and Milhaud went each weekend to escape the scorching heat of the summer of 1917. Since she was a talented artist, Claudel got Parr, following his guidelines, to sketch the sets and costumes for his ballet *L'Homme et son désir*. She constructed a miniature theatre, small enough to sit on a table. 'We would cut out the characters', Milhaud recounted, 'from 15cm strips of coloured paper, and that was how we arranged our whole ballet.'

PERDRIAT, Hélène: French painter and engraver (b.1894). After a spectacularly successful début, she was to abandon her artistic activity quite suddenly. She exhibited at the Salon des Indépendants and the Salon d'Automne from 1919, painting graceful, well-executed works in a *fêtes galantes* vein. She wrote the libretto and made the costumes and sets for the Ballets Suédois' *Marchand d'oiseaux* (1923).

PICABIA, Francis: French painter and writer (1878–1953). He started his career as a successful, latter-day Impressionist, exhibiting works from this period at the Salon d'Automne in 1903. In around 1908, under the influence of Gauguin, he began painting landscapes using broad areas of flat tints and moving away from realistic depiction. Following a trip to Spain, which exerted a powerful impression on him, he discovered Cubism and shifted towards abstraction (as in the 1909 watercolour *Caoutchouc*, frequently considered a pivotal work in the genesis of abstraction). His figures from this period combine the influence of Léger and of Futurism with the Cubism of Picasso and Braque.

A friend of Apollinaire, Jacques Villon and Marcel Duchamp, it was with the latter that Picabia left in 1913 for New York, in order to exhibit at the historic Armory Show, the United States' first introduction to modern art. It was also in 1913 that he began producing his famous mechanistic paintings. This series of works, which was to monopolize virtually his entire pictorial output until 1922, may be regarded as the most significant stage of Picabia's activity as a

painter and was to be echoed by the young artists of the sixties.

In New York once more, he linked up with Duchamp to develop, from 1915, his pre-Dadaist activities (in particular, in Stieglitz's revue *291*, then in his own, *391*) and began publishing collections of poems, which attracted the attention of Tristan Tzara and the Dada group in Zurich, which he joined in 1919. That same year, he went to live in Paris, joined in 1920 by Tzara. Together they were to become the driving force behind the Dada movement in Paris. In 1921, however, Picabia backed Breton against Tzara. He was experimenting by now with new techniques and bizarre materials (collages of feathers, matches, toothpicks and hairpins on canvas). In 1922, he began painting his Monsters series, where the colour and texture are reminiscent of both Masson and Picasso.

His collaboration on *Relâche* and *Entr'acte* (1924) corresponded in effect to the last phase of his Dadaist activity. His resignation to the notion of universal absurdity was channelled into the doctrine of 'instantaneousness', invented for the occasion, and the philosophy of 'cheat to lose' and 'sacrifice one's reputation', the idea of living the way one loves, 'a life without a tomorrow, the life of today, everything for today, nothing for yesterday, nothing for tomorrow' (Ballets Suédois programme).

Picabia is well known for his affluent, flashy life-style, his pleasure-seeking and love of luxury. From 1925, he went to live in the South of France, spending part of his time on various yachts. He returned to Paris in 1945, and, from then onwards, developed a whole range of figurative and abstract styles, which he varied to suit public taste and circumstance.

PIRANDELLO, Luigi: Italian writer (1867–1936). Predating Brecht, he was responsible for systematically renewing the principles on which modern dramaturgy was based. And yet, he was nearly fifty before he began writing plays, which represent only a third of his entire output (he also wrote novels, short stories, essays and poems). His seven novels and 242 short stories were essential to the genesis of his plays, twenty-eight of which were in fact drawn from his earlier writing. This was the case with *La Giara* (staged by the Ballets Suédois as the ballet *La Jarre* in 1924), based on a Sicilian short story.

Those plays which do not actually duplicate the narrative work rely on the use of mirroring as a dramatic technique. Thus, Pirandello's entire oeuvre is a rigorously self-reflective system arranged round the mirror theme and the twinning of images. The trilogy of plays dealing with the 'theatre in the theatre' is the most fully elaborated critical reflection of the conditions determining any theatrical production.

In 1934, Pirandello won the Nobel prize for literature.

PORTER, Cole: American composer (1881–1964). Following the First World War, he moved to Paris, where he continued to live the life of a rich playboy during the twenties. Precociously talented as both poet and musician, he completed a range of eclectic but in-depth studies at the Schola Cantorum, familiarizing himself with Stravinsky's innovations, the Gallic spirit of Milhaud and Poulenc, and American jazz. He made the acquaintance of Gerald Murphy on the Côte d'Azur in 1921 and wrote the first jazz ballet, *Within the Quota*, with him at the Palazzo Barbaro in Venice, in 1923. This satirical, jazz-inspired ballet score predates Gershwin's *Rhapsody in Blue* by several months.

It was during the thirties that Porter composed his greatest works and won wide public acclaim. In 1936, he wrote the score for *Born to Dance*, and the following year, he composed two songs for Réne Clair's film *Break the News*. In 1946, Warner Brothers produced a film based on a biography of Cole Porter, played by Fred Astaire. He broke both his legs in a riding accident in 1937, and in 1958 had to have one of them amputated. He died six years later, leaving behind him more than eight hundred compositions, half of them unpublished.

His work is linked with the golden age of American musical comedy and includes such well-known shows as *Fifty Million Frenchmen*, *Anything Goes*, *Kiss Me, Kate* and *Can-Can* and famous films like *Born to Dance*, *Rosalie*, *Broadway Melody of 1940* and *High Society*.

POULENC, Francis: French composer (1899–1963). He was the incarnation of the Six's most classical tendencies. A musician free of prejudice, an instinctive composer rather than a theoretician, he safeguarded the purity of a French tradition which steered him clear of the reefs of romanticism on the one side and of academicism on the other. In 1920, he composed *Sculpture nègre* for Jean Börlin and, in 1921, collaborated on Cocteau's *Les Mariés de la tour Eiffel*, for which he composed the General's Speech. In his fifties, this apparent devotee of burlesque light-heartedness began composing religious music of a delicately spiritual quality.

R

RAVEL, Maurice: French composer (1875–1937). During his lifetime, he never knew real fame. It was only after his death that his talent was recognized and he was promoted to the dignified rank of a 'classic'. In 1919, he wrote a Viennese waltz for Diaghilev, *La Valse*, although it was performed, not by the Ballets Russes, but by Ida Rubinstein (in Monte Carlo in 1929). He also composed *Daphnis and Chloe* (choreographed by Fokine, 1912) for the Ballets Russes and *Bolero* (choreographed by Nijinska, 1928) for Ida Rubinstein.

In 1920, the Ballets Suédois presented his *Le Tombeau de Couperin*. This delicate and charming evocation of the eighteenth century was something of a light relief for Rolf de Maré's aggressively avant-garde company.

ROLAND-MANUEL, Roland Alexis Manuel Lévy, known as: French composer and musicologist (1891–1966). A pupil of Roussel and of Ravel (of whom he was also a disciple and friend), he presented the daily radio broadcast 'Plaisir de la musique'. Thanks to his eclecticism and extensive knowledge, this programme attracted a remarkably large audience. He also wrote two *opéras bouffes*, three ballets, an oratorio, a piano concerto, chamber music, music for stage and screen, etc. He wrote *Le Tournoi singulier* (1924) for the Ballets Suédois and also orchestrated early works by Satie for use as ballet music.

S

SATIE, Erik: French composer (1866–1925). The first musician for whom musical creation was no longer lyrical, but 'critical', he was profoundly influential in the development of modern music. Bound by the rules that he himself had laid down, his music is music questioning itself. His youthful works, *Gymnopédies* and *Sarabandes* (eighteen-eighties), already contained in embryonic form all the elements of the new harmonic language which Debussy and Ravel were later to adopt and develop.

Parade, his first ever ballet score, written for Diaghilev in collaboration with Cocteau and Picasso in 1917, identified Satie with the Cubist movement. His bizarre little masterpiece *Le Piège de Méduse* (1913), though composed three years before the official birth of Dadaism, unquestionably forestalled the Dada movement, while his last ballet, *Relâche* (which included a remarkable score written for René Clair's *Entr'acte*), composed for the Ballets Suédois – for whom it was also to be *their* last – was regarded as the first piece of Surrealist theatre.

A lover of puns and practical jokes (but also an enthusiastic adherent of Rosicrucianism and a disciple of sâr Peladan), Satie composed three other ballet scores, borrowing as always from the aesthetic of the *café-concert* and throwing in a hint of jazz and a few deliberate malapropisms: *Premier amour* ('morceaux en forme de poire' [literally 'pear-shaped pieces'; the malapropism was presumably 'poire' for 'paire', meaning 'pair']) and *Mercure* for the Comte de Beaumont's Soirées de Paris (1924), and *Jack-in-the-Box* for Diaghilev (1926).

Satie continues to exert – not least through his admirers John Cage and Merce Cunningham – a more profound influence on modern dance than any other composer prior to Stravinsky.

SAUGUET, Henri: French composer (1901–1989). The most famous representative of the Arcueil school. This was the name adopted by those musicians who took the place of the Six and congregated around the composer Satie, now retired at Arcueil. For Satie's voluntarily ascetic simplicity, Sauguet substituted a primitive simplistic fervour and 'naturalism'. Generously launched by Rolf de Maré, who organized a concert for the Arcueil composers at the Théâtre des Champs-Élysées in 1924, as a critic Sauguet was revolted by the bold eclecticism of the Ballets Suédois, whom he violently attacked. Sauguet's expressive and poetic humanism linked him, in fact, with the group Jeune France, which was formed at the end of the thirties.

He was commissioned to write the music for a number of ballets: *Les Roses* (1924) for the Comte de Beaumont, *La Chatte* (1927) for Diaghilev, *David* (1928) for Ida Rubinstein, *La Nuit* (1930) for Cochran's Revue, *Fastes* for Les Ballets 1933, *Les Forains* (1945) and *Les Mirages* (1947) for the Paris Opéra, and *La Rencontre* and *Œdipe et le Sphinx* (1948) for the Ballets des Champs-Élysées.

SINTENIS, Renée: German sculptor (1888–1965). With the rise of Nazism, she was obliged to resign from the Prussian Academy of Fine Arts. Renowned for her animal sculptures, she succeeded in capturing the dynamism of her subjects, accentuating muscular movement in pieces that were close to Cubism. She also did a fine sculpture of Börlin.

SIX, The: group of six French musicians, Auric, Durey, Honegger, Milhaud, Poulenc, and Germaine Tailleferre, who formed their own movement (1920–23). The group received its name, unbeknown to its members, from the music critic Henri Collet, who baptized them 'le groupe des Six' (a name that was to stick for good) in an article that appeared in *Comœdia* in January 1920. It was his way of distinguishing them from the Russian 'Five' (Rimsky-Korsakov, Mussorgsky, Borodin, Cesar Cui and Balakirev). The Six also attracted poets such as Blaise Cendrars and Cocteau, the group's theoretician, who elaborated an aesthetic in response to what Satie called 'l'esprit nouveau'.

Although Cocteau endeavoured to restate the situation – 'There is no Satie school. Satie-ism does not exist. I would earnestly resist such a notion. There should be no slavery in art' – Satie was indeed the spiritual leader and grand precursor of this group of musicians, forebears of all modern French music. As with Satie, the Six's music reveals strains of *café-concert*, music-hall and circus tunes, coupled with a sense of irony designed to dissolve romantic illusions and Debussy-esque charm – as a means of penetrating to essentials. Five of the group (Louis Durey withdrew at the first hint of scandal) mustered round Cocteau in order to produce a joint composition – a unique event – for *Les Mariés de la tour Eiffel* (1921).

STEINLEN, Alexandre: French painter, designer and sculptor, born in Switzerland (1859–1923). At the age of nineteen, he moved to Paris, where he earned a living as an industrial designer, before becoming a regular visitor to the night club the Chat-Noir. From that point on, he began doing illustrations for the major humorous papers and also illustrated a great number of books. From 1893, he exhibited at the Salon des Indépendants, painting the street scenes (Paris suburbs and the Montmartre area) for which he is still famous today.

He had a particular fondness for cats, and his drawings, paintings and sculptures of cats attempt to capture a whole range of attitudes conveying feline suppleness, sensuality and mystique. He also produced some very fine posters (dedicated to Aristide Bruant and Yvette Guilbert, among others), stage sets and a masterly *Portrait d'Anatole France*. The sets he designed and made for *Iberia* amply demonstrate his vigorous style of drawing and the originality of his palette.

T

TAILLEFERRE, Germaine: French composer (1892–1983). She was a member of the Six, then of Jeune France, a group formed in 1936 by Yves Baudrier, Olivier Messiaen, André Jolivet and Daniel Lesur. While the Six had freed music from all Expressionist aims, fifteen years later Jeune France underlined a concern for musical humanism by affirming the necessity for a 'reincarnation of music in man'.

As a member of the Six, Germaine Tailleferre collaborated on *Les Mariés de la tour Eiffel*, for which she composed a burlesque waltz and quadrille. In 1923 she composed another ballet, *Marchand d'oiseaux*, the theme of which was the punishment of false pride. She was one of the first to have a hand in shaping the new aesthetic which arose out of spoken film: by writing music for films, composers like Honegger, Roland-Manuel, Milhaud, Sauguet, Auric, Poulenc and

Tailleferre would, after a fashion, be putting into practice the notion, dear to Satie, of a *musique d'ameublement* (literally 'music as furniture'), composed simply to be heard rather than actively listened to.

TANSMAN, Alexandre: French composer of Polish origin (1897–1986). He won the first prize for composition at the Warsaw Conservatoire and, in 1920, moved to Paris, where his experimental approach to music identified him with the avant-garde. From there he later moved to the United States. Inspired by the music of Ravel and Stravinsky, his work is both prolific and diverse.

TOUCHAGUES, Louis: French painter and scenographer (1893–1974). At the start of his career, he was designing fabrics for Poiret, and theatre sets for Charles Dullin. He made a name for himself by exhibiting at the Salon de l'Araignée organized by Gus Bofa, to whom he had been introduced by André Salmon. Touchagues was *the* portraitist of Paris high society in the thirties: theatre celebrities and famous politicians alike posed for this fashionable painter, whose work reveals the influence of Watteau, Fragonard and Toulouse-Lautrec.

V

VASILIEVA, Maria: Russian painter, sculptor and scene painter (1884–1957). She studied medicine in St Petersburg, and later fine arts. In Paris, she was a student of Matisse, before founding her own painting school, the Académie Vassilieff, which became the meeting place of Picasso, Matisse, Braque, Gris, Modigliani, Cendrars, Satie, André Salmon and Max Jacob, while Léger gave a series of lectures there in 1913.

In 1914, Vasilieva signed up as an ambulance driver in the French Red Cross, and, from 1915 to 1917, she ran a soup kitchen at the academy in order to help out friends in need. Picabia, Valadon, Diaghilev, Friesz, Gide, Poulenc and t'Serstevens used to meet there at that time, along with the regulars from the academy.

Following the war, she designed furniture and décors for Poiret, who introduced Paris to her *Poupées-portraits* (Doll-portraits) of Parisian personalities. She also designed numerous sets and costumes for the Théâtre des Champs-Élysées. At the Arts Décoratifs exhibition of 1925, she showed a set of furniture she had designed and made using precious materials, such as lacquer and gold leaf, and on which she had spent her entire savings.

Her work as painter and sculptress harnessed the influence of Léger and Delaunay, Cubism and popular Russian art. Vasilieva is still famous today for her portraits of friends – Matisse, Picasso, Derain, de Maré, Börlin and Cocteau – and the portrait she did of Stravinsky, with a tapir on his head, is to be seen hanging in the famous Paris restaurant La Coupole. After responding to several commissions from the Rosicrucians, she ended up devoting her skills to religious subjects.

W

WEGENER, Gerda: Danish painter (1889-1940). Born into a French Family who emigrated to Denmark in the eighteenth century, she studied at the Academy of Fine Arts in Copenhagen, before moving to Paris in 1912. She exhibited regularly in different Paris salons, collaborated on a number of newspapers and produced book illustrations that were highly prized in her day. She was married to the painter Einar Wegener, who had a sex change operation in 1930 and subsequently assumed the name Lili Elbe.

BIOGRAPHY OF BENGT HÄGER

Bengt Häger was born in Sweden. In 1950 he founded the Stockholm Dance Museum, which he continued to direct until 1989. From 1977 to 1988 he was president of UNESCO's International Dance Council, of which he had previously been vice-president since its foundation in 1973.

Häger was introduced to dance at the age of fifteen, when he saw his first performance by the Ballets Russes in Monte Carlo. Thereafter, he went back each year during the school holidays, to attend ballet classes (sometimes given by the guest master Fokine). When war broke out in 1939, he was forced to give up his European travels and studied law, economics and statistics at Stockholm University. He then went on to study theatre history and, as the first Swedish dance scientist, was later appointed professor by the Swedish government.

Towards the end of the war, Rolf de Maré enlisted Häger's help in organizing two choreography competitions, which took place in 1945 and 1947, and appointed him general secretary of his Archives Internationales de la Danse in Paris (1947–50).

Married to the famous classical Hindu dancer Lilavati, Häger spent several years studying classical dance cultures in Asia. For twenty-five years he was a dance critic and wrote a weekly dance column in the Swedish government's daily paper. He was responsible for organizing numerous tours by different dance companies throughout Scandinavia and other European countries. During the 1950s and 1960s he brought important companies and artistes over on tour from America and Asia, such as Martha Graham, Merce Cunningham, Alvin Ailey, Alwin Nikolais, Murray Louis, Pilobolus, the Peking Opera, Ram Gopal, Mrinalini Sarabhai, Kabuki, and many others. On behalf of UNESCO, he organized international congresses worldwide. The Swedish government entrusted him with the task of creating a Swedish Dance High School at university level, of which he was the first dean (1964–71). With Marcel Marceau, he founded a Franco-Swedish school of mime; and, for its first twenty years, he was administrative director of the Cullberg Ballet Company, Sweden's leading modern dance theatre.

Häger is also the author of several books and scholarly articles, some of which have been translated into several languages. He was made commander of the French Ordre des Palmes Académiques and has won UNESCO's Picasso medal, Stockholm's St Erik medal, and the Carina Ari Gold Medal.

LIST OF ILLUSTRATIONS

for *L'Homme et son désir,* watercolour glued to green paper.

p. 133: Andrée Parr, design for *L'Homme et son désir,* Indian ink.

p. 134: Andrée Parr, 'Woman', costume for *L'Homme et son désir,* watercolour glued to blue paper, 21.5 × 17.5cm.

p. 135: (top) Irma Calson and Greta Lundberg as the Bells, Kaj Smith as the Pan-Pipes, in *L'Homme et son désir;* (bottom) Andrée Parr, 'Bells', costumes for *L'Homme et son désir,* watercolour and gouache glued to green paper, 22 × 19cm.

pp. 136–37: Photograph of a scene from *L'Homme et son désir.*

p. 138: A scene from *Les Mariés de la tour Eiffel,* pencil and gouache, 28.5 × 31.5cm.

p. 139: Jean Hugo, 'Mother-in-law', costume for *Les Mariés de la tour Eiffel,* pencil and gouache, 28.5 × 21.5cm.

p. 140: Jean Hugo, 'Sailor', costume for *Les Mariés de la tour Eiffel,* pencil and gouache, 28.5 × 21.5cm.

p. 141: Jean Hugo, 'Hunchbacked photographer', costume for *Les Mariés de la tour Eiffel,* gouache, 29 × 22cm, and photograph of Jean Cocteau reading his part.

p. 142: Jean Cocteau, four pointillist drawings showing the dancers' outlines inside their costumes and masks, which were made by Jean Hugo out of papier-mâché for *Les Mariés de la tour Eiffel:* 'Cyclist', 'Father-in-law', 'Huntsman' and 'Trouville bathing girl', Indian ink, 29 × 21cm.

p. 143: Jean Hugo, 'Lion', costume for *Les Mariés de la tour Eiffel,* pencil and gouache, 28 × 21cm.

p. 144: Jean Hugo, 'Trouville bathing girl', costume for *Les Mariés de la tour Eiffel,* pencil and gouache, 28 × 22cm.

p. 145: Jean Hugo, 'Ostrich', costume for *Les Mariés de la tour Eiffel,* pencil and gouache, 28 × 22cm.

p. 146: Jean Hugo, 'General', costume for *Les Mariés de la tour Eiffel,* pencil and gouache, 28.5 × 21.5cm.

p. 147: Jean Hugo, 'Bridesmaid', costume for *Les Mariés de la tour Eiffel,* pencil and gouache, 28.5 × 21.5cm.

p. 148: Jean Hugo, 'Cyclist', costume for *Les Mariés de la tour Eiffel,* pencil and gouache, 29 × 22cm.

p. 149: Paul Witzansky in the role of the General and Eric Viber as the Lion.

p. 151: Jean Hugo, 'Director of the Eiffel Tower', costume for *Les Mariés de la tour Eiffel,* pencil and gouache, 28.5 × 22cm.

p. 152: Jean Hugo, four costumes for *Les Mariés de la tour Eiffel.* From left to right: (top) 'Art Dealer', pencil and gouache, 28 × 20.5cm, and 'Father-in-law', pencil and gouache, 27 × 21cm; (bottom) 'Huntsman', pencil and gouache, 28 × 21cm, and 'Bridegroom', pencil and gouache, 27.5 × 21cm.

p. 153: Jean Hugo, 'Child', costume for *Les Mariés de la tour Eiffel,* pencil and gouache, 28.5 × 21cm.

pp. 154–55: Photograph of a scene from *Les Mariés de la tour Eiffel.*

p. 156: Dancers in *Dansgille.* Top photograph, from left to right: Paul Eltorp, Margit Wåhlander, Jean Börlin, Thorborg Stjerner and

Kaj Smith; bottom photograph, from left to right: Ingeborg Kahr, Margareta Johanson, Jean Börlin, Irma Calson and Siva Blomkvist.

p. 157: Scene from *Dansgille.* From left to right: Helga Dahl, Axel Witzansky and Berta Krantz.

p. 158: Scene from *Dansgille,* 1921. Backdrop based on a painting done at Rättvik in 1848 (currently in Stockholm's Nordic Museum) depicting the parable of the labourers in the vineyard.

p. 159: Gouache based on a popular drawing.

p. 160: Fernand Léger, 'Sailor', costume for *Skating Rink,* watercolour, 15 × 18.8cm.

p. 161: Fernand Léger, 'Man', costume for *Skating Rink,* watercolour, 23 × 15cm.

p. 162: Fernand Léger, two costumes for *Skating Rink.* Bottom left: 'Gentleman in a top hat', watercolour, 22.5 × 15cm; top right: 'Man', watercolour, 22.5 × 14.8cm.

p. 1263: Fernand Léger, 'Man', costume for *Skating Rink,* watercolour, 22.5 × 14.8cm.

p. 164–65: Fernand Léger, curtain for *Skating Rink,* watercolour, 40.5 × 48cm.

p. 167: Fernand Léger, four costumes for *Skating Rink.* From left to right: (top) 'Woman in a hat', watercolour, 24 × 16cm, and 'Woman in a checked skirt', watercolour, 25 × 16cm; (bottom) 'Woman', watercolour, 23 × 14.5cm, and 'Woman', watercolour, 22.5 × 14.5cm.

p. 168: Jean Börlin in *Skating Rink.*

p. 169: Fernand Léger, design for Jean Börlin's costume in *Skating Rink,* watercolour, 30 × 18cm.

p. 170: Fernand Léger, 'Gentleman in a top hat', costume for *Skating Rink,* watercolour, 23 × 14cm.

p. 171: Fernand Léger, 'Gentleman in a top hat', costume for *Skating Rink,* watercolour, 23 × 14cm.

pp. 172–73: Fernand Léger, model for *Skating Rink.*

p. 174: Hélène Perdriat, 'Elder sister', costume for *Marchand d'oiseaux,* gouache, 42.5 × 28.5cm.

p. 175: Hélène Perdriat, painting.

p. 176: Hélène Perdriat, 'Stranger unmasked' and 'Masked stranger', costumes for *Marchand d'oiseaux,* gouache, 35 × 41.5 cm.

p. 177: Hélène Perdriat, 'Young bird seller', costume for *Marchand d'oiseaux,* gouache, 43 × 30cm.

pp. 178–79: Hélène Perdriat, 'Schoolgirls', costumes for *Marchand d'oiseaux,* gouache, 37 × 58cm.

p. 180: Gunnar Hallström, 'Profile of a woman with drinking cup', costume for *Offerlunden,* pencil and watercolour, 26 × 36.7cm.

p. 181: Gunnar Hallström, 'Two white costumes on a green ground' (reproduced here in black and white), costumes for *Offerlunden,* watercolour, 45.5 × 27cm.

p. 182: Gunnar Hallström, 'Gilded cup', design for *Offerlunden,* pencil and watercolour, 36 × 25.5cm.

p. 183: Gunnar Hallström, 'Detail of a headdress', design for *Offerlunden,* pencil, watercolour and gouache, 36 × 25.5cm.

p. 184: Gunnar Hallström, two costumes for *Offerlunden:* 'Woman in grey and black', pencil and watercolour, 34 × 24.2cm, and 'Woman in a black cloak', pencil and watercolour, 29 × 24.5cm.

p. 185: Gunnar Hallström, 'Brown costume', design for *Offerlunden,* pencil and watercolour, 35 × 25cm.

pp. 186–87: Photograph of a scene from *Offerlunden,* 1923.

p. 188: Fernand Léger, 'Woman's costume', design for *La Création du monde,* watercolour, 43 × 25cm.

p. 189: Fernand Léger, 'Divinity', costume for *La Création du monde,* watercolour.

p. 190: Fernand Léger, 'Mask', design for *La Création du monde,* watercolour, 36 × 14cm.

p. 191: Fernand Léger, 'Horned creature', design for *La Création du monde,* watercolour, 36.7 × 20cm.

pp. 192–93: Fernand Léger, set design for *La Création du monde,* watercolour, 39.5 × 61cm.

p. 194: Fernand Léger, three costumes for *La Création du monde.* From top to bottom: 'Coleopteran', watercolour, 15 × 25cm, 'Prehistoric creature', watercolour, 14 × 28.5cm, and 'Coleopteran', watercolour, 15.7 × 25cm.

p. 195: Fernand Léger, figure study for *La Création du monde,* watercolour, 43.5 × 28.5cm.

p. 196: Fernand Léger, two figure studies for *La Création du monde,* watercolour, 35 × 12cm and 32 × 14cm.

p. 197: Fernand Léger, studies for *La Création du monde.* Top: figure study, watercolour; bottom left: 'Large figure', watercolour, 43.5 × 22cm; bottom right: 'Large figure', watercolour, 44 × 24cm.

p. 198: Fernand Léger, 'Bird', costume for *La Création du monde,* watercolour.

p. 199: Fernand Léger, 'Monkey', costume for *La Création du monde,* watercolour, 30 × 17cm.

p. 200: Fernand Léger, 'Bird', costume for *La Création du monde,* watercolour.

p. 201: Fernand Léger, 'Bird', costume for *La Création du monde,* watercolour, 31 × 22cm.

p. 202: Fernand Léger, 'Bird', costume for *La Création du monde,* watercolour.

p. 203: Fernand Léger, 'Monkey', costume for *La Création du monde,* watercolour.

p. 204: Fernand Léger, costume for *La Création du monde,* watercolour.

p. 205: Fernand Léger, costume for *La Création du monde,* watercolour.

p. 206: Fernand Léger, costume for *La Création du monde,* watercolour.

p. 207: Fernand Léger, figure study for *La Création du monde,* watercolour.

pp. 208–9: Photograph of a scene from *La Création du monde.*

p. 210: Gerald Murphy, collage for *Within the Quota,* from the 1923 Ballets Suédois programme.

p. 211: Photograph of Jean Börlin as the Immigrant in *Within the Quota,* 1923.

p. 212: Photograph of Kaj Smith as the Coloured Gentleman in *Within the Quota.*

p. 213: Miguel Covarrubias, portrait of Jean Börlin in *Within the Quota,* watercolour, 34.5 × 22.5cm.

p. 214: Gerald Murphy, three costumes for *Within the Quota,* pencil and watercolour.

p. 215: Gerald Murphy, 'Millionairess', costume for *Within the Quota,* pencil and watercolour.

pp. 216–17: Photograph of a scene from *Within the Quota.*

pp. 218–19: Photograph of a scene from

Within the Quota.

p. 220:   Aleksandr Alekseev, costume for *Le Roseau*, pencil and watercolour, 47 × 31.5cm.

p. 221:   Aleksandr Alekseev, 'Flute player', costume for *Le Roseau*, pencil and watercolour, 47.5 × 31.5cm.

p. 222:   Portrait of Daniel Lazarus by Boris Grigorin, taken from *La Danse*, November–December 1924.

p. 223:   Aleksandr Alekseev, costume for *Le Roseau*, pencil and watercolour, 47.5 × 31.5cm.

pp. 224–25:   Aleksandr Alekseev, stage set for *Le Roseau*, in imitation of a Persian miniature, pencil and watercolour, 24 × 32cm.

p. 226:   Aleksandr Alekseev, costume for *Le Porcher*, pencil and Indian ink, 35 × 24cm.

p. 227:   Page from *La Danse*, November–December 1924.

p. 229:   Aleksandr Alekseev, costume for *Le Porcher*, pencil and Indian ink, 35.5 × 24cm.

p. 230:   Foujita, 'Folly', costume for *Le Tournoi singulier*, pencil and watercolour, 24.5 × 15.5cm.

p. 231:   Foujita, 'Eros', costume for *Le Tournoi singulier*, pencil and watercolour, 20 × 11cm.

p. 232:   Foujita, portrait of Roland-Manuel, taken from *La Danse*, November–December 1924.

p. 233:   Foujita, preliminary décor design for *Le Tournoi singulier*, pencil, 17 × 24cm, and self-portrait, 1924, Indian ink, 19 × 13cm.

p. 234:   Two scenes from *Le Tournoi singulier*.

p. 235:   Foujita, 'Zephyrus', costume for *Le Tournoi singulier*, pencil and watercolour, 23.5 × 15.5cm.

p. 236:   Giorgio de Chirico, 'Peasant woman', costume for *La Jarre*, gouache, 33 × 25cm.

p. 237:   Giorgio de Chirico, 'Jar', gouache for the ballet *La Jarre*, 33 × 25cm.

p. 239:   Giorgio de Chirico, 'Hunchback', costume for *La Jarre*, gouache, 33 × 25cm.

p. 240:   Giorgio de Chirico, 'Boss's daughter', costume for *La Jarre*, gouache, 34 × 26cm.

p. 241:   Giorgio de Chirico, 'Peasant', costume for *La Jarre*, gouache, 33 × 25cm.

p. 242:   Giorgio de Chirico, four costumes for *La Jarre*: peasant and three peasant women, gouache, 33 × 25cm.

p. 243:   Giorgio de Chirico: (top) preliminary décor design for *La Jarre*, gouache, 25.5 × 33.5cm; (bottom) preliminary décor design for *La Jarre*, Indian ink, 15 × 23.5cm.

p. 244:   Giorgio de Chirico, self-portrait, Indian ink, page taken from *La Danse*, November–December 1924.

p. 245:   Giorgio de Chirico, portrait of Luigi Pirandello, Indian ink, page taken from *La Danse*, November–December 1924.

pp. 246–47:   Photograph of a scene from *La Jarre*, 1924.

p. 248:   Photograph of a scene from *Relâche*, 1924.

p. 249:   Jean Börlin and Edith Bonsdorff in a scene from *Relâche*.

p. 251:   Two extracts from *La Danse*, November–December 1924: the 'Picabia page' (detail) and the 'Erik Satie page' (detail).

pp. 254–55:   Francis Picabia, stage curtain for *Relâche*, pencil and watercolour, 31.3 × 48cm.

p. 258:   Extract from No. 391 of the *Journal de l'Instantanéisme*, November 1924.

p. 259:   Francis Picabia, figure for *Relâche*, Indian ink, 18 × 14.5cm.

p. 260:   Francis Picabia, figure for *Relâche*, Indian ink, 18 × 14.5cm.

p. 261:   Francis Picabia, figure for *Relâche*, Indian ink and wash, 24 × 19cm.

p. 262:   Photograph taken during the shooting of René Clair's film *Entr'acte*, shown in the entr'acte of *Relâche* (1924). The figure on the right is Jean Börlin.

p. 263:   Film still from René Clair's *Entr'acte*.

p. 266:   Michel Simon in René Clair's film *Entr'acte*.

p. 267:   A scene from René Clair's film *Entr'acte*. The figure in the coffin is Jean Börlin.

p. 268:   Scene from René Clair's film *Entr'acte*.

p. 269:   Scene from René Clair's film *Entr'acte*.

p. 270:   Francis Picabia, self-portrait, 1924, Indian ink and wash, 26 × 20cm.

p. 271:   Page taken from *La Danse*, November–December 1924.

pp. 272–73:   Photograph of the stage set for *Relâche*.

p. 274:   Serge Gladky, poster.

p. 275:   Serge Gladky, portrait of Jean Börlin in the ballet *Cercle éternel*.

p. 276:   Jean Börlin in some of his roles, page taken from the 1923 Ballets Suédois programme.

p. 277:   Photograph of Jean Börlin.

p. 278:   Photograph of Jean Börlin in his dressing room.

p. 281:   Darius Milhaud (at the piano) and Jean Börlin.

p. 282: Nils Dardel, 'Jean Börlin in Danse siamoise' (this dance was not part of the Ballets Suédois' repertoire), 1919, oil on canvas, 116 × 82cm, Dance Museum, Stockholm.

p. 283:   Roger Chastel, drawing of Jean Börlin performing a Swedish dance, taken from *La Danse*, November 1920.

p. 284:   Per Krohg, poster and cover for *La Danse*, November 1920.

p. 285:   Paul Colin, poster, 1925.

pp. 286 and 287:   Jean Börlin as Harlequin.

p. 288:   Jean Börlin and Ebon Strandin in 1915.

p. 289:   Francis Picabia, 'Portrait of Jean Börlin', press cutting, 1924.

p. 290:   Page from the 1923 Ballets Suédois programme, with portrait of Jean Börlin superimposed on a collage of press cuttings.

p. 291:   Drawing by Francis Picabia with text by Blaise Cendrars, taken from *La Danse*, November–December 1924.

ACKNOWLEDGMENTS

Some of the texts quoted in this book are drawn from *Les Ballets suédois* (Trianon, Paris, 1932) published by Rolf de Maré. A few texts without references are taken from various of the Ballets Suédois' programmes and from contemporary press cuttings. The publishers reserve all rights concerning these texts.

The photographs and illustrations which appear in this book are taken from Stockholm's Dance Museum archives. The publishers reserve all rights regarding these photographs. The stills from René Clair's film *Entr'acte* are the property of the Bibliothèque Nationale, with the exception of those appearing on pages 263 and 266, which were lent by Roger Viry-Babel. Jacques Sassier was responsible for the reproductions of pages taken from *La Danse* and from the Ballets Suédois' 1923 programme.

Works by Pierre Bonnard, Jean Cocteau, Giorgio de Chirico, Valentine Hugo, Roger de La Fresnaye, Pierre Laprade, Fernand Léger, Francis Picabia, Alexandre Steinlen and Louis Touchagues: © SPADEM, Paris, 1989 and 1990.

Works by Pierre Bonnard, Paul Colin, Léonard Foujita and Francis Picabia: © ADAGP, Paris, 1989 and 1990.

The publishers reserve all rights concerning the works of the following: Aleksandr Alekseev, Roger Chastel, Miguel Covarrubias, Nils Dardel, Lucien Daudet, Eldsten, Serge Gladky, Boris Grigorin, Gunnar Hallström, André Hellé, Jean Hugo, Per Krohg, Gerald Murphy, Einar Nerman, Andrée Parr, Hélène Perdriat and Maria Vasilieva.